MY UNCLE JOHN

J. M. Synge 1906
Crayon portrait by James Paterson in the possession of
Mrs. L. M. Stephens

MY UNCLE JOHN

Edward Stephens's Life of
J. M. Synge

EDITED BY
ANDREW CARPENTER

LONDON
OXFORD UNIVERSITY PRESS
1974

Oxford University Press, Ely House, London W.1

GLASGOW   NEW YORK   TORONTO   MELBOURNE   WELLINGTON
CAPE TOWN   IBADAN   NAIROBI   DAR ES SALAAM   LUSAKA   ADDIS ABABA
DELHI   BOMBAY   CALCUTTA   MADRAS   KARACHI   LAHORE   DACCA
KUALA LUMPUR   SINGAPORE   HONG KONG   TOKYO

ISBN 0 19 211718 1

© Lily M. Stephens 1974

PRINTED IN GREAT BRITAIN
BY W & J MACKAY LIMITED, CHATHAM

CONTENTS

ILLUSTRATIONS

frontispiece
J. M. Synge 1906, by James Paterson
Crayon portrait in the possession of Mrs. L. M. Stephens

between pages 94 and 95
The Synge family

Wicklow houses: Glanmore Castle, Roundwood Park, Castle Kevin, Tomriland House

At Castle Kevin: Claire and Edward Stephens with their dogs; Synge with his mother, Rosie Calthrop, and Annie Harmar, 1900

Florence Ross
Courtesy of Mrs. Doreen Farrington

Cherrie Matheson
Courtesy of Miss Winifred Matheson

Crosthwaite Park: Nos. 31 and 29, with one of the sitting rooms

between pages 190 and 191
The Stephens family, with Synge

Synge's Paris: his room in the Hotel Corneille; bookstalls
Reproduced by permission of the Board of Trinity College, Dublin

A wool-buyer in the west of Ireland; Synge's photograph of Aran Islanders at Kilronan pier, Aranmore
Reproduced by permission of the Board of Trinity College, Dublin

Molly Allgood in *Riders to the Sea*

Rehearsal room of the Irish National Theatre Society, 1903
Courtesy of Mrs. Doreen Farrington

Photographs by The Green Studio, Dublin

MAP
facing page 3
Dublin and Co. Wicklow

FOREWORD

My husband, Edward M. Stephens, was devoted to his uncle J. M. Synge and spent many years writing his biography. Knowing the Synge family's dislike of publicity, he realized that there could be no question of an early publication. In spite of this difficulty, my husband, with perseverance and enthusiasm, collected a vast amount of material relating not only to his uncle but also to the branch of the Synge family which had settled in Co. Wicklow in the eighteenth century.

In addition to the material he had collected, my husband added his personal recollections of his Synge relations and friends, and of the yearly holidays he spent with his grandmother and uncle in Co. Wicklow. Being by training a lawyer, he believed in the importance of detail and of the written word. At the same time he realized, as the biography grew in size, that it was too long as it stood for publication, and he had always intended to revise and condense the material; unfortunately this was prevented by his sudden death in 1955.

For some years before his death, my husband had been in touch with his friend Professor David Greene of New York University. David Greene had read the typescript and had given my husband much helpful advice and encouragement. After my husband's death, I wrote to David Greene asking if he would be interested in writing a biography of J. M. Synge using as a basis the material in my husband's typescript. This suggestion resulted in the publication, in 1959, of *J. M. Synge: 1871–1909*.

When the book appeared, I was delighted that much of my husband's work was available to students of Synge and lovers of his plays. However, the amount of material from the typescript which David Greene was able to incorporate in the book was small in comparison to what was left, and, as he said in his Introduction, he had written a book 'quite different from the one Edward Stephens projected'. He also made it clear that though my husband would probably have endorsed a good deal of the book, some of the judgements found there were very different from those in the typescript. For this reason, I had always hoped that one day it might be possible for a new book, made up entirely from my husband's typescript and reflecting his particular views, to be published. I was particularly pleased when Oxford University Press suggested just such a project and proposed Dr. Andrew Carpenter as editor. I am sincerely grateful to Mr. John Bell of the Press and to Dr. Carpenter.

LILO M. STEPHENS

Dublin, 1973

INTRODUCTION

EDWARD MILLINGTON STEPHENS was born in November 1888 when his uncle, J. M. Synge, was seventeen years old. The Synge and Stephens families occupied houses next door to each other in the Dublin suburbs from that time onwards until shortly before Synge's death in 1909, and during most of this period Edward Stephens lived in close contact with Synge. Later Stephens entered the legal profession and had an eventful and distinguished career in Irish public life: after acting as a secretary to the committee which drew up the Irish constitution, he became assistant registrar to the Supreme Court, and finally registrar to the Court of Criminal Appeal. Throughout his life, he always maintained a devotion to the memory of his uncle and an awareness that he was himself uniquely qualified to be Synge's biographer. In addition to his own very considerable and vivid recollections of his uncle, Stephens could understand with particular clarity the background from which Synge came, the tensions of his home life, and some of the peculiarities of his character. Furthermore in 1939, on the death of Synge's brother Edward (who had preferred not to make Synge's private papers available for study), Stephens became the custodian of all Synge's unpublished manuscripts, notebooks, and papers: he was thus presented with sole access to as great a quantity of primary material as any biographer of Synge could ever hope to see.[1]

During the next ten years, Stephens worked with immense care and diligence assembling every available scrap of information on the life of his uncle and preparing the biography. He was inspired by the belief that a sober, factual account of Synge's family life would prove to be of far greater value to anyone wishing to understand the man and his plays than any analysis or literary comparison. 'I see J.M. and his work as belonging much more to the family environment than to the environment of the theatre,' he wrote to Professor David Greene.[2] Thus the family background was of paramount importance and Stephens felt that the reader who understood Synge's everyday life would come to appreciate his character, which would in turn lead to an appreciation of

---

[1] The papers held by Stephens as trustee of the J. M. Synge Estate are now in the library of Trinity College, Dublin.

[2] Stephens to Greene, 1 July 1954 (unpublished).

his writings. So strongly was Stephens's work based on these assumptions that his typescript became, in places, more a history of the Synge family and a detailed chronicle of Stephens's own childhood than an objective biography of Synge.

In spite of this, the typescript is obviously a work of very considerable interest to anyone concerned with Synge's life and writings. For without some knowledge of the forces which moulded Synge—his family (particularly his mother), his home, his religion, his love of the Irish countryside and country people, his social background—one can hardly understand the energy and bravado of his plays. Edward Stephens, more than any other commentator on Synge, was in a position to provide this knowledge. He had been a member of the household, had received his religious instruction from Mrs. Synge, had been taught to love the countryside by Synge himself, and had also experienced the same kind of religious and cultural crisis as his uncle. His memories of family life and of Synge's part in it illuminate the playwright in a remarkable way, particularly as Stephens saw Synge entirely in the context of the family and believed that his genius was a perfectly logical, if perhaps unexpected, flowering of the family genius of the Synges.

However, the public and artistic side of Synge's life is hardly illuminated at all by Stephens's typescript. Stephens never saw Synge's plays on the stage during his uncle's lifetime and knew so little of the theatre that he was unable to recognize Synge's literary and theatrical friends at his funeral. After Synge's death, of course, Stephens read all his works and became an expert on them; but his first-hand knowledge was entirely of Synge's family life. This, he felt, gave his interpretations strength and a perspective lacking in the work of other commentators on Synge, particularly as he saw Synge as a fundamentally autobiographical writer who used every detail of his life as material for his art.

It was ⟨Synge's⟩ ambition . . . to use the whole of his personal life in his dramatic work. He ultimately achieved this . . . by dramatizing himself, disguised as the central character or, in different capacities, as several of the leading characters, in some story from country lore or heroic tradition. It is in this sense that his dramatic work was autobiographical and that the outwardly dull story of his life became transmuted into the gold of literature. . . .[1]

Today few scholars would, I think, accept so simple an explanation of Synge's personal involvement with his work, but Stephens's adherence

[1] Stephens TS. 658; see below pp. 87–8.

to this belief was instrumental in the conception and working out of his biography.

Such a theory brings with it a logical concern with every detail of Synge's personal life and background, and Stephens's typescript shows that he found it difficult, if not impossible, to omit anything which came to his attention.[1] He transcribed in full many family papers dating back to the eighteenth century; he copied any letters, notes, reviews, articles, fragments of plays, or other documentary evidence connected, even remotely, with Synge. He also recounted, with a precision which is truly astonishing, the events of Synge's life: the weather on particular days, the details of views Synge saw on his bicycle rides or walks and the history of the countryside through which he passed, the backgrounds of every person Synge met during family holidays, the food eaten, the decoration of the houses in which Synge lived, the books he read, his daily habits, his conversations, his coughs and colds—and those of other members of the family. Few biographers have attempted so detailed an account of a man's life, and Stephens's biography must stand as a monument to his devotion to the memory of his uncle and to his own patience, care, and determination.

However, the price paid for this inclusiveness, in literary, artistic, and practical terms, is great—as indeed it must have been in personal terms. By 1950, the typescript was in fourteen volumes, containing 3,287 pages and nearly three-quarters of a million words. The publishers to whom it was sent agreed that it was a work of great interest, but deplored its extreme length. As one reader put it: 'This enormous manuscript is the hillside from which must be quarried out the authoritative life of Synge.'[2]

Edward Stephens retired in 1950, and it appears from his correspondence that he was aware of the justness of the comments made to him by publishers and intended to undertake the task of editing and condensing the biography himself. However he died suddenly in 1955 and the typescript remained unpublished. It was made available by Stephens's widow to Professor David Greene, with whom Stephens had been planning to collaborate on a biography of Synge, and Greene was able to incorporate much of Stephens's work in his book *J. M. Synge: 1871–1909*,

---

[1] 'What I was trying to do was to build up a picture of the context of his life, which was quite different from that of other writers in the literary movement. I tried to create a picture of a class or group in Irish society that has almost vanished.' (Stephens to Greene, 1 July 1954.)

[2] File of correspondence (January 1951) in the possession of Mrs. L. M. Stephens.

which appeared in 1959. He also credited Stephens as co-author, but explained in his introduction:

. . . Telling the story of Synge's life has been my responsibility. The interpretations and conclusions in this book, and the actual writing, are my own. I am sure that my collaborator would have endorsed a good deal that I have written, but I am equally sure that he would not have agreed with some of my judgements. I can only say that in producing a book quite different from the one Edward Stephens projected I have used the same freedom any biographer would have considered essential.[1]

Thus although he is cited as co-author of *J. M. Synge: 1871–1909*, by no means all of Stephens's work on Synge appeared in that book, and much of the text of the typescript, particularly passages of detailed reminiscence and of family history, has remained unpublished.

Stephens's interpretation of Synge's life and his 'accumulation of ordered material'[2] are both interesting in themselves but, of course, the typescript itself is quite inaccessible to the general reader on grounds of its length. An additional problem is posed by Stephens's decision to deal with his material, particularly transcripts of correspondence and criticism, in strictly chronological order, often without himself providing any commentary. Thus the casual reader of the typescript finds it almost impossible to see any coherence, particularly towards the end of the work. The strictly chronological order will juxtapose items that are completely unconnected and the lack of comment makes it hard to see connections between items on the same subject. The last three volumes of typescript are hardly more than notes and transcripts of material to be used in the later book Stephens was planning.

My aim in constructing this edition of the typescript has been to concentrate on fairly long passages in which Stephens was writing from his first-hand knowledge of Synge. Originally, I had intended to eschew continuity and to provide short bridge passages between these long extracts; but as I worked with the typescript, I found that the web of interlocking references in each major passage grew so large that I would have had to provide extensive footnotes to each extract or to edit out irrelevant references—neither of which seemed desirable. If, however, I abandoned the notion of 'selections' and included many short passages as well as a few long ones, I could adhere to a rough continuity,

[1] David H. Greene and Edward M. Stephens, *J. M. Synge: 1871–1909* (1959), p. ix.
[2] Stephens to John Cullen of Methuen & Co., 18 January 1951 (unpublished).

bridge the gaps between extracts with Stephens's own words, and reduce the appearance of editorial activity. This has seemed the most satisfactory way of presenting the essence of Stephens's work despite the fact that what may appear to be a continuous narrative is somewhat uneven in tone and texture. However the sense of continuity is true to Stephens's original intention as biographer, and any unevenness a fairly accurate reflection of the typescript itself.

In at least one important respect, Stephens's account of Synge's life appears to have been coloured by his own views. In his early years, Stephens was strongly influenced by the religious teaching of his family and seems to have been happy to accept, as his uncle John had before him, most of the tenets of evangelical Protestantism. Later in life, Stephens's attitude changed, and there are many references in the typescript to the narrowness, bigotry, and humourlessness of Irish evangelicalism. Stephens assumed that Synge, since he too had deviated from the strict path of regular church attendance, would have endorsed these views; equally, he assumed that Synge would have felt as he did himself about politics, morals, and social behaviour. In one passage, Stephens asserts that Synge found Cherrie Matheson's views on religion 'fantastic' and that he thought the social system in which he and his family lived 'wholly absurd'.[1] There is no evidence however that Synge would have described the evangelicalism of his family or friends or their way of life in such terms. On the contrary, he always respected the integrity of his mother and brothers and expressed very little criticism of their way of life or of their attitudes. He was deeply sensible of his mother's devotion to him and once explained to a friend that she was 'much better than her theories'; he told his fiancée, Molly Allgood, that his brothers and sisters 'could not be kinder' and referred to his brother Sam as 'one of the best fellows in ⟨the⟩ world'—adding however that Sam was so religious that 'we have not much in common'.[2] Obviously Synge and his family were aware that his views differed from theirs on many matters, but there seems to have been a tolerance and generosity in the family relationship which is not always fully brought out in Stephens's typescript.

The greater part of Stephens's work was done during the 1940s, before the resurgence of interest in Synge which has taken place in recent years. There is now a large body of valuable critical commentary on

[1] Stephens TS. 799–800.
[2] *Letters to Molly: John Millington Synge to Maire O'Neill, 1906–1909*, ed. Ann Saddlemyer (1971), pp. 291, 43.

Synge, as well as a definitive edition of his work[1] which provides extensive documentation on his creative methods and on his sources. With the benefit of these critical and textual studies, one can see that many of the conjectures and suggestions made in the Stephens typescript about Synge's sources of inspiration and methods of work, as well as about the dating of particular notes and poems, are not entirely accurate. I am sure that, if Stephens were writing today, he would wish to incorporate into his biography many of the findings of recent scholarship; however I have not felt it within the scope of this edition to refer the reader to modern studies which suggest interpretations different from those in Stephens's typescript, nor to point out instances where he differs in matters of detail from scholars today. In a few places where I have omitted entirely Stephens's rather detailed treatment of events which are by now familiar—the rise of the Abbey Theatre and *The Playboy* riots, for instance—I have included references to modern essays which provide useful summaries.

The main body of the text is taken directly from Stephens's working copy of the typescript, with spelling, punctuation, and capitalization normalized. The connecting passages, enclosed in square brackets, [ ], are paraphrases of Stephens's text and all the judgements—as well as many of the phrases—in these passages come directly from the typescript. Editorial insertions of words or phrases in the main text are enclosed in angle brackets, ⟨ ⟩. If a word or phrase in angle brackets replaces one in the text, no ellipsis has been inserted; otherwise all omissions are noted. Footnotes taken directly from the typescript are followed by Stephens's initials in brackets, (E.M.S.); all other notes have been prepared for this edition.

ACKNOWLEDGEMENTS

I am very grateful to Mrs. Lilo Stephens for her patience, enthusiasm, and hospitality during my work on her husband's papers. Professor David Greene's book has, of course, been invaluable to me and I should like to thank him also for his help and advice. Several members of the Synge family have been kind enough to read the book through before publication and to correct errors, particularly Mr. John S. Synge and Dr. V. M. Synge. I should like to express thanks to Miss Honor Betson, Mrs. Doreen Farrington, Professor A. N. Jeffares, Miss Winifred Matheson, Mrs. Shirley Milligan, Professor Weldon Thornton, and the librarians of Trinity College, Dublin. The late Mrs. Sybil le Brocquy

[1] *J. M. Synge: Collected Works*, 4 vols. (1962–8).

gave her enthusiastic support to the project and helped to get it under way. Professor Ann Saddlemyer has been very helpful in many ways, and Miss Catharine Carver of Oxford University Press has given me invaluable assistance. My wife, Mary-Jean Carpenter, has been a source of constant encouragement.

ANDREW CARPENTER

Dublin, 1973

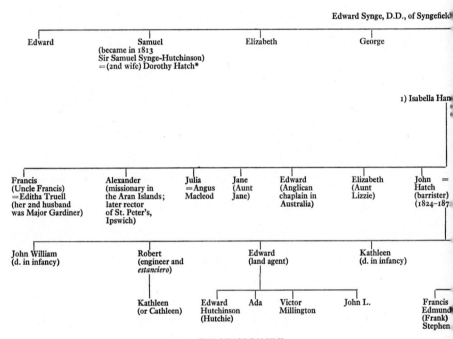

Edward Synge, D.D., of Syngefield

Edward | Samuel (became in 1813 Sir Samuel Synge-Hutchinson) =(2nd wife) Dorothy Hatch* | Elizabeth | George

1) Isabella Ham

Francis (Uncle Francis) =Editha Truell (her 2nd husband was Major Gardiner) | Alexander (missionary in the Aran Islands; later rector of St. Peter's, Ipswich) | Julia =Angus Macleod | Jane (Aunt Jane) | Edward (Anglican chaplain in Australia) | Elizabeth (Aunt Lizzie) | John Hatch (barrister) (1824–187 =

John William (d. in infancy) | Robert (engineer and *estanciero*) | Edward (land agent) | Kathleen (d. in infancy)

Kathleen (or Cathleen) | Edward Hutchinson (Hutchie) | Ada | Victor Millington | John L. | Francis Edmund (Frank) Stephen

THE SYNGE FAMILY

A simplified chart showing only those sides of J. M. Synge's family mentioned in this book. The family can be traced back eight generations before Edward Synge, D.D., to a Milling or Millington who lived in the fifteenth century. Dates have only been supplied for the direct ancestors of J. M. Synge. I am grateful to Mr. John S. Synge for checking this chart.

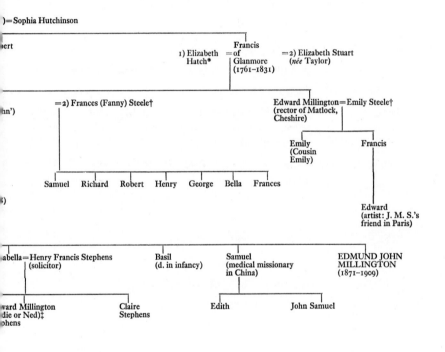

)=Sophia Hutchinson

ert   1) Elizabeth =of   =2) Elizabeth Stuart
                                          Hatch* | Glanmore   (*née* Taylor)
                                                    | (1761–1831)

                                                              Francis

hn')   =2) Frances (Fanny) Steele†   Edward Millington=Emily Steele†
                                                   (rector of Matlock,
                                                   Cheshire)

                                                        Emily   Francis
                                                        (Cousin
                                                        Emily)

        Samuel   Richard   Robert   Henry   George   Bella   Frances

)

                                                              Edward
                                                              (artist: J. M. S.'s
                                                              friend in Paris)

abella=Henry Francis Stephens   Basil   Samuel   EDMUND JOHN
       (solicitor)   (d. in infancy)   (medical missionary   MILLINGTON
                                                  in China)   (1871–1909)

vard Millington   Claire   Edith   John Samuel
die or Ned)‡   Stephens
phens

                                    * sisters, daughters of John Hatch
                                    † sisters
                                    ‡ author of this book

ABBREVIATIONS AND CONVENTIONS

used in text and footnotes

C.W.	*J. M. Synge: Collected Works* (General Editor: Robin Skelton), in 4 vols. (London: Oxford University Press, 1962–8): Vol. I, *Poems*, ed. Robin Skelton Vol. II, *Prose*, ed. Alan Price Vols. III and IV, *Plays*, ed. Ann Saddlemyer
E.M.S.	Edward M. Stephens
GS	David H. Greene and Edward M. Stephens, *J. M. Synge: 1871–1909* (New York and London: Macmillan, 1959)
Letters to Molly	*Letters to Molly: John Millington Synge to Maire O'Neill, 1906–1909*, ed. Ann Saddlemyer (Cambridge, Mass.: Harvard University Press, 1971)
T.C.D.	Trinity College, Dublin
TS.	E. M. Stephens's typescript
[ ]	paraphrase of E. M. Stephens's text
⟨ ⟩	editor's interpolation

PART ONE

1871-1892

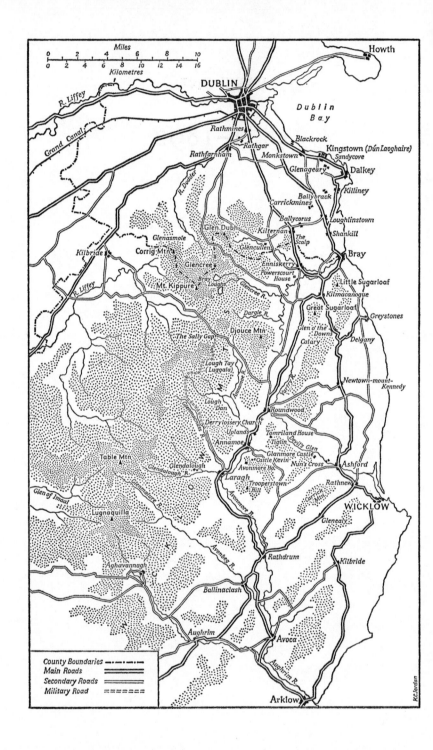

JOHN MILLINGTON SYNGE, as a writer, transcended race and epoch. A certain common quality which gives permanence to folk-lore, to the epic tales of the Greeks, and to the poetry of the Chinese, gives eternal life to *The Playboy of the Western World*. Though his art was in this sense cosmopolitan, John Synge, as he was generally called, used material which was strictly local while his education and environment belonged to a peculiar moment in Irish history. His life lacked incident of the kind that furnishes startling narrative; its story is of simple events which acquire significance only by reason of their effect on his mind and work. He was not one of those writers who are unrelated to particular places because their characters are dream images, false forms from the Ivory Gate.[1] He drew his material from the wealth of his immediate surroundings, rendered peculiarly accessible to him by an accident of birth.

The landlord class to which he belonged had retained all its self-esteem, some of its education, but very little of its moneyed influence. It had with the people of the country an association which had often been hostile but was more intimate than any group of townspeople could hope to establish. For the members of that class who, like John Synge, had not inherited its riches, that association had increased in intimacy. He came of a branch of his family which, at the date of his birth, had been settled in Co. Wicklow for almost a century. Though his home was in the suburbs of Dublin, he drew his inspiration from Co. Wicklow and a part of Co. Dublin that was physically one with the Wicklow hills. He looked on himself as a Wicklowman and his approach to the county and its people developed from childhood under the influence of a potent family tradition.

The understanding of John Synge's work as cosmopolitan art is open to 'strong men, and thieves, and deacons'[2] in any country to the end of time. The understanding of the writer himself, and of how his works came to be written in their unique mode depends on understanding the very soil out of which he grew. . . .

I

[Wicklow is a mountainous county on the east coast of Ireland immediately south of the city and county of Dublin. The part of

---

[1] Virgil, *Aeneid* vi. 895. (E.M.S.)   [2] *C.W.* I. xxxvi.

Wicklow which John Synge knew best, and in which his ancestors had lived for several generations, was the eastern part. This consists of a fertile plain, known as the Golden Belt of Ireland,[1] and a range of high granite hills, still desolate and uninhabited, known as the Wicklow Mountains. Between these two extremes lies a bleak and windswept plateau, separated from the Golden Belt by a range of smaller hills which form a retaining wall or rampart for the plateau.[2] The people of this plateau, and of the upper valleys opening on it from the hills above, have always lived in almost insular isolation despite the fact that they are only about twenty miles from the city of Dublin. It was to this part of the county that the ancestors of John Synge, John Hatch and Samuel McCracken, moved in the middle of the eighteenth century.

[John Hatch was the son of a successful land agent from the north of Ireland; with the assistance of his cousin, Samuel McCracken, he purchased land near the village of Roundwood and McCracken himself bought the large house and demesne of Roundwood which probably incorporated one of the small castles of the dispossessed O'Tooles. On McCracken's death, John Hatch inherited the whole Wicklow property and, as he already possessed substantial estates in Co. Meath and in Dublin, became a landowner of considerable importance. In 1765, when he was approaching middle age, he proposed marriage to Barbara Synge, a member of a distinguished Protestant family, and the possessor of a dowry of £4,000. He was accepted and thus married into an ancient and respected family which had the unique distinction of providing, in a mere three generations, five bishops for the Church of Ireland. One of these bishops, George Synge, Bishop of Clogher, who died in 1660, was described in his epitaph as *Vir gravis admodum et doctus*[3]—an inspired phrase which described not only the dead bishop but a type of character which was to persist in the family for at least two hundred years.

[It was natural that the new Mrs. Hatch, belonging to a family of some importance, should hope for sons who would inherit some of

---

[1] The term was first used by Sir Jonah Barrington in his *Personal Sketches of his Own Times* (London, 1827), II. 149.

[2] Throughout the TS., Stephens refers to this range of hills as 'the retaining wall'.

[3] 'A man of Singular Gravity, and great Learning. . . .' *The Whole Works of Sir James Ware . . .*, revised by Walter Harris (Dublin, 1764), I. 579.

the gifts of their episcopal forebears and also make good use of the opportunities that wealth affords. But she had only two children, both daughters. The girls were likely to inherit considerable property when they grew up, and there was therefore the problem of finding for each of them a suitable match. In the event, they married their cousins, the brothers Francis and Samuel Synge, sons of their mother's brother Edward Synge D.D., of Syngefield, Birr, in Co. Offaly. Some years later, Samuel Synge inherited a baronetcy from his uncle, Sir Francis Hutchinson, and changed his name to Hutchinson; his branch of the family remained in Co. Offaly. Francis Synge and his bride moved to Co. Wicklow soon after their marriage in 1786 to live on the estate at Roundwood, and thus became the first holders of the Synge name to settle in the area. Ten years later, when John Hatch died, it was decided that, since Francis Synge was already in possession of the house and farm at Roundwood, the whole Wicklow estate should form part of his wife's share of her father's property. It was in this way that Francis Synge inherited the lands in Wicklow which were to form the basis for a great estate.

[The property he now controlled ran from the rich lands of the Golden Belt up into the waste lands of the mountains. Experience had taught him that the hardy but ill-fed stock from the plateau improved very profitably on the farms of the Golden Belt and that mountain ewes would thrive in spring if they were brought down for lambing to the sheltered fields. He intended to form an estate lying partly in each district and, with the help of his uncle Sir Francis Hutchinson, who was a leading landlord in the area, managed to purchase various parcels of land suitable to his purpose. The most important of these were the hill farm of Upper Tiglin and the lands on the southern side of a famous beauty spot, the Devil's Glen. Here the Vartry River had cut a spectacular rift through the hills of the retaining wall on its way from the plateau to the coast.]

The Devil's Glen was one of those natural features which were most prized by the demesne makers of the period. ⟨At the end of the eighteenth century,⟩ it had just become accessible to visitors, and was regarded as a beauty spot of sufficient importance to deserve special comment from the topographer of a then fashionable guide book, *The Post Chaise Companion*. After describing the beauties of Dunran the topographer continued:

The curious traveller should venture still farther into these awful scenes of majestic nature. By the attention of the late Lord Rossmore and Charles Tottenham Esq., he may have an opportunity of exploring the long concealed beauties of the Devil's Glen, a road being carried from Dunran to the farther end, where the river Vartry falls about one hundred feet with astonishing fury into the Glen. . . . Opposite to the boldest promontory, but in a spot finely embosomed with wood, Mr. Tottenham has built a rustic temple admirably adapted for contemplation, and equally well suited to the gayer purposes of rural entertainment.[1]

These embellishments of nature were on the northern side; the southern side still awaited development and was easily accessible from the large house, then called Glenmouth, which stood on high ground overlooking the river. The house had a pleasant view to the distant sea and was reached by a long avenue winding up an open sunny lawn while at its northern end was a great square of stables and outhouses built on the plan of an artillery barracks, for which it may at one time have been used.

Francis Synge believed that only by metamorphosing the house could he make it a fitting residence for the owner of the estate which he was consolidating. Unhappily he undertook this wer'; twenty years too late; the tide of culture had turned. The landlords, feeling that their self-assurance was in danger, were growing ostentatious. Not only did ⟨Francis Synge⟩ enlarge the house, but he built towers at each of its corners overlooking the glen, hid its roof with a crenellated parapet, and renamed it 'Glanmore Castle', the Castle of the Great Glen.[2] To this house ⟨he⟩ moved as soon as the work was done, and for some years Roundwood was but little used. . . .

[By the end of the first decade of the nineteenth century, Francis Synge had carried out his plans for the development of the estate with apparent success.] Taking into account all his lands in Wicklow, irrespective of their tenure, his estate stretched with little interruption for about ten miles, from the heights of Djouce

---

[1] William Wilson, *The Post Chaise Companion* . . ., 3rd ed. (Dublin, 1803), col. 426.

[2] Glanmore Castle, a notable example of Gothic-revival architecture in Ireland, is still standing. Until recently it was in a state of disrepair, but its present owners are restoring some of its features. Other buildings mentioned in this section have also been preserved, including Kilfee schoolhouse, Nun's Cross church, and many of the slate-built farm buildings of the Glanmore estate. The Devil's Glen is now open to the public.

Mountain across the plateau, down the ⟨hills of the⟩ retaining wall and up again to Carrick, a long jagged hill lying parallel with the coast and breaking unexpectedly the undulating contours of the Golden Belt. A large part of the estate was let to tenant farmers whose rents provided a steady income. The portion which Francis Synge retained in his own control consisted firstly of the farm including about three hundred acres at Roundwood, secondly, in view from Roundwood but in the distance, on the coping of the retaining wall, the hill farm of Tiglin, of about the same extent, and thirdly, adjacent to the castle, some fifteen hundred acres, an area great enough to provide a demesne with pleasure grounds, a home farm, and deer park.

The development of the demesne was work which Francis Synge loved. His expenditure was extravagant, but his results were successful. He planted trees carefully chosen to suit different situations, and so arranged as to give beautiful combinations of foliage in spring and autumn. For the sake of their white blossoms among the young leaves he scattered cherry trees through the woods. The formation of the ground afforded him wonderful opportunities. There was the steep retaining wall where trees would grow one above another from behind the garden at Glanmore to the fences of Tiglin farm; there was the glen with jagged outcrops of rock to provide platforms from which there would always be a view over the highest tree-tops; and there were sheltered slopes to the river where it ran gently in the valley below the lawn. . . .

Large as was the estate, the rents of the tenants would not have been sufficient to meet its expenses, and it was not free from encumbrances . . . [since some of the land was still held on mortgage]. Francis Synge thought himself secure because part of the property which he had derived from his father-in-law consisted of well-secured rents and good building sites in the city of Dublin. He seemed to regard this wealth as inexhaustible ⟨and⟩ in 1814 he purchased, as his town house, the magnificent Georgian mansion built by Lord Ely and generally known as No. 8 Ely Place. . . .

[As his schemes progressed, Francis Synge realized that he should educate his heir to maintain the position in which he hoped to establish the family. He sent his eldest son John to both Trinity College, Dublin, and Magdalen College, Oxford, after which he

arranged for the young man to go on an extended tour of the
Continent. Between the years 1812 and 1815, John travelled in
Portugal, Spain, Italy, and Switzerland: he took his travels seriously
as part of his education, recorded them in a journal, and made
sketches of the places he visited with the accuracy of a skilled
draftsman. Undoubtedly the most important event of the tour was
John's meeting with the famous Swiss educationalist, Pestalozzi;[1]
he was soon completely converted to Pestalozzi's system of 'natural'
education and returned to Ireland fired with the twin desires of
advancing the evangelical movement of the Protestant Church and
the educational methods of Pestalozzi. He set up a private printing
press at Roundwood to further these aims and also took his place as
one of the leading figures in the evangelical movement in Wicklow.
Perhaps the most interesting products of the printing press were the
lesson-sheets printed according to the principles of Pestalozzi, and
a series of edifying reading exercises for children.[2]]

John Synge was to put faith in his educational theories to the
severest test, for he became the father of a long family. There is no
reason to suppose that he ever doubted the wisdom of his convic-
tions, and it is certain that his teaching had a profound effect on the
lives of his children. . . .

[In 1818, he married a young heiress named Isabella Hamilton
who brought a fine property into settlement;] John's father made
over to him the old house at Roundwood so that the young couple
might make their home on the Wicklow estate. After living at
Roundwood for the first nine years of his married life, John removed to Devonshire in 1827. . . . It was said that Mrs. Synge was in
bad health and that the hope of her being cured by a milder climate
was his principal reason for uprooting his family: but there can be
little doubt that [his motive was a religious one] ⟨and that⟩ he was
drawn to the south of England by the gathering there of 'the
Brethren'.[3] On leaving Roundwood, ⟨John Synge⟩ dismantled his

---

[1] Johann Heinrich Pestalozzi (1746–1827), Swiss educational theorist.

[2] Details and excerpts are given in Stephens's TS., 85–90.

[3] The Plymouth Brethren, as they are usually called, are a community of Christians of evangelical beliefs. The movement started in Dublin in 1825 but took its
name from Plymouth where the first English congregation was established in
1831. John Nelson Darby (1800–82), a clergyman of the Church of Ireland active in
Wicklow and supported by John Synge (Stephens TS. 55–6), became the leader of
the movement; after a disagreement in 1845, his followers broke away from the
rest of the company and formed the Exclusive Brethren.

printing press and took it with him to Devonshire, hoping to devote it to the service of God.

His move to England was an important event in John's career. It meant that for some years, when his father was growing old, he turned his back on all responsibility for the large Irish estate and, in company with other religious enthusiasts, immersed himself in dreams of the Kingdom of Heaven. . . .

[In 1831, on Francis Synge's death, John became master of the Irish estates. Though he would undoubtedly have preferred to remain in England, John acknowledged that 'a desmesne of 1600 acres, in the midst of a property of 4000, will require attention and labour, and indeed, were I disposed to cast it all behind my back tomorrow, justice to others would oblige me for some time to labour at it.'[1] Thus when he had taken the necessary steps for giving up his home in Devon, John Synge returned to Wicklow bringing his household goods, his printing press, the family servants, and his seven children, three daughters and four sons, the third of whom became the father of J. M. Synge.]

In spite of his pious resolutions to labour at the estate for some time in justice to others and to treat the work as 'mere duty', John Synge soon found himself carried away by the magnitude of his undertaking. No less than his father he longed to make the demesne of Glanmore a place for visitors to admire. He found a system of avenues leading from the castle into the Glen, but the work of continuing a wide path, high along its steep side to its further end, is attributed to him.

From the pleasure grounds at the castle, the Upper Glen path passed beside the garden wall and then along the side of the more open part of the valley, winding up through beech trees, which stood in an undergrowth of laurels. Having climbed steadily for about half a mile it reached a great outcrop of rock, which, facing a cliff on the opposite hill, formed one side of the entrance to the narrow glen. Here the path turned abruptly and passed through a cutting in the rocks into dank shadows which seemed deepened by the sunshine when it struck the tree-covered hillside beyond the river. For the next mile or more the path, rising gradually, was built along the precipitous side of the glen. In many places it was carried on a wall of uncemented masonry as thick as the rampart of a

---

[1] Letter of 29 December 1831, John Synge to Miss Bridson, the family governess. Stephens TS. 73.

prehistoric fort. . . . At places where promontories afforded the best viewpoints, the path was widened into small platforms, and at one point, where it reached a perpendicular cliff, it was carried through an arch cut in the solid rock. Beyond this arch the path continued rising into the upper end of the glen, until it came to a place where the noise of the waterfall could just be distinguished from the ordinary sound of the river, and emerged on the smooth high fields of Tiglin.

John's second wife[1] loved the glen, and used to go often to a place near its entrance where there was a cottage hidden among the rocks and trees. At this cottage, known to her descendants as 'The Grand-mother's Tea House', tea used to be prepared on summer after-noons for parties from the Castle. Near the cottage a path with rustic stone steps at its steeper points led up to a seat at the top of the great outcrop of rock, which marked the entrance to the narrow part of the glen. The seat was sheltered with stones and bushes, and the moss-covered top of the rock sloped south. It was a sheltered, sunny place where butterflies spread themselves in the warmth, and from which there was a wonderful view across the Golden Belt to the sea. Behind the seat there was the dark green of the oaks and the shady glen rich with the smell of damp ferns and sedge.

To connect the River Avenue with the Upper Glen path, near the Grandmother's Tea House, John Synge built a great flight of five hundred rustic steps, winding up like a goat track among the trees on the steep side of the glen. His great-grandchildren, nearly a century later, used to delight in finding the flagstones one by one among the moss and undergrowth, and in clearing each stone as they climbed.

John Synge might not have undertaken his costly engineering works in the glen if he had not had skilled quarry men on the estate for a wholly different purpose. About half a mile from the Castle, cut in the foot of the retaining wall, there was an old slate quarry which he hoped to make profitable. He brought from Wales men skilled in cutting roofing slates, and began the development of the quarry on a large scale. Metal lines were laid to carry trucks for a mile or more to a small stream by which a watermill was built for

[1] His first wife, Isabella, died in February 1830. Miss Bridson brought up the large family and supervised the removal to Ireland. After the return to Glanmore, John followed the family pattern and married the sister of his brother's wife, Fanny Steel. She, like her predecessor, presented him with seven children.

dressing slates, flags, and gravestones. The loaded trucks ran down by their own weight to an arch under the public road and with little or no assistance through it and down to the mill along the track of the disused Wicklow road. Horses drew the empty trucks back to the quarry. The system was well planned and the work well done, but the grain of the slate was not satisfactory for cutting. The roofing slates proved too small, and the demand for tombstones was not sufficiently brisk. The enterprise was a failure, so the story goes; but no written accounts of the quarry and its output have been preserved.

At this time the economic depression which followed the Napoleonic wars was affecting all markets. The tenant farmers were suffering heavily. Even in times of prosperity they lived from hand to mouth, and, as prices fell, the collection of the rents that they paid for their holdings became increasingly difficult. In all parts of Ireland, landlords, blind to the drying up of the sources from which they could have hoped to repay their creditors, borrowed large sums.

John Synge's position was not exceptional. The farming and forestry of his estate were unprofitable and the rent collection poor. Though he would have shrunk from spending money in profligate living, as many of the landlords were doing, his mind was so preoccupied by religion that in matters of finance he was reckless. He met deficits by borrowing, and maintained his estate in apparent affluence while drifting towards inevitable catastrophe. . . . He seemed to regard retrenchment as impossible, and as his sons came of age, he asked them to sink in Glanmore money secured to them by family settlements. They advocated economies and stoutly refused to sign away property that their father was unable to encumber. Heated arguments followed, but there was no compromise. In 1845 the inevitable crash came. Judgements were put into execution, and the bailiffs were in the house when John died.

Tradition has it that he and his faithful butler had previously buried the family silver which has never since been found, and that the total ready money in the house was seven shillings and sixpence. It is said that faced with this situation the infuriated bailiffs seized the corpse in the hope of selling it for dissection, but that it was recovered by the family on the avenue and safely buried ⟨in the graveyard of the church built by his father at Nun's Cross⟩.

[On John Synge's death, his eldest son, Francis, inherited the estate. It] was loaded with a crushing burden of debt and in April 1847 a petition ... was filed in the ... High Court praying for the sale of the Synge estates. The matter was transferred to the Encumbered Estates Court and the usual tedious investigations were made and accounts taken. Meanwhile Francis lived at Glanmore as tenant under the court and with him two of his sisters, Jane and Julia. It was difficult to live a frugal life in a big house surrounded by a large demesne, but their minds were set on saving the Wicklow estate. Under family settlements, John Synge's children were entitled to some money which enabled Francis and his two sisters to live quietly in their old home and to continue joining in the social life they had enjoyed with their neighbours. ...

In the course of two years, the proceedings in court were nearing completion. ... Francis offered £40,000 to the Commissioners of Encumbered Estates, but the offer was refused and he was compelled to await in suspense the result of a public auction. ... [When this took place in December 1850, all interest in Roundwood House and in much of the land around it passed out of the family. However, the plans laid by Uncle Francis—as he was generally known in the Synge family—were partly successful.] He was declared the purchaser of Glanmore, Tiglin, and a large portion of the adjoining property for the sum of £25,000.

The furniture of the castle was put up for auction, but most of it seems to have been bought in by members of the family. There is a local tradition that in spite of their religious teaching, the Synges were popular with the people of the district and that good feeling manifested itself in the crisis. It is said that the blacksmith, a huge man, attended the auction and, by backing any unwelcome bidder against the wall, smothered efforts to raise prices. It is said too that on the night after the Glanmore estate was knocked down to Uncle Francis, there was a torchlight procession and a party at the foot of Ballymoroghroe Hill in the 'proppy house'—so called because of the timber supports which kept its walls from falling. ...

[Uncle Francis was now head of the family and, as such, he took seriously the responsibility of Glanmore and the estate; under his careful management, the property began to recover and by the middle of the 1850s, it was again prospering in a small way. His brothers, though, were forced to enter the professions. Alexander decided to seek ordination and he became the first Protestant clergyman to take up regular duties in the Aran Islands: John

Hatch Synge (father to the playwright) was called to the Bar, and the other son, Edward, also became a clergyman and spent his life as a missionary in the Australian bush.] Of the girls, Julia (the eldest) married a seafaring man from the Hebrides called Angus Macleod who, on account of his great piety, was forgiven by some members of her family for his lack of social position. Jane, afterwards known to our family as 'Aunt Jane', and her sister Elizabeth died spinsters. . . .

John Hatch Synge often visited his brother Francis⟨at Glanmore⟩ and during vacations worked on the estate as he had done in his youth. He had established a small practice at the Bar and his earnings [with the rents from a property which he had inherited in Co. Galway] provided him with an income which enabled him to marry.

It happened that a widow, Mrs. Traill, used to take her four daughters and three sons to spend each summer . . . within a short distance of Glanmore. The girls were clever and handsome and had been brought up in the same religious tradition as inspired the Glanmore household; but they unfortunately lacked dowries. It was said that Francis was very much attracted by Agnes Traill, but after the financial crisis through which his estate had passed, a match with her seemed impossible. ⟨However,⟩ his brother John fell in love with her sister, Kathleen, and married her ⟨in 1856⟩ when she was eighteen. Of their children five survived infancy, one daughter and four sons, of whom the youngest was John Millington Synge.

2

Kathleen Traill's parentage and birth are recorded in her father's ornate handwriting on the front page of his large family Bible. First is entered his marriage:

The Rev. Robert Traill, son of the Venerable the Archdeacon of Connor, married to Anne, eldest daughter of Sir Samuel Hayes, late of Drumboe Castle, Co. Donegal, Bart. in the parish church of St. Peter's Dublin by the Rev. John Sweeney, Rector of Cleenish, on the 11th day of February 1829.

There follow records of the births of three daughters and a son and then the entry:

Kathleen their fourth daughter, born 25th March 1838, baptized April

15th following being Easter Monday, and registered in the parish of
Schull in the diocese of Cork.

As years passed and Kathleen grew up and married, the similarity
which developed between her life and her mother's clearly indicated
that she both inherited Mrs. Traill's gifts and adopted her philosophy. Mrs. Traill was one of those clever women who in the last
century found employment for their genius in rearing and educating
large families. In the eighteen years of her married life she had nine
children, four sons and five daughters. As in turn they grew old
enough for lessons, they were taught under her supervision, by the
governess, Miss Osborne, who shared the evangelical beliefs of
Dr. and Mrs. Traill. . . .

In common with most mothers of large families, Mrs. Traill
felt the grief of casualties among her children. It was not until she
had three daughters that her first son was born, and he lived for
only a fortnight. Her eldest daughter Elizabeth died from diphtheria
and her third daughter Anne became incurably deaf as a result of
suffering from scarlatina. These and many other sorrows Mrs.
Traill met with the belief that they formed part of a Divine plan,
of which the wisdom would be revealed to the blessed, in a life
beyond the grave.

Her care of her children was not of a kind likely to undermine
their independence. The seven who survived childhood grew up
self-reliant and enterprising and though events compelled some to
scatter, none of them ever lost the sense of family unity which her
force of character had created. She was afterwards to be an important influence in the early life of her youngest grandson, John
Millington Synge, and was to see her great-grandchildren receive
their first instruction in the faith she taught her own children from
their infancy. . . .[1]

[Her husband, the Revd. Robert Traill, had been born in 1793 in
Co. Antrim. His beliefs had thus originated in the harsh political
Protestantism of the northern counties and it was the evangelical
movement which caught his enthusiasm. This enthusiasm became
part of his life and, though he was a man of considerable talents—
he was, among other things, the translator of Josephus' *The Jewish
Wars*—Dr. Traill had great difficulty in securing for himself any

---

[1] These great-grandchildren included Edward Stephens, his brother, and his
sister.

clerical appointment: his zeal was too great. He spent his life, as he put it, waging war against popery in its thousand forms of wickedness, which did not always endear him to his ecclesiastical superiors.[1] At last, in 1830, his search for a living was successful and he became rector of Schull on the south-west coast of Co. Cork.]

His parish was thickly populated: from the time of his appointment, he worked among the poverty-stricken people consciously under the shadow of impending calamity. In the winter of 1846, when he had been rector for fifteen years, came the famine, which he had believed inevitable, caused by the failure of the potato crop. The next year, when his translation of Josephus was going through the press, was a second year of famine rendered more horrible than the first by increasing pestilence. Dr. Traill died of the fever, caught from the people among whom he worked, and was buried in the graveyard overlooking the Atlantic.

At the time of his marriage, provision had been made for his wife: but unfortunately hopes of large returns had led those responsible for the trust funds to invest unwisely in copper mines near Schull. Dr. Traill had expended a large sum in obtaining original drawings of historic places in ⟨the Holy Land⟩ as illustrations for his translation of Josephus. In the famine years, he had devoted much of his own money to the relief of his neighbours and parishioners. When he died, his widow ⟨had, of course, to leave the rectory: she also⟩ found that only by the strictest economy could she meet the expenses of her family from her small income. . . .

Mrs. Traill settled in the neighbourhood of Blackrock, some four or five miles south of Dublin, in 1848. Ten years earlier D'Alton, in his *History of the County of Dublin*, had described the place as 'one of the most ruinous suburbs of the metropolis . . ., a collection of deserted lodging-houses and bathing villas'.[2] But following the construction of the Dublin-Kingstown[3] Railway, between 1832 and 1834, came a change in the character of the district, which at the time of Mrs. Traill's arrival was a developing residential suburb of Victorian propriety.

The general fall in the incomes of country estates, having reduced many to insolvency, and rendered many others unable to support

[1] Long and vigorous passages from Dr. Traill's notebooks, including the remark about popery, are included in the Stephens TS. 118–27.
[2] John D'Alton, *A History of the County of Dublin* (Dublin, 1838), p. 863.
[3] Kingstown is now known by its Gaelic name of Dún Laoghaire.

dower houses or to provide portions for younger children, was causing a migration of people belonging to the landlord class. This migration tended to increase the growth of the Dublin suburbs, and to fill them with a population fantastically incongruous with its new surroundings. One by one houses in long stucco terraces facing across small front gardens to the public road were occupied by people who had lived in mansions looking out on gravel sweeps, wide lawns, and fine trees. These people, who had lost much of their money and most of their libraries and learning, increased their class-consciousness in self-defence. They clung together like members of a secret society, and refused to mix with the prosperous townspeople whose neighbours they had become. Their emotions had suffered violence; their beliefs had become restrictive; if anyone among them chanced to inherit the genius of their race, he found himself unhonoured by his kin. In suburban life there was no outlet for the energy of their children, who, cut off from their traditions, tended to seek abroad scope for their enterprise.

For Mrs. Traill, marriage had meant exchanging her life at Drumboe Castle for life in a remote country rectory. . . . On the walls of the rectory she had hung, in gilt frames, sketches of her old home, of its avenues and trees, and of its gate lodge with a background of distant hills. As her elder children had learnt to understand pictures, it was from these they had first known their mother's home.

Though there was a great contrast between the demesne in the hills near Strabane and the surroundings of the rectory in the seaside parish of Schull, the contrast was not of a character that could do violence to feeling. The Dublin suburbs were so out of harmony with both that the move to Blackrock impressed with a lasting sense of loss not only Mrs. Traill but those of her children who could remember Schull. In their new surroundings, the Atlantic shore and the graveyard where Dr. Traill lay buried seemed strangely far away, while the places recalled by Mrs. Traill's pictures acquired a yet greater distance.

Mrs. Traill's money affairs proved to be in a very confused state after the death of her husband, and it seemed uncertain that her income would be sufficient for her very modest needs. She was advised to take her family on the Continent, where she could live cheaply while her affairs were being put in order. Many women would have hesitated, but she saw the wisdom of a step which would effect a necessary economy, and afford her family an opportunity of learning French. Mrs. Traill accordingly set out for Bordeaux with her governess Miss Osborne and her seven children, the youngest of whom was at that time only three years old.

After about twelve months she was securely in receipt of a small regular income, and was able to return to Blackrock in 1850, the year in which Francis Synge redeemed Glanmore from the control of the Encumbered Estates Court. It was in the following summers that Mrs. Traill and her children went regularly to stay for their holidays in Wicklow, and became intimate friends of the Synge family. In 1855 Mrs. Traill moved from Blackrock to the neighbouring parish of Monkstown, where she took a house in Montpelier Parade, a tall eighteenth-century terrace on the main road from Dublin to Kingstown. From this house in the following year her daughter Kathleen at the age of eighteen married John Hatch Synge.

3

Mr. and Mrs. Synge lived first at No. 1, and afterwards at No. 4, Hatch Street, one of the wide residential streets made through John Hatch's property as Dublin spread to the south and west. Here were born Mrs. Synge's two elder sons Robert and Edward, and Annie, her only daughter to survive infancy.

Mr. Synge's practice as a barrister consisted mostly of conveyancing, the branch of law to which he was temperamentally most suited. He was not one of those men who try to separate their business from their home lives, and often in the evening his young wife helped him to compare documents which seemed to her endless and unintelligible. From time to time Mr. Synge left home for his usual visits to his Galway estate. When he went in winter, he took his gun for duck shooting on the western bogs. Robert used to say that one of his earliest recollections of Hatch Street was of being shown the birds that his father had shot in Galway, and looking at the iridescent plumage of a mallard's neck lying on the shining mahogany of the hall table.

Mr. and Mrs. Synge had no wish to move in society. They would not have enjoyed social functions or diplomatic dinner parties, and would have shrunk from seeking through society preferment for themselves, or, in later years, advancement for their children. Their circle of friends would have extended but little beyond the few with whom they were associated in religious belief had they not, in common with most Irish people, kept contact with their relations no matter how remote.

By living very quietly, people like Mr. and Mrs. Synge did not in any way detach themselves from the privileged minority, the Protestant governing class, which was held together by inter-marriage, by tradition, and by fear of the Roman Catholic majority in the country. This minority controlled the opportunities for rising professional men in Ireland. Its members were quick to recognize among their number, and to advance by their support, the conventional clever young men who were likely to prove useful in upholding their privileges. Its members were willing to strain their resources in providing for those of their sons who could not be absorbed at home, an education which would fit them for the services of the British Crown, or for professions by which they might earn their livings abroad.

It often happened that men who had spent their best years pioneering in foreign countries returned to Ireland in later life, and of these some retired with considerable fortunes. Those who returned rich were enthusiastically welcomed by the Protestant minority, as people who would contribute to the sporting social life of the country, and who would revive the frozen prejudices of their youth if they felt in need of political opinions.

The people of the Protestant minority were slow to inquire into the losses resulting from the export of their professional men, but they were quick to recognize the danger of independent genius in any member of the rising generations. These people were often kindly and complaisant, and were usually incapable of seeing any anomaly in their position. Most of them assumed that any of their kin who questioned their values forfeited all right to their support. As the children of John Hatch Synge grew up it was on this group that they depended for their opportunities, and under pressure from its public opinion they formed ideas of their position in society and of the careers that they should adopt. . . .

As the revenues of the landlord class continued to diminish, the tendency for its younger men to emigrate steadily increased. The chances of Mrs. Synge's three brothers finding work in Ireland had been greatly reduced by their father's early death, and the occupations regarded by their family as suitable for gentlemen were very limited. None of the three remained at home.

Basil, the eldest, went to India, as an engineer, but soon became dangerously ill. In an attempt to return home he reached Cairo, but could travel no further. His mother, who used to throw all her energy into every family emergency, met him in Cairo. There she and her deaf daughter Anne, whom she had taken as her companion, nursed him until he died.

His brothers Robert and Edmund were more fortunate. They went as pioneers to the Argentine, and established themselves on adjoining ranches in north Santa Fé. Their nearest town, Rosario, was two days' journey south, as the railway that afterwards developed the district had not then been completed. Land could be bought for about sixpence an acre, but it was in its natural state without houses, road, or fences, and still in danger of being raided by Indians.

For Mrs. Traill this time was overshadowed by the unhappiness of partings, but she was not a jealous mother who would hold back her children from enterprise or marriage. She had not brought them up to cling round their home, though her influence gave them a sense of family unity, and led them to maintain their contacts with her and each other. Her daughters Agnes and Harriet were married, Agnes to William Steward Ross, a northern clergyman, and Harriet to Cathcart Dobbs of the Indian Civil Service, while her sons Robert and Edmund, when they were established in the Argentine, brought out wives to their ranches.

In this way it happened that Mrs. Synge's children grew up to regard cousins who arrived from the Argentine or from India as part of their family circle, and themselves as belonging to a large though scattered clan. From it they derived almost all their experience of people and remained quite unaccustomed to strangers. They did not resent their isolation which seemed to them natural. Children often adopt the tacit assumptions of their elders even when contrary to experience, and both Mr. and Mrs. Synge tacitly assumed that they were only visitors to Dublin, and that, as their real associations were with Glanmore and Co. Wicklow, they did not need friends among their neighbours.

Glanmore did not remain many years without a mistress, for on 7 November 1861, Francis Synge married Editha Truell, daughter of Robert Holt Truell who lived at Clonmannon, a large house near the sea some three or four miles from Glanmore. She had a dowry of £10,000 and a reputation for great piety. Mrs. Synge's children

regarded their Uncle Francis and Aunt Editha, the master and mistress of the big house in Wicklow, as the most important people in
their circle. . . .

[Aunt Editha was a conscientious and devoted member of the
'Brethren'; she had been brought up in the faith by her mother]
who held firmly to a belief in evangelical religion and in homeopathic medicine. These beliefs seemed closely related in her mind,
for she was often heard to say: 'I hate allopathy and the Church of
England.' Both mother and daughter, while they had retained the
manners and prejudices of their family, had lost its culture.

Aunt Editha was tall with a good carriage and a large mild face.
To people whom she knew personally, she was kind. She came to
Glanmore full of enthusiasm for change. Neither she nor Uncle
Francis attended the church ⟨at Nun's Cross⟩ that his grandfather
had helped to build; ⟨they⟩ went instead to meetings of the 'Brethren' at Kilfee schoolhouse. Under her direction the house was
renovated; small window-panes were replaced by plate glass, old
furniture was sold, and tradition everywhere brushed aside. Aunt
Jane and Aunt Julia soon left, although before her marriage Aunt
Editha had always said that Glanmore should continue to be their
home.

Uncle Francis cared little about Aunt Editha's innovations; his
mind was fixed on the management of the estate and for his predecessors, who brought it to ruin, he had no reverence. He rarely
spoke of their mistakes but once, when a guest asked whether the
portraits in the dining-room were of his ancestors, his nephew
Robert heard him say: 'If they were, they wouldn't be there.'

He was a good practical farmer and well known as a driver of a
four-in-hand. He had learnt his skill in managing four horses from
the driver of the stage-coach when, as a student in Trinity College,
he was frequently a passenger between Ashford and Dublin. An
old man in Glanmore used to say: 'I often saw the master drive
eight hundred pounds' worth of horses up to the door under the
one whip.'

Uncle Francis aimed at making his estate as self contained as a
feudal manor. The old quarry had been unprofitable for supplying
roofing slates but he utilized its durable stone for great new farm
buildings by the public road. He developed an intensive system of
agriculture, cultivated a large walled garden, and maintained a
forge and carpenter's shop on the estate. To secure cheap supplies

of coal, he joined with a local skipper in paying the expenses of a schooner which brought direct shipments to Wicklow harbour. Working on the farm, there were up to a dozen 'bothy' boys—young unmarried labourers for whom lodging was provided in one of the older buildings. Uncle Francis used to hold a Bible class for them every Sunday morning and when it was over used to watch them march down before him to public worship. At times when it was not under supervision, life in the bothy was wild; on the arrival of a new boy, his comrades used to take him into a field at the back and ring him like a horse, with a long whip to keep up his pace. Once when a boy found a sod of turf in a pot where he had left a lump of bacon boiling, he threw the scalding sod at the first suspect and nearly killed the wrong man. . . .

Aunt Editha interested herself in the management of the estate school at Kilfee and provided a bedroom at the Castle for Miss De Lion, the new teacher. 'Dear Martie', as Aunt Editha called her, was a half-caste from the West Indies and knew nothing of Pestalozzi and his methods of education. She had the simple faith that inspired Negro spirituals and Aunt Editha felt sure that under her tuition the children at the school would have no temptation to wander towards popery. When she was not engaged in teaching, she was Aunt Editha's companion and lady help and used to come to a whistle that hung from Aunt Editha's belt.

In the work of the estate, there was increasing evidence of energy and co-ordination. Uncle Francis had the capacity for controlling a large undertaking; his personality so impressed the people of the neighbourhood that stories of his doings lived in local tradition half a century after his death. Once at a fair, when sales were slow, he bought all the animals and was cheered by the people as his procession moved off. His work as a Protestant evangelist naturally excited resentment in the district, but the people mostly forgave him for trying to undermine their religion because he believed sincerely in his own. He had succeeded in re-establishing the fortunes of Glanmore and was justifying, in a reduced form, the plan that his grandfather had made for a great estate depending partly on rents from tenants on the plateau and partly on a farm in the Golden Belt drawing supplies of sheep and cattle from the higher districts.

Meanwhile his brother grew weary of living in the city and about the year 1865 moved from Hatch Street to Newtown Villas, a group of houses in the country on the southern outskirts of Dublin. Their site was on the high ground by the right bank of the river Dodder near the demesne of Rathfarnham Castle, and they had a clear view to the Dublin Mountains across the quiet dairy farms that supplied milk to the city.

At Newtown Villas two more children were born to Mr. and Mrs. Synge, on 15 March 1867 a son Samuel and on 16 April 1871 another son who was christened Edmund John Millington. The name Edmund seems never to have been used; for his mother called him 'Johnnie' and, when he grew up, his usual signature was 'J. M. Synge.'

4

During John's first year, the household at Newtown Villas was plunged in continual mourning. . . . [Four of the seven children brought by John's grandfather to Glanmore in 1832 died within twelve months of his birth: Aunt Betty caught typhoid fever while nursing two of John's cousins; his Uncle Edward, who had spent his life as a clergyman in Australia, and his uncle Alec who had begun his ministry in the Aran Islands, both died in England.] The worst shock for the household at Newtown Villas was however still to come, for on 13 April ⟨1872⟩ John's father died. He had called to inquire for a neighbour who was suffering from smallpox. The neighbour recovered but Mr. Synge caught the infection, which for him proved fatal. He was nearly forty-nine years of age and had been steadily gaining at his profession a reputation for legal knowledge and sound judgement. Mrs. Synge used to speak of her short married life as having been singularly happy and of her husband as a man of few words and deep religious conviction—*vir gravis admodum et doctus.*

Shortly before Mr. Synge's death, Mrs. Traill had moved from Monkstown to No. 3 Orwell Park, a small house near Newtown Villas on the opposite side of the river Dodder. It happened that Mrs. Synge, on being left a widow, was able to obtain a letting of No. 4, and so had the consolation of her mother's help in bringing up her children. Her income from the Galway estate was about £400 a year which, with the income from . . . money that Uncle Edward had left to her children by his will, enabled her to give them a good education.[1] For sixteen years Mrs. Synge lived at No. 4

[1] Uncle Edward had left John £100: together with a small legacy from his aunt Jane, it provided him with a modest private income for the rest of his life.

Orwell Park which was John's home from infancy until he was a student in Trinity College. . . .

[Orwell Park was situated on the very edge of Dublin; a stone's throw from the house, the road from Dublin dipped and crossed the Dodder bridge. Beyond the bridge, a by-road turned up by the unfenced grassy bank of the river, past the gate to the demesne of Rathfarnham Castle. The bank of the Dodder and the grounds of Rathfarnham Castle[1] were John's playgrounds in childhood and were the places where he first became interested in natural history. But the countryside of Co. Wicklow, particularly the area around Glanmore, also played an important and continuing part in his childhood. Mrs. Synge first brought John to Glanmore in his infancy; she used to travel by rail with her children to Rathnew where Uncle Francis met the train with his four-in-hand to drive them the four miles to the house.]

Uncle Francis and Aunt Editha, though themselves childless, were singularly tolerant of children and imposed no unnecessary restrictions upon their visitors. The elder boys were free to go out walking for a whole day whenever they wished and to fish and shoot on the estate. The younger children played in the shrubberies and pleasure grounds near the house with very little supervision. All the children accepted their elders' belief that neither the company of other children nor the playing of organized games was necessary to their enjoyment.

Mrs. Synge and her family delighted in being at Glanmore: life there seemed happy without regularly planned amusements, but it was not without its special occasions. Sometimes Uncle Francis would leave the work of his estate for a day to take a party for a picnic in the four-in-hand. He used to drive to Glenmalure or one of the valleys opening on the plateau or . . . to one of the popular resorts—the Meeting of the Waters at Avoca, or the Dargle, a deep rift (like the Devil's Glen) among the foothills at the northern end of the retaining wall. The brake made a stir in passing; the people looked out of the doors to watch the horses, the men touched their hats and everyone made way on the narrow roads.

Two of John's brothers were old enough to stay at Glanmore without their mother. Robert, the elder, adapted himself very easily to his uncle's methods and at the time when he left school,

[1] The owner of Rathfarnham Castle, a Mr. Blackburn, gave Mrs. Synge's children leave to play and walk in the estate.

assisted in the overseeing of the Glanmore woods. The boys were good walkers and came to know not only the estate but all the surrounding country on foot. They enjoyed talking to the country people with whom they mixed on easy terms when they were young enough not to feel interrupted by class distinctions. The Wicklow dialect, with its extravagant similes and fantastic metaphors, was to them so ordinary that it affected their own speech unnoticed.

When John was still too young to join in his brothers' sports and excursions, Glanmore suffered another change. In 1878, when the estate was at the height of its prosperity, Uncle Francis fell ill. Aunt Editha, being much concerned, kept him quiet in his room and excluded visitors. Instead of calling in a doctor, she prayed for his recovery and, in accordance with instructions which she received on mysterious postcards from England, administered medicine in homeopathic doses. This treatment proved unsuccessful and Uncle Francis died, leaving Glanmore to Aunt Editha for her life. His widow was overwhelmed with grief and it seemed to some of her friends that unless she had a complete change of scene, she would settle down to a life of inconsolable melancholy. It was arranged that she should be invited to London, whence she returned in the following year married to Major Theodore Webber Gardiner, known afterwards to the Synge family as 'the Major'.

The Major was a member of the Exclusive Plymouth Brethren,[1] and was precluded by his religion from attending Nun's Cross church or praying with any person about whose salvation he entertained any doubts. He knew nothing of farming in Ireland and had no money with which to finance the estate. From the time of his coming, the prosperity of Glanmore began to decline.

After giving the estate to Aunt Editha for life, Uncle Francis had by his will settled it on the eldest of his brothers, Alexander Hamilton Synge, and on his sons in tail. Alexander had become rector of St. Peter's, Ipswich; his children lived in England and were strangers to Wicklow; there was no one of the Synge name living at Glanmore. Mrs. Synge no longer went to stay there with her children in a family party. Her elder sons retained their associations with the estate, but these associations underwent a subtle

[1] The Exclusive Brethren, followers of John Nelson Darby, believed, in Darby's words, that 'Separation from evil is God's principle of unity.' Thus some of them refused all collaboration with Christians outside their circle.

change. Aunt Editha invited the boys to spend holidays at Glanmore as she had done in their uncle's lifetime; they met the people on the estate as old friends, but no longer as if they were members of the owner's household. John, who was only seven years old when Uncle Francis died, had never shared in their work at Glanmore nor had he learnt to deal as an employer with the men on the farm. When in a few years he knew the estate and the adjoining country as well as his brothers, and was on friendly terms with the people of the district, conditions had changed: he was accepted by the people as a boy belonging to a local family, but he was free from the formality which necessarily surrounded the near relatives of Uncle Francis when he held a position of importance in the neighbour-hood. . . .

[Even though she no longer took her whole family to Glan-more, Mrs. Synge continued to move with her household to the country for the summer months; this removal was, for all of them, the great event of the year. Mrs. Synge's plans for it were made months in advance and were always determined by the same considerations.] She disliked popular summer resorts, and usually chose some quiet place in Wicklow where she could find an inex-pensive lodging or where she and her mother could share with relations in paying the rent of a large house. While avoiding places where she would be likely to meet strangers, Mrs. Synge saw in the summer holidays an opportunity for the social intercourse that she enjoyed with relations and religious friends. . . .

[It was in 1874 that Mrs. Synge first took her family to Grey-stones, a small fishing village in Co. Wicklow which was slowly developing following the opening of the railway from Dublin in 1850.] Mrs. Synge found the neighbourhood of Greystones such a suitable resort for her family that she returned there for sixteen summers, which were consecutive but for the summer of 1882 when her sister Anne died. She loved the beauty of the district and delighted in being near the hills while at the same time giving the children the advantage of a seaside holiday. She was glad to be within visiting distance of Glanmore, which was about twelve miles south of Greystones. In addition, she was attracted through her religious feelings to a place where the neighbours were, almost exclusively, Protestants[1]. . . .

[1] The parish of Delgany, which included Greystones, had been strongly under the influence of a rich Huguenot family, the La Touches; some of them, like John

The annual removal to Greystones, or to its neighbourhood, was part of the routine of John's life from his fourth to his twenty-first year. Such regularity was, in itself, an important condition of his development, but still more important was the uniformity of social environment that it secured. Moving annually to a place in every way different from Orwell Park, and finding there people with the faith and reactions that he had known at home, led him to mistake the small fabricated world of a privileged minority for a real universe. It protected him, even in the holidays, from forming impressions of people outside the limited circle of evangelical society. So complete was this protection that, except for occasional distress about the idea of Hell, his mind was free from serious conflict until he was old enough to read scientific books. . . .

[The idea of Hell, however, which had been implanted in him by the teaching of his mother, did cause him great distress. He recounted in his autobiographical notes[1]:]

I was painfully timid and while still very young the idea of Hell took a fearful hold upon me. One night particularly I thought I was irretrievably damned and cried myself to sleep in vain yet terrified[2] efforts to form a conception of eternal pain. In the morning I renewed my lamentation, and my mother was sent for. She comforted me with the assurance that my fears were caused by the Holy Ghost who was now convicting me of sin and thus preparing me in reality for ultimate salvation. . . .

The only one of John's brothers young enough to join him in childish games was Sam, who was nearly four years older than he. This difference in their ages made Sam necessarily the leader. They played well together; with minds free from the confusion caused by complicated toys, they dramatized their own ideas, absorbed in games of make-believe. . . .

Synge, had been prominent in the evangelical revival. Greystones was one of the centres of Protestant religious fervour in the nineteenth century.

[1] The extracts from Synge's autobiographical notes are taken from the version in T.C.D. MS. 4382 (previously No. 15 in Professor Ann Saddlemyer's listing), ff. 55v–59. Stephens used only this version of the autobiography. The text entitled 'Autobiography' in C.W. II. 3–15, is a composite one constructed by Dr. Alan Price from all available autobiographical fragments, including the notebook used by Stephens.

[2] The MS. indicates as alternative wording 'fearful' and 'terrible'.

We had several elaborate games which were not, I think, usual. There was a legendary character we called 'Squirelly'[1] who was a sort of folklore creation and we used to spend hours inventing adventures for him to pass through.

I have a hazy recollection of a piece of paper on which we kept a sort of chronicle of his doings but I have entirely forgotten the nature of his adventures. Then we had a number of 'men' mostly spools with red flannel belts sewed round them, who lived a most complicated life with war and commerce between our opposite settlements. I believe I sometimes gained in the war but in the commerce I was lamentably at a loss[2]. . . .

Sam loved pets and John, as he grew old enough, gradually shared with his brother the care of dogs, cats, pigeons, rabbits, and canaries. It was in this way that the two boys created the centre of interest to which their cousins, the Ross children, were drawn when they lived next door. . . . [It was with the youngest of these cousins, Florence, who was about his own age, that John struck up a friendship of great intimacy and lasting influence. He wrote of it:]

We had a large establishment of pets, rabbits, pigeons, Guinea pigs, canaries, dogs, which we looked after together. I was now going to school but ⟨I⟩ had many holidays from ill health—six months about this time especially which were recommended on account of continual headaches, that I suffered from—which gave us a great deal of time to wander about among the fields near our houses.

We were left complete liberty and never abused it . . . She was I think a very pleasant featured child and must have had an excellent character, as for years I do not remember a single quarrel—with ⟨my⟩ brother of course I had plenty, sometimes of considerable violence. . . .

Strange though his early environment may have been, John drew from it immeasurable benefit. He could write as he looked back to his childhood: 'This period was probably the happiest of my life. It was admirable in every way.'[3] The assured faith of his elders imparted a sense of stability. They inflicted no harsh punishments, made no heated scenes, used no hasty words. They were not over-anxious about business, nor did they impose a strain on children by stimulating worldly ambition. If her children discussed the making of money, Mrs. Synge always quoted the text: 'Seek ye

[1] Stephens read this word as 'Squirrlly'.
[2] 'lamentably at a loss' is deleted in the MS.; the words substituted are illegible.
[3] *C.W.* II. 7.

first the Kingdom of God and His righteousness, and all these things shall be added unto you.'

When John was ten years old, he was sent with his brother Sam to a Dublin day-school, Mr. Harrick's Classical and English School, No. 4 Upper Leeson Street. . . . From Orwell Park on fine days, John and Sam could walk to school in about half an hour. On wet days they travelled part of the way by the horse tram. John's attendance proved to be very irregular as he suffered often from colds and his schooling was soon for the time abandoned.

His mother did not believe in any particular method of instructing young children. She thought that a teacher should be kind but firm, a person who would make children understand that they were 'meant to be seen but not heard', and that answering back was being 'pert to their elders'. She was sorry that John, through doing lessons at home, should lose the companionship of other children but for this, it seemed to her, there were compensations. She could not feel certain that other children at school were well brought up and John, while he remained at home, was under the good influence of her household, and had the company of his sister, his brothers, and his cousins.[1]

John received religious instruction from both his mother and his grandmother. They were in complete accord in carrying on the teaching of the evangelical revival, as it had been preached by the Revd. Dr. Traill at Schull. They did not believe that its adherents suffered by their dissociation from the ordinary life of society, regarding those who accepted salvation as a community of saints— 'in the world yet separate from the world'. They were concerned with salvation, not with managing society which, according to their belief, was to remain under the domination of the Evil One until the second coming of Christ.

Mrs. Synge conducted her household by a rule as strict as that of a religious order and supposed that her children would acquiesce without question. She was very well versed in the doctrine to which she adhered and could support every tenet by citing scriptural authority. She believed the whole Bible to be inspired and its meaning to be clear to anyone who read with an open mind and faith in the Holy Ghost.

If John had been a child who depended on variety and amuse-

[1] See Samuel Synge, *Letters to my Daughter: Memories of John Millington Synge* (Dublin and Cork, 1931), for many details of Synge's childhood.

ment, he would have been dulled by his surroundings. But having a spontaneous interest in everything he saw and an active imagination stimulated by his mother's religious devotion, his isolation tended rather to heighten his sensitiveness. Doing lessons at home without any companions of his own age did not make him bored or listless, but it provided an unusual opportunity for brooding over problems and imaginings and was likely to induce a morbid outlook as he grew older. John's mind afterwards went through a morbid phase, but he did not reach the period of his literary productiveness until it had passed. The peculiarity that was afforded an unusual opportunity of developing in his boyhood, and that was to remain dominant to the end of his life, was his power of digesting experience. In the tranquillity of his home, he learnt to focus his imagination on distilling essentials from happenings that to an outsider might have appeared trivial.

Most boys measure the stages of their growing up by competition in games, swimming, and other sports. As John did not go regularly to school and was not allowed to bathe—because of his tendency to catch cold—he had no opportunity for the usual trials of strength; yet he felt one powerful incentive to increasing effort. . . . Sam did not join in school games, but used to enjoy taking very long walks with his other brothers and some of their friends; for John, the test of his growing powers was in walking to some valley where his brothers used to fish or to the top of some mountain that they used to climb.

The country surrounding his home at Rathgar[1] and the district around Greystones became associated for him with the delight of reaching the goal of the hills for the first time on foot. Nothing ever dimmed that association and the hills remained significant for him to the time he last saw them from the top window of the tall Dublin house where he died. Sam was very good-natured and often brought John on excursions before he could walk as fast or as far as his elder brothers. John's reaching a place of which they had often talked delighted Sam and he sometimes noted the event in his diary. . . .

[In the summer of 1882, Mrs. Synge decided not to go to Co. Wicklow but to take her family to stay with her sister-in-law, Julia Macleod, in the Isle of Man.] ⟨John⟩ found Douglas a contrast to the only seaside resort he knew. Instead of a few families of old

[1] The Dublin suburb which includes Orwell Park.

friends and relations, there were dense crowds; instead of a lonely shore winding for miles along the coast, there were piers, esplanades and amusements. Though everything outside was strange, John soon found that in his aunt's house, he felt at home; everything there seemed familiar. ⟨His aunt⟩ spoke of most visitors to the Isle of Man collectively as 'trippers' and never thought of the people of the multitude as having individual existences. . . . She talked with ⟨John's⟩ mother and Mr. Macleod[1] in the same way as the grown-up people talked at Orwell Park. All three regarded an Irish crowd as composed mostly of Roman Catholics who believed in something that was definitely wrong. The Isle of Man crowds they looked on as composed mostly of Protestants who were indifferent as to what they believed—careless about God. Their stay in ⟨their aunt's⟩ household tended to confirm in the minds of John and Sam the tacit assumption that they belonged to a minority which was in the right, entitled to regard most people as forming the majority which was in the wrong. John's creed suffered profound changes as years passed, but this assumption remained unshaken.

The days passed pleasantly except that for the older members of the party the holiday was overshadowed by [the illness in Dublin of Mrs. Synge's sister, Anne Traill.][2] Early in August a telegram recalled Mrs. Synge and her children and on 23 ⟨August⟩ her sister died.

It was at this time that John was sent with his cousin Florence Ross to spend, in the demesne of Rathfarnham Castle, the days of which he afterwards wrote:

I suppose I did not realize what death meant. The days when the house was darkened—it was August—I spent in some woods near Rathfarnham with my little friend. They were wonderfully delightful, though I hardly remember what we did or talked of. I was passionately drawn to nature and was now busy in the study of birds—a matter which I afterwards carried a good way. She took fire at my enthusiasm and we devoted a great deal of our spare time to observation and reading books on ornithology. . . .[3]

[Since Sam was now going each day by train to school at Bray—eight miles away—and John was continuing to receive lessons at

---

[1] Stephens explains (TS. 196) that Synge's aunt always 'referred to her husband as "Mr. Macleod" instead of "Uncle Angus" because, being only a sailor, even a marriage with her did not bring him effectively within the family circle'.

[2] Anne Traill had been living with her mother at No. 3 Orwell Park.

[3] Stephens quotes only 'I suppose . . . talked of'.

home, he and Florence were inevitably thrown closely together. They kept, for a time, a written record[1] of their doings—daily visits to feed the birds in the woods, observations of squirrels, rabbits, plants, and birds. This period was one of the happiest of John's life.

[During the summer of 1883, it was decided that John's eldest brother, Robert, would go to Argentina to work on the ranch of one of his uncles and to seek his fortune. His second brother, Edward, had become a land agent so that the two boys were safely settled into careers suitable to their position. The third brother, Sam, was sixteen and planning to enter Trinity College, and the only girl, Annie, was now of marriageable age. She was favoured with the attentions of two young men, both of whom had been school friends of her eldest brothers and both of whom proposed marriage to her.] John Joly ⟨the unsuccessful suitor⟩ was interested in science and had a private income sufficient to relieve him from any urgent necessity for earning money. Harry Stephens, whom she married in January 1884, was an ambitious young solicitor with no income except his professional earnings. . . .

In making arrangements for her daughter's marriage, Mrs. Synge showed her peculiar form of parental wisdom. . . . It was arranged that ⟨Annie⟩ should have a marriage settlement . . . ⟨which secured⟩ an insurance on the life of the husband and a charge on the Galway estate to take effect on Mrs. Synge's death,[2] and so provided security for maintaining children of the marriage in their station in life. Though Mrs. Synge would not stand in the way of enterprise that led her sons to leave Ireland, she tried to secure that those of her family who remained at home should live in the closest association, and that the next generation should be brought up in the same tradition and under exactly the same influences as her children. It did not seem to her that there was anything necessarily unwise in arranging that a young married man should be under the supervision of two generations of mothers-in-law. It was accordingly arranged that the young couple should live next door to her in Orwell Park as tenants of part of Mrs. Traill's house, where my brother Frank and I and our sister Claire were born. . . .

[1] T.C.D. MS. 4369, transcribed in whole by Stephens, TS. 202–6.
[2] By this procedure, the estate would have a liability to provide funds for the children's maintenance in the event of Mrs. Synge's death.

5

[John was still devoting much of his energy to the study of natural history. His notebooks contain many details of birds and also his own descriptions of the behaviour of those he could observe.] In February 1884, for example, ⟨he noted:⟩ 'I saw Pied and Grey Wagtails dipping their feet into the white foam of the river while flying. . . .' [In April 1884 he wrote:] 'I found a water-ouzel's nest in a hole in the rocks of a waterfall so that the bird had to fly through a sheet of water to get to its nest, which was made of moss—eggs pure white.'[1]

In writing notes like these, ⟨John⟩ expressed a feeling that he did not mention. Gradually, without the conscious intention of doing it, he established a mode of expressing his emotions through writing descriptions of what he saw in the field and by the river. Later in his life the realism of his plays was often to draw its force from significant details of the kind that he described in his notebook. These references to nature are so frequent that they form part of the structure of his works. For example ⟨in *Deirdre of the Sorrows*⟩ Conchubor says to Deirdre:

. . . and yet this last while I⟨'m⟩ saying out when I'd see the furze breaking and the daws sitting two and two on ash-trees by the Duns of Emain, 'Deirdre's a year nearer her full age when she'll be my mate and comrade,' and then I'm glad surely.[2]

The symbol of love and marriage was furnished for John by the conspicuous jackdaws sitting on the ash, a tree still bare in the late spring when other trees are hiding the birds with their fresh foliage, and the smell of furze is in the air. . . .

[The summer of 1884 was spent near Greystones again, this time] at Rathdown House where Mrs. Synge organized a large family party. . . . John was becoming very familiar with the part of the Golden Belt adjoining Co. Dublin and staying from time to time at different houses widened his knowledge of the district. As he grew older, his intimacy with the country and with country people was increasing. It was an intimacy that had begun earlier than memory and was to grow until he knew south Co. Dublin and east Co. Wicklow as most people might know the vicinity of

[1] T.C.D. MS. 4370.   [2] *C.W.* IV. 193.

their own homes. Though he lived at the edge of the city he spent in the country most of his time out of doors. As a result of his bird-watching, he knew every field near Orwell Park; he was gradually growing familiar with the Dublin hills and with as much of the land lying between them and the sea as he could reach on foot. . . . He knew the fields round each of the houses where he stayed in summer . . . and on his longer walks he linked his knowledge of different areas. . . .

[The countryside of south Co. Dublin and north Co. Wicklow was particularly suitable for the type of exploration which John found so enjoyable. During the late eighteenth and early nineteenth centuries, new, straight roads had been constructed in many parts of Ireland. In level country, many of the old roads were improved and incorporated in the new system. In a mountainous county like Wicklow, this was impossible. The old roads often crossed valleys at right angles where the banks were steep and dry as the early road-makers had found it difficult to build roads through bog land.] This plan not only adapted the roads to physical conditions but suited the traffic of the time which consisted of unsprung vehicles, pack animals, and horsemen. For these, the directness of the route was more important than opportunities for speed. The engineers who began the improvement of the roads towards the end of the eighteenth century were working in the days of the stage-coach and the well-equipped private four-in-hand. They chose the easiest gradients and followed the courses of rivers leaving the old roads to degenerate into lanes and byways narrowed by encroaching overgrowth and used by few but the local farmers and the tinkers who camped on the wide grass margins.

The new roads usually ran through cultivated lands, but the old roads on their course across hills and valleys passed through varying country. They were little assisted by engineering works and took the character of the ground they traversed, turning sharp corners and dipping steeply to cross streams by fords or small arched bridges. Where they ran by demesnes, they were shaded by fine trees and fenced with old walls overgrown with moss and ferns. The walls took their colours from the surprisingly varied stone of Wicklow. In some districts they were purple with slate, in others russet with sandstone, grey with granite, or white with quartz. Where the old roads ran through the fields they were usually edged by unkept hedges, banks, and ditches and where they reached the higher parts of the hills were often unfenced, running through the open heather.

John never lost his delight in the roads that became his familiar walks when he was staying at Rathdown House in 1884 and years afterwards ⟨he⟩ seemed always to find a special pleasure in their early associations. . . . The people he met usually wished him the time of day and sometimes stopped for a chat as they passed. He used to go with Sam to the farm houses and cottages to fetch eggs for their mother or to buy pullets for their hen run. The pleasant intercourse with country people near his home resulted afterwards in his mixing at his ease not only with them but with the people of Aran and Kerry.

In his boyhood, he never went to the west of Ireland; but he heard of Galway so often that it seemed to be a place he knew. His mother frequently spoke of the estate near Tuam; ⟨his great-uncle⟩, the Revd. Edward Synge, had begun his ministry in that district, ⟨and⟩ Eugenia, one of Uncle Alec's daughters, who was staying at Rathdown House, used to talk of her father's work in Aran.

John's inspiration depended on the emotions stirred by intimate understanding of familiar life and places rather than on feelings produced by the shock of newness. He preferred following threads of association to making random experiments. It was natural for him afterwards to seek in Galway a wider knowledge of the life on which, in Dublin and Wicklow, he had from childhood set an increasingly conscious value. . . .

At this time, a boy of fourteen, ⟨John⟩ had outgrown the games that interested him as a child. When he was at home, he was taught by a tutor three times a week, but when he was in the country no special provision was made for his education. The routine of his home offered no variety; he was quite unacquainted with town amusements and had never seen either a pantomime or a circus. His environment was in every way likely to stifle a boy's mind with boredom. In overcoming this difficulty and adapting himself to solitude and monotony, John passed a crisis in his development and formed habits of mind which afterwards affected his work. . . . His mother's teaching, like a running commentary on all that happened, emphasized the importance of searching out and utilizing every opportunity that his life might afford. John applied her wisdom in a way that she could not understand and found in an outwardly prosaic life events so dramatic that they ultimately contributed to the inspiration of his plays. . . .

⟨By⟩ the spring of 1885, John . . . had begun a collection of butterflies, moths, and beetles and was giving most of his attention to this branch of natural history. His new work led him to give up going out bird-watching in the early mornings and to go instead in the dusk and the dark in search of insects, a practice that he said gave him 'a great fondness for the evening and the night'.[1] Gradually he was finding by experience that out of doors there was always variety—the alternation of day and night, the passing of the seasons—and that in his home there was uninteresting routine. He was beginning to see the world he knew out of doors as a symbol of inspired life and the house as a symbol of dull method. This antithesis emerged from current experience and existed in his mind without rancour or dislike of his mother's home.

Mrs. Synge lived gracefully: she did not intrude unimportant domestic affairs nor drown the intelligence of her family with her simple routine. Towards it her attitude was definite: she sought to perform ordinary duties conscientiously to the glory of God without allowing them to absorb her mind as if they were important in themselves. For instruction on this subject, she used to read aloud to John the story in Bunyan's *Pilgrim's Progress* about the man with the muck rake. In her copy there was a picture of him intent on collecting straws and filth while, if he had looked up, he could have seen an angel high above his head offering him a crown of glory. John's way of solving the problems arising from the monotony of his life by distilling profundity of feeling from ordinary experience was in accordance with this teaching, but it was an application of Mrs. Synge's philosophy which she could not recognize nor he explain. The relation that she maintained with her world did not necessarily exclude the experiences that are the basis of creative art, but they had no synthesis in her system. Feelings of importance had a meaning for her in terms of religion only. She did not claim to understand science or art, but classified them as phases of worldly wisdom—very good in their way provided they were pursued for the glory of God, but paltry next the wisdom that is alive to salvation. . . .

John gradually grew conscious of art, and related to it the qualities in his understanding that seemed to him spiritual. Though ultimately he became a writer, by the time he was a student, he

---

[1] T.C.D. MS. 4382, f. 53v. Dr. Price (*C.W.* II. 9) read the phrase as 'for the eerie and night'.

had formed the ambition of devoting himself to music. His interest in it was aroused . . . through his brother Sam learning to play a concertina. . . . Within the next three years he followed Sam in learning to play the violin, an instrument which fully aroused his enthusiasm. He needed no further stimulus and soon not only devoted himself whole-heartedly to the study of music, but focused his mind on becoming a professional musician. . . .

John in his recollections of his early life seems to indicate ⟨the summer of 1885⟩ . . . as the time of a sudden crisis in the development of his religious beliefs.[1] This crisis marked the beginning of a successful struggle for intellectual honesty and independent judgement. It was brought about by an event which, like many events important in his life, was insignificant in itself, drawing its force solely from his private experience.

One of the works of natural history that he had taken to the country for his summer reading ⟨in 1885⟩ was Darwin's *Origin of Species*. . . . The book chanced to open in his hand at a place in the last chapter where he began to read:

The similar framework of bones in the hand of a man, wing of a bat, fin of the porpoise, and leg of the horse,—the same number of vertebrae forming the neck of the giraffe and of the elephant,—and innumerable other such facts, at once explain themselves on the theory of descent with slow and slight successive modifications.[2]

For John, Darwin's words instantly related to each other facts with which he was familiar through his study of natural history and made them vivid with a new meaning. Never before had he doubted the explanation of the universe furnished by his mother's religious teaching. Her beliefs formed such a closely-knit system that they were not susceptible of modification. The story of the creation, of man's fall in the Garden of Eden and of his subsequent redemption by the atonement formed one consecutive history. Mrs. Synge's teaching provided no symbols for the interpretation of undefined spiritual vision. She regarded symbols, such as the sacrificial lamb, as having importance before the Christian revelation, but as having lost their usefulness when the atonement, which they represented, had become an accomplished fact. The validity

[1] T.C.D. MS. 4382, f. 54.
[2] Charles Darwin, *On the Origin of Species* . . . (London, 1859), p. 479.

of her doctrines could not be tested by their value for the purpose of synthesizing emotional experience, but by theological argument. It seemed to John that the foundation on which her system of belief rested had been destroyed by the meaning that Darwin gave to familiar facts. John's own words, written more than ten years later, are filled with the intensity of his feelings:

I flung the book aside and rushed out into the open air—it was summer and we were in the country—the sky seemed to have lost its blue and the grass its green. I lay down and writhed in an agony of doubt. Till this I had never doubted and had never conceived that a sane and wise man or boy could doubt. I had of course heard of atheists but as vague monsters that I was unable to realise. My memory does not record how I returned home nor how long my misery lasted. . . . In a few weeks or days I had regained my composure, but this was the beginning.[1]

When he was fourteen, an age at which boys are generally supposed to be preoccupied with their games and their food, John regarded questions of faith as matters of life and death; if the words he read had raised only the familiar conflict between revealed religion and secular science, he might have contented himself with the belief that the provinces of religion and science are separate. . . . [But that was not possible in the religious system that he had accepted.] He had been taught the virtue of faith and at the same time the virtue of an honest search for truth. His mother had told him that the Protestant faith was free from superstition and depended on 'The Open Book' and the use of private judgement. She had often repeated: 'Seek, and ye shall find, knock and it shall be opened unto you.' His research appeared to be disclosing facts contrary to his faith: the dilemma seemed insoluble. ⟨Furthermore,⟩ John saw that if he arrived at the logical conclusion of Darwin's argument, as it now appeared, he would be faced not only with religious difficulties but also with the outraged feelings of almost everyone he knew. . . .

Outwardly ⟨his⟩ life ⟨might be⟩ sheltered and tranquil, but inwardly . . . the conflict between ⟨John's⟩ ideas was increasing. Though he was suffering from no definite illness and his general health was improving, he was still far from robust. His nervous energy was absorbed by mental conflicts and the fact that he was

[1] T.C.D. MS. 4382; cf. C.W. II. 10–11. (Dr. Price's conflation differs slightly from this version.)

not allowed to go to school impressed his mind with the idea that he was an invalid. This impression, at a time when he was affected by the tendency to anxiety usual at adolescence, filled his mind with forebodings. Something like a nightmare quality in his thoughts is suggested by the part of his notes in which he wrote:

This ill health led to a curious resolution. . . . Without knowing, or as far as I can remember hearing, anything about doctrines of heredity, I surmised that unhealthy parents should have unhealthy children—my rabbit breeding may have put the idea into my head—therefore I said I am unhealthy and if I marry I shall have unhealthy children. But I will never create beings to suffer as I am suffering so I will never marry.[1]

This note [like others among his autobiographical jottings], seems to indicate that he had a difficulty in thinking of himself as different at different ages. He was in many ways undeveloped, and cannot have been more than twenty-six when he made this entry in his notebook describing a resolution about marriage formed before he was fifteen as in some measure explaining all his subsequent evolution. His account of his vow of celibacy does not lose importance for this reason: for him his resolution represented a dreadful reality forced upon him by a sense of responsibility which his mother's teaching had trained. It implied isolating himself and avoiding intimacies. Though it appeared to him to have been arrived at logically, it probably expressed a feeling of being misunderstood by the members of his family of whose affection he had no doubt and furnished him with an explanation of his increasing aloofness. . . .

[John's isolation from the outside world was partly broken in December 1885 when he joined the newly-formed Dublin Naturalists' Field Club. Most of the members of the club were distinguished scientists or elderly amateurs and John was too young to take a very active part in the meetings;[2] but he attended many lectures on various aspects of natural history and also went with the club on field trips, including one in May 1886 to Howth.]

John's intense interest in the study of natural history had a very marked effect on his general education. Except when he was living

[1] T.C.D. MS. 4382; cf. *C.W.* II. 9.

[2] Stephens states (TS. 259) that about half the members of the club were professionally interested in science and that about half were Quakers who, 'though they followed other avocations, were careful and accurate naturalists'.

at Orwell Park and working with a tutor, the amount he learnt of ordinary school subjects, which he tended to regard as of secondary importance, was left to his own discretion. He read difficult works on natural history and theology, fixing his mind on their matter and mode of expression but giving no attention to their spelling and punctuation. He spelt badly and his handwriting was a scrawl, but he was gaining a good knowledge of English and a knowledge of history and geography, so far as they were necessary to understanding the subjects in which he was more directly interested. Latin, Greek, and mathematics he learnt with his tutor and, though quite willing to bring his knowledge up to the standard necessary for entering the University, ⟨he⟩ made no attempt to treat any of them as honours subjects.

Meanwhile his religious education was producing unobserved effects on his development. His mother, aware that he had not definitely accepted her faith, intensified ⟨both⟩ her efforts to interpret the gospel and her prayers that his understanding should be enlightened by divine revelation. Knowing that, because John was accustomed to her exposition, he might not feel its force, she did not allow him to miss any opportunity of hearing her teaching in fresh words at Zion Church, or at the curate's Bible classes.[1]

All John's religious teachers adopted the same technique, which, since it utilized one of the best established paths of human feeling, seemed—in their experience—continually to prove its efficacy. Their first aim was to produce in the mind of each of their hearers 'a conviction of sin' or deep sense of personal guilt. Once this was established, they sought to show the sinner that for him only two courses lay open; the first, to stagger to final perdition through a miserable life in which every enjoyment would be interrupted by the sting of conscience; the second, to be 'washed in the Blood of the Lamb'. John's teachers at Zion Church continually reiterated the doctrine that the salvation purchased for mankind, by the vicarious sacrifice of the Redeemer, is a free gift to any individual who by acceptance makes it his own. They said that the acceptance of such a gift carries with it the moral obligation to renounce the world, and John knew from his experience of his relations what a renunciation of the world implied. In his environment, scepticism was out of place. The beliefs of the members of his family seemed to be in

---

[1] Zion Church, Rathgar, was the parish church for Mrs. Synge and her family. It still maintains an evangelical tradition.

harmony with those of the other people he knew. Eminent
Quakers, who attended the meetings of the Field Club, saw in a
scientific examination of nature new and unexpected evidence of
the infinite wisdom of the Creator. The professors of science when
they addressed these meetings refrained from raising questions
associated with religious controversy. In this way his fellow members of the Field Club, though they did not hold in detail to one
creed, seemed to give general support to his mother's teaching,
which attached blame even to honest doubt.

During the imaginative sensitiveness of his adolescence, John
was continually under the pressure of this teaching. He could not
at once decide what he ought to believe. Sometimes he had
thought himself 'saved', but 'never for very long at a time'.[1]
His teachers read, as if directed to each of them, the instructions of
St. Paul to Timothy: 'Preach the word; be instant in season, out of
season; reprove, rebuke, exhort with all longsuffering and doctrine'. These they interpreted by adding to the simple rhythm of
John's routine life a suggestive refrain of powerful declamatory
words: 'You are an unforgiven sinner; your righteousness is as
filthy rags; you are guilty in the sight of God; the thoughts of your
heart are infinitely wicked.' Into the web of his reactions a great
dread was being inextricably woven. It manifested itself at that
time in increased anxiety and forebodings and led him to think of
himself as 'a low miscreant' as he became increasingly aware of
normal sexual impulses. . . .[2]

6

[John's interest in music continued to grow and in the autumn of
1887, he persuaded his mother that he should start violin lessons;
in October she engaged a music master, Mr. Griffith, to give him
lessons.] Those who remember Patrick J. Griffith say that he was
large and burly, in appearance more like a boxer than a violinist.
At the time John began lessons with him, he was becoming well
known in Dublin orchestras as the leader of the second fiddles, and
was one of the best teachers in the city. By him John was not only
taught the violin, but introduced to people interested in music and
more concerned with art than with intellectual conclusions. This
group of musicians, with whom John gradually became acquainted,

[1] T.C.D. MS. 4382; cf. *C.W.* II. 4.
[2] T.C.D. MS. 4382; cf. *C.W.* II. 12.

formed a strange contrast with his family circle engrossed in theology, and ⟨with⟩ his fellow-members of the ⟨Dublin⟩ Naturalists' Field Club engrossed in the study of natural science. . . . [The world of music was to prove far more stimulating and exciting than that in which he had moved until now.]

[During the winter of 1887-8, Mrs. Synge began a series of letters to her son Robert, now in Argentina, which inevitably contain many frank and revealing comments on John's behaviour. For example, her letter of 14 February 1888[1] was almost entirely taken up with an account of his current activities, beginning with his progress in music.]

Johnnie's ear is wonderfully good now, he hears if the piano is at all out of tune. . . . ⟨He⟩ and I play together sometimes. I have to practise the accompaniments as they are not easy: there are so many chords and incidental sharps and flats. He is greatly improved in time; at first he never kept with me and still *runs away* when he ought to rest, so I have to try and watch him as well as play my own part. We played some nice slow melodies last night, and it sounded wonderfully nice. . . .

John intends to go in for honours in literature; he wants to go in for a prize for literary composition in Autumn. His tutor thinks he would have a very good chance and is much pleased with the compositions he writes. He gives him very difficult subjects to write on. Johnnie certainly is the literary man of the family. I never saw such a love of reading as he has—he would spend any amount of money on books if he had it. . . . I think Johnnie takes after my father. He was a *very* literary man. . . .

[In another letter to Robert, written later in the same month, she continued her comments on John's behaviour and made some revealing comparisons between him and his brothers.]

Sam is beginning to look forward to Greystones already and hopes I will be able to go. He has got some little songs suitable for singing walking home from picnics! 'Never too late to mend' and 'Don't judge a man by his coat': both point good morals and I am sure will be appreciated. He is very busy at his lectures. Johnnie looks down on Sam's slowness and ignorance very much. Johnnie has read so much more and has much greater general knowledge. Sam can't help being slow. He is

[1] Mrs. Synge's letters to Robert, with other family papers, have recently been donated by Mrs. L. Stephens to the library of Trinity College, Dublin. Stephens's transcription of Mrs. Synge's letters was not as accurate as his transcription of Synge's own work; these extracts have been newly edited from the holographs.

very like his dear father in that as well as other things, more like him than any of you and his virtues make him a comfort to me. It is a great pity for Johnnie to have such a good opinion of himself. He is more like Ned than any one and Sam and you have many points alike though you have not his calm patient spirit, but you have greater powers of reading and writing than he has. . . .

[On John's birthday, she wrote again to Robert and her mind turned naturally to a retrospect of his childhood and to her worries about his spiritual health.]

This is Johnnie's birthday. I can hardly fancy he is 17. I have been looking back to the time he was born. I was so dreadfully delicate and he, poor child⟨,⟩ was the same. How much mercy has been shown to him in his wonderful restoration to health, and Oh! that I could see him showing in his life that he has a due sense of all the mercy vouchsafed to him. I see no signs of spiritual life in my poor Johnnie; there may be some, but it is not visible to my eyes. He is very reserved and shut up on the subject and if I say any thing to him he never answers me, so I don't know in the least the state of his mind—it is a trying state, *very* trying. I long so to be able to see behind that close reserve, but I can only wait and pray and hope. . . .

[John was now working hard towards the entrance examination for Trinity College.] This year, for the first time in his life, ⟨his⟩ enjoyment of the month of May was seriously restricted by his work. Out of doors again, spring was changing into summer. Through the open window he could hear the birds singing, but he had no leisure for lying hidden in the bushes to watch their movements. When he went out, it was to take necessary exercise and his mind was full of the subjects that he was learning under pressure of an impending examination. He had a clear visual memory and understood mathematics easily. Sometimes he revised Euclid when he was out on his bicycle, glancing from time to time at a small book that he carried in his pocket. He told Sam that on one bicycle ride, he had gone over nearly a whole book as he went along.[1] Greek and Latin he found difficult. He had not at this time evolved a settled system of learning languages; the strain of remaining at work, while he was filled with an unquenchable longing to be in the open air, disturbed his thoughts and he had no teacher to focus his

---

[1] *Letters to my Daughter*, p. 17.

attention on his books. History and geography interested him greatly and in his . . . notebook, among scraps of poetry and entries about literature and philosophy, he wrote the dates of the fall of Troy and of the crowning of Charlemagne and notes about land tenure in Ireland. This interest in essentials did not, however, lead him to gain much familiarity with simple textbooks and for the purpose of a special test his work was unsatisfactory. The entrance examination of Trinity did not impose a high standard of know-ledge and would not have presented difficulty to any boy of John's ability who had prepared for it at school. For John, the answering of set questions in a silent hall with more than a hundred other candidates was to be an entirely new experience, and as the date approached he grew nervous.

In a letter to Robert on the first of June Mrs. Synge wrote:

Johnnie is very busy reading as his examination is on 18 June. He is getting rather anxious now, and not quite so confident as he was at first. He rode on his bicycle to Enniskerry[1] and back before lunch yester-day morning, an hour and 10 minutes going and an hour coming back. He said it looked lovely down there. I wish I could take a fly[2] down and enjoy it for a few hours. Johnnie did it as a medicine he said, as he had not gone to sleep till 3 the night before. He came in very warm and changed his clothes. . . .

Every student entering Trinity College is required to place himself under the tutelage of one of the Junior Fellows, who remains responsible for his guidance and discipline during his college course.[3] John, following the example of his three elder brothers, arranged to enter under Anthony Traill,[4] and on the morning of the 18th presented himself before nine o'clock at his tutor's rooms. When Anthony Traill had assembled his four or five other new pupils he led the party through the front square

[1] An attractive small town in the foothills of the Dublin Mountains, about ten miles south of Dublin.

[2] A light, one-horse carriage.

[3] This is still the case today, although the academic regulations which enabled Synge to obtain credit for one or two terms each year by examination only have been changed.

[4] Anthony Traill (1839-1914) was a cousin of Mrs. Synge; she used to recall her memory of him as a child—'an ugly boy in funny, tight clothes' (TS. 137). He was at this time a distinguished Junior Fellow and later became Provost of Trinity College. See GS, p. 17.

and up the steps of the Dining Hall where other tutors and their pupils were arriving for the Entrance Breakfast. . . .

Attending the breakfast that used to be given each year for the candidates at the entrance examination marked very pleasantly, for those who were successful, the beginning of their college careers. John took his place among Anthony Traill's group of pupils. His enjoyment of the meal may have been spoiled by the idea of the impending examination, but the strain heightened the intensity of his impressions. Besides the candidates for entrance, there were in the party a few older students, mostly elder brothers or friends of candidates who had introduced them to their tutors and had been invited to enjoy the breakfast free from the oppression of an examination. All sat in lines on both sides of long tables, the tutors sitting here and there among the company. The high panelled hall was made the more impressive by the June sunlight striking in shafts through the windows near the ceiling. The door shut with a heavy sound echoing in the vestibule. The liveried menservants hurried up and down carrying trays and serving, in addition to usual breakfast dishes, large slices of Sally-Lunn and saucers of strawberries and cream.[1]

After breakfast the candidates were free to walk for a short time in the College grounds and to assemble in a leisurely way at the Examination Hall. The examination lasted two days. On the first it was entirely in writing, but on the second candidates were examined orally in classics and Euclid. It was difficult for John, coming from the seclusion of his home, to make full use of his knowledge in his first university examination. His fortunes varying in different subjects and with different examiners, he left the hall uncertain of the result, but soon heard that he had passed. His entrance fee of £15 was paid at once, and his name placed on the College books in the junior freshmen class. . . .

The books that John took to Greystones in 1888 for his summer reading were literary textbooks and examples of English classics, recommended in the college calendar to candidates for the Entrance Prize Examination in composition and English Literature, held each October. His literary education was no less orthodox than his religious training. He had little opportunity for careless sampling of good and bad styles, ⟨since⟩ neither a magazine nor a cheap novel was to be found in Mrs. Synge's house. His introduction to

[1] Stephens is here recalling his own experience of the breakfast in 1908.

literature consisted in reading steadily through works which were either known to his family to be classical or prescribed by the college authorities. At this time, he accepted the judgement of his elders; but reviewing his education afterwards, in the light of his subsequent experience, he regarded as pedestrian the courses prescribed by the Board of Trinity. . . .

John's experience of spoken English may have delayed the development of his powers of criticism. His mother had made language one of the special subjects of her religious instruction. She taught that to refer to God in any but a strictly religious manner was a sinful taking in vain of the Holy Name, that to use expletive oaths or curses was a breach of St. James's injunction 'Let your yea be yea; and your nay, nay', and that to exaggerate was to lie. Mrs. Synge sought divine aid in confining within the closest limits the already restricted speech of the Victorian period, praying fervently, 'Set a watch O Lord, upon our lips'. So strict was her rule that it almost paralysed language as an expression of feeling. It was possible afterwards for the effect of her teaching on John's diction to mingle inextricably with the effects of other influences, but it seems never to have disappeared. Though he used the imaginative words of the country people in his plays, there was in his ordinary prose a realistic truthfulness which appears to owe something to her teaching. . . .

Side by side with this restricted language, he knew from childhood the rich, imaginative, rhythmical dialect common to east Wicklow, and preserved among the people of the plateau and the hills, as safe from outside influence as if they lived on an island. He was familiar with it in all its phases, whether in current conversation with the country people, or in the wild curses of brawling tinkers fighting when he happened to pass, or in the blessing of some tramping woman, who begged a penny as he pushed his bicycle up a hill. It was nothing strange if such a woman stopped to pronounce in benediction with ecclesiastical solemnity: 'The blessing of Jesus on you, and may the Lord Almighty keep you from a sudden or an unprovided death.'

Among the . . . books that John brought to Greystones ⟨that summer,⟩ there was one that gave a new meaning to the familiar contrast between the speech of his family and the speech of the country people. The book was *English Past and Present* by Archbishop Trench. From it John learnt of the process by which languages gradually become dull and meaningless, and of how they may be revitalized. He read the Archbishop's eloquent summing up of his theory of deterioration:

We have seen how words wear out, become unserviceable, how the glory that clothed them once disappears, as the light fades from the hills; how they drop away from the stock and stem of the language, as dead leaves from their parent tree.[1]

He knew what a language of dead words was like, . . . [and the idea must have struck him as] illuminating. Earlier in the same paragraph, after reading of a few less important sources from which a language may recruit its vocabulary, he found one of the Archbishop's most memorable passages:

A time arrives for a language when, apart from the recoveries I have just been speaking of, its own local and provincial dialects are almost the only sources from which it can obtain acquisitions such as shall really constitute an increase in wealth.

This was a new light on the value of the curious local dialect to which he was accustomed, a dialect containing words borrowed from English provincial speech on the one hand, and Gaelic on the other, and using a syntax that was partly English and partly Gaelic in origin. His family regarded it as the amusing speech of the uneducated classes, but John began to note with greater attention than before the force and meaning of the phrases he heard, when he was walking or cycling through the country. . . .

⟨During the summer holidays of 1888,⟩ as John went his usual ways . . . [walking, fishing, or making excursions from Greystones on his bicycle,] his mind remained constantly concerned with religion. He had learnt to regard uncertainty about matters of faith as inevitable, but about morals he had no doubts. Towards behaviour, he felt as he had been trained to feel, and on the teaching of morals remained not only fully assured but filled with missionary zeal. He embodied his reflections and aspirations in juvenile verse in all of which he differentiated morality from religion. . . .

> You know that sin can be withstood,
> And yet you will not bend your mind
> To relieve our fallen kind.

[1] Richard Chenevix Trench, *English Past and Present* (London, 1855), lecture II.

Religion is, I fear, the cause:
You think you're right who keep her laws
And preach an unavailing creed
Which history tells us fills no need.[1]

There were no words in which John could convey ideas of this
kind to his mother, and his decision on some of the problems that
they created for him necessarily affected her intimately. The most
difficult of these concerned his attending church on Sundays. He
hated any word or act that might be regarded as untruthful: if he
went to church, he would seem to endorse, by a public act, a faith
in which he did not believe; but if he refused to go, his absence might
create even greater misunderstanding. Reluctantly he still continued
to conform, but was ready to seize the slightest pretexts for absent-
ing himself as often as possible. On 21 July, his mother wrote to
Robert:

. . . I have been reading and praying while they are at church—indeed
Sam is the only one there today as Johnnie got a cold in his head this
morning from 5 till 7. The wind was on his window, and blew in the
damp air, as it is always open. His cold seems to have passed off again,
but he is not sorry for an excuse to stay at home, poor boy. It is fine now,
but blowing *very* hard. I hope I shall go to church in the evening. . . .

[Mrs. Synge and her family returned to Dublin in September and
John's first academic year as an undergraduate at Trinity College
began that autumn. He did not have to attend lectures during the
first term and he continued taking violin lessons and doing what he
called 'vague private reading', some of which was to be of importance to him later.] From the time he had begun to take long walks
and bicycle rides in Dublin and Wicklow, he had been interested
in ancient graves, churches, and castles scattered through the district, and at this time began to read books on Celtic antiquity. It was
a subject in no way connected with his academic course, for Trinity
had no chair of Irish Archaeology. As the small notebook in which
he wrote his verses and personal reflections was nearly full, he
began a larger book more definitely devoted to his studies.[2]

[1] T.C.D. MS. 4371, ff. 31–31v. Stephens punctuated the poem and altered MS.
'your' (l.5) to 'you're'. Synge has scribbled over the poem in pencil the word
'Bosh' and initialled it.
[2] T.C.D. MS. 4373.

Twenty pages he used for his literary notes and set apart the next fifteen for entries about archaeology. He wrote neatly in ink, made a marginal drawing of the doorway in the round tower at Kildare and carefully copied Irish inscriptions, although at the time his knowledge of Irish cannot have extended much beyond the alphabet. His information was not derived from romantic books of patriotic lore but from scientific authorities such as Stokes and Petrie.[1] The last page of these notes on archaeology was devoted to Glendalough where, in a remote valley in the Wicklow hills, were the remains that he had known from childhood of one of the most famous monastic centres of the Celtic church. This new study remained one of his interests for the rest of his life and had an important effect on his literary work. It illuminated freshly for him the whole district that he knew intimately in Dublin and Wicklow, and gave him a new understanding of the traditional religious feeling of the country people.

Unlike his early interest in natural history, John's study of Irish archaeology did not receive his mother's approval. Though at times she countenanced it by asking him to show English visitors antiquities in Wicklow, her usual attitude was deprecatory and discouraging. The popular traditions and folk-lore that surrounded ancient ruins she dismissed as foolish stories invented by local guides to obtain money from tourists. The reverence of the people for ancient monuments she regarded as superstition, and thought it better to forgo historical research than to awaken, round relics of antiquity, memories which might inspire disturbances of the law and order that the Protestant minority was trying to enforce throughout the country. There was no open conflict of opinion between John and his mother on the question, but in silence it was accepted as a new subject on which their opinions differed.

It was through John's interest in archaeology that he began consciously to accept and to associate himself with Irish tradition. From archaeology he was to pass on, stimulated by events and by the people he met, to studying folk-lore, history and the Irish language, and finally to take his place in the national literary movement.

In spite of his having been able to continue his accustomed routine

---

[1] G. T. Stokes, *Ireland and the Celtic Church* (London, 1886); George Petrie, 'The Ecclesiastical Architecture of Ireland', in *Transactions of the Royal Irish Academy*, xx.

almost unbroken, there was one question which had been raised by his entering college and was being pressed upon him continually by his family: What profession was he going to choose? His relations talked of the various opportunities which they could provide for him, and he found it impossible to convey to them any conception of his ambitions. He had decided to devote himself to one of the arts, and at this time music was his principal focus. If he even suggested that he might make music his profession, his relations treated the idea as quite impractical and he soon changed the subject. They were satisfied by his silence, because they thought that talking nonsense confirmed him in foolish opinions, and that a little experience of the world would show him how necessary it was for gentlemen, without private means, to earn suitable incomes.

The ambitions that at this time shaped themselves in his mind found definition in the verse that he used to write in his notebook. His fixed purpose is clear from a few crude lines beginning 'Art I would serve in future without pause',[1] and suggests doubt only as to whether he was doing all that could be done and would be able to recognize the truth when found. . . .

In the year 1888 John's health had been good, he had entered Trinity, and found his holiday at Greystones pleasant, but the background of all his thoughts had been so filled with conflict and perplexity that he looked back on the old year as a time of unhappy strain. His active mind was unable to accept contradictory ideas, and he struggled for consistent beliefs. . . . Decision about religion seemed a pressing necessity, but nowhere could he find the repose of a sure faith. His solitary life exposed him to the onset of haunting doubts and morbid forebodings. The close of the year suggested thoughts of death, and on 27 December he wrote a youthful aphorism, sententious and melancholy:

We fear death it seems to me much as we fear getting an old tooth out. Life and old teeth are unquestionably misfortunes, but dentists and deathbeds are horrible.

Gloomy reflections of this kind did not impair, or even for the moment exclude his healthy love of everything vigorous, for a few days later he wrote:

[1] T.C.D. MS. 4371, f. 39v.

We all of us delight in strength, whether we see it in other things, or feel it in ourselves. There is joy in the rush of a mountain torrent, in the flying foam of waves in a storm, and in the storm itself, when it comes rushing to us through the terrified pine trees.[1]

Between these two entries, some pages of the notebook contain an explicit account of the arguments that weighed with John in trying to choose his future work. His mode of approach to the choice was one of which his mother approved, but the conclusions he arrived at were at variance with hers. His method was first to review abstract principles, and when he believed that he had found an applicable rule, to test its validity by relating it to particular facts.... His first premises were strictly orthodox. Pride in achievement he regarded as the most foolish of human passions, because man made neither himself nor the material on which he works. The use of opportunity he believed virtuous, and doing nothing to be 'desperate evil'. So far it was easy for the members of his family to agree with his view, but he found his beliefs in conflict with theirs when he concluded that everyone is under a moral obligation to choose his work according to his abilities.

The evangelical movement had substituted the ambition to possess theological knowledge for the Christian ideal of living to the glory of God. This produced for John one of his chief difficulties. As his reflections led him to believe that theology is a matter for trained minds and that the duty of the individual lies in making the best use of his faculties, he began to think of work as vocational. Although he cannot at the time have realized its immense importance to his future career, the practical example that he selected for testing his theories was the work of the stage. He had been taught that the theatre is worldly and displeasing to God, a belief commonly accepted by the people he knew. *The Merchant of Venice*, *Richard II*, and *Macbeth* he had read with delight. Now, he asked himself, how, if they renounced the theatre, could gifted dramatists and actors fulfil the will of the Creator? This question he reached after first considering how far writers should devote their talents to religion, and wrote:

If minds like those ⟨of⟩ Shakespeare or Newton were applied exclusively

---

[1] T.C.D. MS. 4371, ff. 41v, 50v–51. (A corrected version of Stephens's transcript.)

to theology their power would be terribly misdirected. Instances of this misapplication can ⟨be⟩ adduced. I will mention one. Addison had a remarkable genius for writing light essays. He was a fervent Christian. He considered that he did not fulfil his obligations to Christianity by writing. He therefore set about writing a work on Christian evidences, which was, as might have been ⟨expected⟩, an absolute failure.

The Common idea of God, among religious people, is a Being supremely good, delighting in virtue and in nothing else. But, if God did, as is generally believed, make man in the state ⟨in which⟩[1] he now exists, and if He guides and directs humanity at the present moment, if He gave us our intellects, can we believe that He does not require us to use them? Did He give Shakespeare or Garrick their abilities and not intend them to write and act? If He gives us our minds it is clear to me at least, that He wishes us to use them. It is a sin not to do so, and a virtue to fulfil his wish.[2]

7

[John never entered fully into undergraduate life at Trinity and later in life he dismissed his time in College as time wasted. Certainly his first experience of lectures—during the Hilary term 1889 when he had to attend ordinary arts lectures to obtain credit—must have seemed to him unprofitable.] His fellow-students had been accustomed to mix with boys of their own age, and many found themselves working with old school friends; to John they were all strangers. Among them there was nobody whose companionship in study he could enjoy and what he heard at lectures interested him but little. The sudden change, from thinking of himself as a member of no group—outside his family clan—to thinking of himself as a university student, imposed on him a strain that he could not understand. He became more whimsical and more perplexing to his mother who, on 2 March ⟨1889⟩, wrote to Robert:

Johnnie is gone in to college on his bicycle through all the rain without a coat or umbrella of course! He hates walking in and out of town to lectures, so he goes in his knickerbockers on his bicycle no matter what the weather is, snowing or raining and roads covered with water and mud; he gets well splashed. . . . He does not know how to take care of his clothes and won't take advice; he has much to learn, poor boy; he is very headstrong. . . .

[1] MS. reads 'that' for Stephens's 'in which'.
[2] T.C.D. MS. 4371, ff. 46v–48v. (Stephens's transcript corrected.)

[As soon as his lectures ended,] John wrote a letter to Patrick Griffith arranging to recommence his violin lessons. He had obtained credit for his first academic year and was free for some months to occupy his time as he chose. Instead of embarking on any of the honours courses open to him in college, he relapsed at once into his usual routine, studying music and reading alternately. He was now nearly eighteen; his philosophy was assuming a settled form and he was shrinking increasingly from outward conformity with the religion of his family. . . .

[The most important event of the summer was probably the short visit which John and his mother paid to Glanmore where they stayed with relatives who had rented the castle from Aunt Editha. For Mrs. Synge, in particular, the visit was full of excitement;[1] for John, the impressions of the collapsing estate, its treasures about to be sold and its grounds to fall into decay, were of lasting value. They formed the background for the article he wrote ten years later, 'A Landlord's Garden in County Wicklow'.[2]]

Summer over, John returned to his usual life. He was at the beginning of his second academic year but, as he was not required to obtain credit in it for more than the work of two terms, he deferred serious thought of his college course until after the following Christmas, recommenced his violin lessons . . . and devoted himself to music. [In the autumn, he began attending classes at the Royal Irish Academy of Music where he was to remain a student for the next three years.]

As months passed without any answer to her prayers for his conversion, Mrs. Synge found faith and hope difficult to maintain. She could not remember having left undone anything that ought to have been done on his behalf, and yet he seemed to be drifting further from belief. In her perplexity she asked advice of the Revd. John Dowse, curate of Zion Church, with whom she had sometimes discussed her trouble. On 17 September Mr. Dowse called and, after a discussion with Mrs. Synge in the drawing-room, interviewed John separately in the parlour. Both were sincere, but their tacit assumptions differed so widely that no agreement was possible. Mr. Dowse asked John to put away all intellectual pride and to accept, with simple faith, the teachings of the evangelical

[1] Stephens quotes from Mrs. Synge's diary (TS. 386).
[2] The garden in the essay is that at Castle Kevin, but the third paragraph (C.W. II. 230-1) seems to refer to the decay of Glanmore.

movement. John tried to explain that he could derive no spiritual advantage from pretending to believe something that he found incredible. If the discussion had any effect on him, it was to foster his growing conviction that an open declaration of his unbelief was necessary. He still hesitated to take an irretrievable step, but before the end of the year he was definitely to abandon attending church. . . .

Gradually there had been growing in his mind a conviction that the theology in which he had been taught was a dead and restrictive theory which he must renounce openly. Even after he had abandoned trying to talk with his mother about religious matters, he sometimes spoke of them to Sam. The two brothers occupied the same bedroom and had endless opportunities for undisturbed discussion. Sam had accepted the beliefs of their parents and grandparents, and had adopted a fundamentalism which made the natural history of the Old Testament as much a part of revelation as the Gospel itself. Thinking of this period more than thirty years later, Sam wrote to his daughter:

It was about those closing years of our time at Orwell Park that your Uncle John and I used to have great discussions on theology. I was very conservative in my way of taking or explaining many of the passages, for instance, in the Old Testament. I now see that I should have been far more help to him if I had said to him to take them either way he liked, either as actual historical accounts, or else as parables, so long as he got from them the lessons they were meant to teach, and could see that the Holy Scriptures were written for our learning. For instance, take the story of Jonah and the great fish, although this is not a story that we ever discussed. Some may take the story as a parable, others as a true historical account. It matters very little which way you take it: the lesson it teaches is the same. For people to argue, though, that a whale could not swallow a man is foolish. Some whales could not, but plenty of whales could.[1]

John had been driven to the conclusion that further discussion would be fruitless and had lost belief in religion. Before Christmas, he told his mother that he could no longer conscientiously attend church. Praying, waiting and hoping for his conversion, she felt this decision deeply, but she could not ask him to conform for the sake of appearances. On Sunday 23 December she wrote in her diary: 'Fine, damp, mild day—church very hot—I felt

[1] *Letters to my Daughter*, p. 76.

overpowered. Johnnie would not come, very sad;' and, with mixed
emotions on Christmas Day: 'Very peaceful, happy day; went to
church—my only sorrow Johnnie—he did not come.' Her words
were restrained and conveyed no sense of shock, for John's drawing
away from her beliefs had been gradual. She was deeply distressed,
but her belief in prayer prevented her from regarding John's
decision as final. In it she saw a new trial, in face of which to be
disheartened would have seemed to her sinful.

The members of Mrs. Synge's family clan spoke of her trouble
in subdued tones, and from this time looked on John as different
from any of them. They found the problem that confronted them
more difficult than any that would have been raised if he had fallen
into obvious sin. They knew exactly how they should deal with a
prodigal son, but John did not offer them the opportunity of
reclaiming him from vice. They were sure that his failure to accept
their beliefs indicated spiritual pride, but outwardly his life was
ascetic and conscientious. He was oppressed by a sense of tension
in his mother's house and took refuge in silence. . . .

The crisis through which John had passed had ended a half-
hidden phase in the process by which his mode of thought was
diverging from that of the other members of his family. He had
proved strong enough openly to deny belief in their religious
theories, in spite of the misery into which he was plunged by adopting the role of the infidel. The stress of his unhappiness seems to have
prevented him from realizing that his unwillingness to suffer
isolation was not inspired by simple scepticism. He had a growing
faith in the validity of new conceptions which had been taking
shape in his mind, built up by solitary contemplation from the
results of experience.

John did not differ in type from his kindred with whom he could
not agree. While he rejected their religious teaching, he adopted the
fundamental principles of their Protestant philosophy and applied
in his dealings with them the methods which they advocated for
dealing with the world. He did not engage in any self-assertive
provocative talk nor did he open unnecessary theoretical arguments. When he differed from them on matters of faith, he claimed
the right to think for himself and applied the individualistic
principle, which they supported by the text: 'Come out from
among them and be ye separate.'

Open differences of opinion about religion between him and his relations were followed by differences about social philosophy and politics. They took shape from time to time as beliefs about either subject chanced to be put in issue by the current happenings of his life. He seems to have regarded his political opinions as originating in an exchange of religious for national enthusiasm when, some years later, he wrote:

Soon after I had relinquished the Kingdom of God I began to take a real interest in the Kingdom of Ireland. My patriotism went round from a vigorous and unreasoning loyalty to a temperate nationalism and everything Irish became sacred.[1]

This development took place gradually, but on the subject of social philosophy an issue was raised, at the beginning of the year 1890, by the necessity for his choosing some settled method of earning his living. His mother and the other members of his family had assumed that, by the time he was in his second academic year, his need for an earned income, appropriate to his inherited position in society, would appear as obvious to him as it was to them. They were shocked and bewildered when they found that he would discuss no vocation except music. His mother did not know what to do and turned to Edward and to my father for practical advice. [My father spoke to John warning him against making music a profession but, as Mrs. Synge admitted in a letter to Robert, this advice had not 'the least effect' on him. Edward wrote to his mother offering to take John into his office and train him to be a land agent. On 7 January 1890, Mrs. Synge replied: 'By all means write and advise him to give up the idea of living by music, and offer him a place in your office and a prospect of living as a gentleman. . . .'[2] But this advice, too, fell on deaf ears and during the spring John resolutely continued both his study of music and the work of his college course.]

[At the beginning of April, the even tenor of family life was suddenly overturned when his grandmother, old Mrs. Traill, who had been ill for a short while, died of bronchitis.] Although for some years she had not been able to take an active part in the life of Mrs. Synge's family, her death ended an epoch in its history. While she lived, the members of the family clan, grouped at

[1] T.C.D. MS. 4382; cf. C.W. II. 13.
[2] Quoted in her letter to Robert, 6–7 January 1890.

Rathgar, were reluctant to leave. My father and mother, with their three children, shared her house which had been connected with Mrs. Synge's by a door in the dividing wall ... [and my great-uncle Edmund and his family lived close by. As soon as his mother died, Edmund began to make plans to take his family out to his ranch in Argentina and] my father, whose practice as a solicitor was growing, thought of moving to some neighbourhood more fashionable than the quiet blind alley of Orwell Park. .... On 13 April, Mrs. Synge wrote to Robert:

Harry is going to leave this neighbourhood in September D.V. so I leave too. He says he does not dislike the place, but he wants to be among people he can know and make friends of, to further his business. I shall feel very sorry to leave; I have been so many years in this neighbourhood —25 years is a long time—nearly half my life-time—and I feel rooted here. .... However I could not stay here without any of my dear ones near me. Annie and the children are my great companions and pleasure. The boys are always busy reading and hardly ever come and sit with me. Dear Sam is always a comfort when I see him. My poor Johnnie is not a comfort yet. I am leaving it all in the Lord's hands and asking Him to guide us and to lead Harry and Annie to choose a good place for our future abode. I am also asking Him to find us two houses together as we are here. He can do all things, so if He pleases to do that for me it is quite easy to Him. ....

My father had expressed himself in favour of a move to the neighbourhood of Kingstown, one of the districts that had developed quickly after the opening of the railway in 1836. .... On 28 June, Mrs. Synge and my mother went ... and called at the office of Mr. Talbot Coall, the local land agent, to inquire whether two adjoining houses were available in any of the residential terraces of the neighbourhood. Mr. Coall said that adjoining houses were rarely vacant at the same time but that a tenant in Crosthwaite Park West would shortly be leaving a house next to an empty one, which he invited them to inspect.

Crosthwaite Park West was a tall ugly terrace built some thirty or forty years before. .... The houses bore odd numbers up to 31 and confronted, across a plot of ground, another terrace of smaller houses which bore even numbers up to 32. The plot or park, was surrounded by a line of trees and, outside them, by a spiked iron railing. Many features of the place pleased Mrs. Synge and my mother; the small front gardens were well cared ⟨for⟩, and many of them were bright with flowers formally arranged. The plate-glass windows were polished and decently veiled by lace curtains. The tennis courts in the park were well rolled and neatly marked. Every detail indicated that Crosthwaite Park was socially satis-factory.... [The vacant house, No. 29, had an ample return which made it one of the largest houses in the terrace: this suited my mother as Aunt Jane[1] had promised to pay part of the rent if two rooms of our house could be allotted to her. No. 31, the last house in the terrace, would suit Mrs. Synge, and] Mr. Coall had said that if my father took 29, temporary accommodation for Mrs. Synge could be provided in one of the other houses until 31 became vacant....

[During the summer, the arrangements were completed and it was decided that we would all move in the autumn. Workmen were engaged to prepare No. 29 for our arrival and early in September—after the usual summer holiday at Greystones—our family moved from Rathgar to Crosthwaite Park. Soon Mrs. Synge was given accommodation in No. 9, and she and John were able to move early in October.

[John was faced, almost immediately, with further examinations at Trinity College[2] for which he was ill-prepared, as usual; but he succeeded in obtaining a third class mark and promptly turned his energies back to music. He was now studying theory and composi-tion at the Academy under the distinguished teacher, Sir Robert Stewart[3] who, Mrs. Synge told Robert,] 'the last day . . . put 'A1' on Johnnie's composition, which greatly pleased John—poor boy. I am so sorry for him, he looks unhappy. He has not found the Saviour yet and until he does, how can he be happy? . . .'

While John continued to evolve an independent outlook which detached him from his relations, he found at least one interest within the family circle. My sister was an infant, but my brother was beginning his first lessons and I was old enough to be played with. John's natural love of children was mixed with a sort of scientific curiosity. He had never taken part in school or college life for long enough to acquire a knowledge of boys, and his interest

[1] Aunt Jane, the spinster sister of Synge's father, lived with the Stephenses until shortly before her death.

[2] Little Go, or the Final Freshman Examination.

[3] Sir Robert Stewart (1825–94). Synge heard of his death when he was in Germany, and was very distressed. GS, p. 40.

in the development of children had been violently awakened by the
contrast that he found between himself and the children fighting in
the streets of the Cathedral close.[1] In one of his notes made later,
when he was trying to review his early life, he wrote: 'The objective
study of childhood is full of difficulty' and in another:

If, as I believe, we find in childhood perfect, though rudimentary,
traces of the savage, the whole expression of a fine personality will
reveal to us human evolution from before history to beyond the
science of our epoch.[2]

Later in the same note, reverting to this idea, he continued:

With the same presumption that we show in forcing civilization on
the savage, we teach the child how to be childlike, and for this reason
the most interesting type of childhood is perhaps the uncultivated arab
of the streets.

My brother and I were being brought up under restraints
exactly similar to those that had been imposed on him and he now
had the opportunity of watching their effects in the light of his
own experience. His interest in street arabs did not lead him to
think that children should be uncontrolled or untaught. Although
he was continuing to diverge from the traditional beliefs of his
family, he did not revolt against authority, or regard its use in
education as a violation of the personalities of children. In writing
of him to Robert from Orwell Park, his mother had said: 'He tries
to keep little Frank in great order.' Now that Frank was six, John
was beginning to teach him natural history and music and any
miscellaneous knowledge that he could understand. . . .

[John's life among his family] was as usual rendered more difficult near Christmas, for Advent thoughts increased his mother's
longing that he should worship with his family. . . . On 7 December
she wrote in her diary: 'Went to church with Sam—sat in the top
pew' and added sadly: 'Poor Johnnie spent the day walking up the
Three Rock—hard frost up there.'

⟨On Christmas Day 1890,⟩ my mother invited all members of

[1] In his autobiographical notes, Synge recalled coming out of St. Patrick's
Cathedral and being fascinated by the sight of children from the slums around the
cathedral. A version of his account appears in C.W. II. 5.

[2] Stephens's text is a conflation of two versions of this passage found in T.C.D.
MS. 4353 (formerly item 21); cf. C.W. II. 3.

the family party at Crosthwaite Park to midday dinner . . . and so began a regular usage which she followed in each succeeding year. Every Christmas we had for dinner a fine turkey, often one of several that came as presents to my father from grateful clients in the country. Once both a turkey and a goose arrived alive but, as nobody had the heart to kill them, they lived with our few hens until my mother gave them to a friend who owned a farm-yard. The roast turkey on Christmas Day was always served with potatoes and celery and followed by a large round plum pudding that had hung for a long time in a bulging cloth from the store-room shelf.

John enjoyed a good and satisfying dinner and found these Christmas gatherings free from the embarrassment that was often caused by his divergence from family tradition. Everyone wore Sunday clothes, looked conventionally pleasant, and avoided controversial topics of conversation. My father had a gift for appearing cordial on festive occasions and carved a turkey with a sententiousness that seemed to focus everybody's mind on food. . . .

On returning to the Academy in January 1891, John . . . took a step which was afterwards to prove of peculiar importance to his development. In addition to continuing his study of the theory of music and his lessons on the violin, he joined the students' orchestra. . . . He was shy at first when he began practising with his fellow-students but he soon lost all self-consciousness and felt that, in the orchestra, he had become part of a composite body with one mind and one ideal. It was when he achieved this sense of identity with his fellow-students that he seemed to enter on a new stage of his life. Until then he had been developing his aesthetic powers alone, isolated by the cold doctrine of his family from sympathetic society, yet believing that somewhere there must be people who shared his emotions. He had been working assiduously in the hope of fitting himself for a musical career, when suddenly his ambition seemed to be miraculously realized. It was on looking back to the time in this year when he felt himself fully incorporated in the orchestra that he wrote in his black notebook:

It is not surprising that when I found in the orchestra the world of magical beauty I had dreamed of, I threw aside all reasonable counsel and declared myself a professional musician. . . .[1]

[1] T.C.D. MS. 4382; cf. *C.W.* II. 15.

8

[At the end of April, Mrs. Synge was able to move from No. 9
to No. 31 Crosthwaite Park; her arrangements for making the
family group as consolidated at Kingstown as it had been at Orwell
Park were now complete except for the making of a door between
the two houses. From this time onwards, we lived again in very
close touch with Mrs. Synge and with John.]

At the time of Mrs. Synge's move in 1891 I was two-and-a-half
years old, and it is from some time in that year my memories dimly
begin. Every morning in the back parlour after breakfast, when
my father had gone to his office, my mother used to read family
prayers. Although we did not understand what was being read, my
sister and I were brought down to them from the nursery so that the
care of us might not prevent the attendance of our nurse or either
of the two maids. They were all Protestants, because my mother
thought it essential that we should be under the care of a Protestant
nurse and feared religious differences among the servants. The
nurse dropped me once when she was drunk—so I was afterwards
told—but because of her faith she was not dismissed.

At prayers I felt such a stern disapproval of any movement that
I usually remained quiet, but if, any morning, I chanced to be
intractable, my mother, before she began to read, gave me long
fingers of bread and marmalade to keep my attention occupied. She
read first a portion of scripture and, when she closed the large Bible,
there was a shuffling noise and all knelt at their chairs. Then instead
of asking, as her mother did, for anything she might happen to want,
she read a set prayer out of a book specially written for family
use. . . .

It was not until some years later, after Aunt Jane had moved
from her rooms in 29 Crosthwaite Park, that the wall dividing Mrs.
Synge's house from ours was pierced by a doorway, but in the
meantime the want of this final link interfered very little with the
intimacy between the two households. My brother and I used very
often to run across, by a passage behind the front gardens, from one
kitchen door to the other and, as we spent much of our time at 31,
we knew our grandmother and John as well as if we were all living
in the same house. In this way she was afforded an opportunity for
undertaking our religious education, which our mother left
entirely in her hands. The passing of time had not altered her faith

and she taught us from the Bible in the very words that she had received in her own childhood from her father, her mother, and Miss Osborne at the rectory of Schull.

After the move from No. 9 she was very busy for a week in arranging the rooms, but by the first of May was finally settled in her new home. It was always well swept and dusted, and had in its general arrangement a quality that interpreted her character with peculiar force.

The hall was furnished with a small table, a chair, and a hat-stand, all of polished mahogany, and its floor was covered with dark oilcloth. It echoed the sound of the clock ticking at the top of the kitchen stairs and the bang the front door made in closing. Two rooms opened off the hall, the front parlour or dining-room, lighted by a large bow window, and the back parlour overlooking a small patch of garden.

At the top of two flights of stairs carpeted in dull red was a landing, lighted by the only window that had an uninterrupted view of the hills. Mrs. Synge slept in the back room on this floor. The front room was her drawing room. The doorway was covered inside by a heavy red plush curtain, which used to pull its rings back, squeaking on a brass rod, as the door opened. The room was long and overlooked the park from two windows, one over the hall door and the other, a large bow window, over the dining room. Its furniture conformed to no pattern but seemed to have come together fortuitously. There was a semi-grand piano along the inner wall and a large circular table at the window opposite the door. On this table were family photographs, some books in a carved stand, a stuffed owl under a glass shade and many other things which were never moved except for dusting. Mrs. Synge used to sit in a comfortable high-backed arm chair opposite the fireplace. Next her chair, draped in a tapestry cloth, was a round table for everyday use. On it she kept her key basket, her writing materials, her Bible, the current numbers of *The Life of Faith* and *The Church Missionary Gleaner*, and, after the light failed each evening and the maid had drawn the blinds, a double-wicked oil lamp.

The chimneypiece was of white marble. On each end of it stood a large pink glass candlestick from the lip of which hung long prisms reaching almost to the base. I was never allowed to touch the prisms but when I grew tall enough I often stood on my toes and blew on them without being noticed. As they swung they made a very low tinkling sound and, if the day were bright, coloured lights shimmered on the wall. There was a black marble clock in the centre of the chimneypiece. It had a low tick measured by a little pendulum so devised that as it swung, it caught a gilt cog-wheel first at one side and then at the other, stopping and releasing it for alternate half-seconds. In the years of childhood I watched it for hours as my grandmother read and explained the Bible, and I half-consciously wondered if it would miss a cog, knowing that it never could.

On the walls there were a few pictures hung because Mrs. Synge liked to think of the subjects they brought to mind and not because of their artistic value. A print in a gilt frame hung over the clock. It was of two children in white nightgowns kneeling on a black cushion, their faces illuminated by a shaft of light. A water-colour of the gate lodge of Drumboe, her mother's home, hung near the piano.

About the room were several light chairs of different ages and designs and in the corner of the room, behind the table on which the stuffed owl was sitting, some toys were concealed: a box of bricks, another of ABC cubes, some spring acrobats, a simple jig-saw puzzle, and—for use on Sundays when other toys were forbidden—a Noah's Ark.

When they first lived at 31 Crosthwaite Park, John and Sam shared a long front bedroom over the drawing-room, but later, when Sam was rising early to attend medical lectures, John moved into a back room over his mother's bedroom. This room remained his until three years before his death when he and his mother moved from Crosthwaite Park to a house in Glenageary.

By the time family routine had been established in the new house and John was free from the work of laying carpets and hanging curtains, the month of May had begun. After that the weather was warm enough to enable him to practise by the open window of the front bedroom, instead of practising by the parlour fire. For a short time he devoted himself to music with such intensity that his work in the early summer of 1891 made a special impression on his memory. [Years afterwards he described the 'morbid assiduity' with which he played and remembered]

. . . particularly the long days of a June, that I spent looking out over the four strings of my violin into the filling leaves and white erect florescence of a chestnut and a wilderness of plants beneath it, that crushed and strangled each other in a green and silent frenzy of expansion.[1]

The chestnut tree grew opposite Mrs. Synge's house in the park, the end of which was separated by a narrow road from a small field, where in the early summer, dairy cows used to stand up to their knees in grass and buttercups. This field was fringed with lilac bushes planted at intervals inside a spiked railing like that surrounding the park. The corner nearest to the house was partly shaded by trees and bushes and there the vegetation grew rank and tangled. It would have been impossible for John to have identified the wild flowers separately from his high window, but he had often peered from the footpath among all the different species of plants that were struggling for existence.

Another field, separated from the side of the house by the stable lane, looked sordid and neglected. In the corner a clump of brambles grew over some spare fragments of building stone, which nobody had troubled to remove. The wires in the fence by the road beyond the terrace hung slack and some of the posts leant sideways. Sometimes this field was used by a butcher, and a man in a blue striped overall used to come and take beasts away one at a time for slaughter. Beyond its furthest fence, to the west, in open country rising towards the hills, large houses among fine trees stood in their own grounds. Behind them in the distance were the Dublin Mountains, giving to the horizon the undulating curves that form the skyline of granite hills.

The members of the family group felt themselves to be socially superior to many of their neighbours, and were very careful to avoid making friends quickly with anyone. Their new home, on the outskirts of the suburb of Kingstown and at the end of a terrace, was well suited to the maintenance of their aloofness, except that our mother found an unforeseen difficulty in preventing my brother, my sister, and me from picking up young acquaintances. To her it seemed much more important that we should understand and be guided by class and religious differences, than that we should enjoy naturally the company of other children. The Revd. Mr. Dowse[2] very kindly allowed her to send us with our nurse into the

1 T.C.D. MS. 4382; cf. *C.W.* II. 14.

2 The Revd. John Dowse, previously curate of Zion Church, Rathgar, had been appointed rector of St. Paul's, Glenageary—one of the four Church of Ireland

rectory garden, where we might be safely alone, or play sometimes
with the children of the house. This she considered the best arrangement, but even if it had been convenient to send us often as far as the
rectory, good taste would have imposed a limit on our visits. It was
inevitable that we should be taken frequently into the park, across
which the houses of the two terraces confronted each other. Here
we found nurses and other children with whom we should have
been delighted to have played. The park was kept strictly private
for the people who lived in the houses by which it was overlooked.
To them alone keys were issued, but our mother thought that some
of their children might be vulgar, and a few might even be Roman
Catholics. She discussed the problem with our grandmother, who
on 21 June wrote to Robert:

Annie sends the children out into the park opposite our houses as they
like playing about on the grass much better than walking on the hot
roads. The only difficulty is to keep them from being with the other
children she does not know. There is one family of six children she knows,
and allows hers to play with them, but nurse likes to talk with any nurse
who happens to be near, so Annie has to tell her her wishes. . . .

    After having recently settled in a new district, the members of
the family group at Crosthwaite Park did not organize a general
removal to the country for change of air in 1891. . . . [Instead, Mrs.
Synge and Sam visited friends in Co. Tipperary and my father and
mother went for a tour of Galway and Mayo taking my brother
with them. John remained at home all summer studying music
and learning German which he had taken up in the hope of gaining
new inspiration from a foreign literature.]
    [The differences between Mrs. Synge's two youngest sons
became even more marked at this time.] Sam was planning to
devote himself to foreign missions and had decided to become a
doctor of medicine in addition to taking holy orders. He had just
completed his divinity course but postponed seeking ordination
until he should have left the medical school. From the time he
entered Trinity College he had been continually under the influence
of the extreme evangelical party and had become increasingly

---

churches near Crosthwaite Park—shortly before the Synge and Stephens families
moved to Kingstown. Stephens wrote that Mrs. Synge 'was to find in Glenageary
the same evangelical teaching that she had loved in Rathgar . . .' (TS. 434).

zealous in supporting his mother's rule of life. She was thankful
that he shared her faith and relied on his help in her efforts to convert
John to her political and religious opinions. Both she and Sam liked
to read ... the *Daily Express* which uncompromisingly upheld the
landlords' class privilege. John preferred the *Irish Times*, another
unionist paper, because it seemed to him to represent more reasonable political thought. His mother consented to take it for a time
but abandoned it because it praised Daniel O'Connell who, although
a loyalist to the British Crown, was classified by her as a rebel,
because more than half a century before, he had won political
emancipation for Roman Catholics. ...

[John was now in his last year at Trinity College. He later wrote
of this period:]

When I realized that the life about me could not give me any real satisfaction, my desire for study came on me again. I ran through history,
chemistry, physics, botany, Hebrew, Irish, Latin, Greek, something of
French and German and made a really serious study of the history and
theory of music.[1]

His taking up the study of Irish in Trinity College met with no
opposition from the members of his family because it had for them
no political significance. They regarded both Irish and Hebrew
as Divinity School subjects, Hebrew because it was the language of
the Old Testament and Irish because it was the medium through
which the Irish Church Missions sought to convert the Roman
Catholics of the western coast to the Protestant faith. The text from
which beginners were to be taught was not prescribed by the calendar: but the Protestant version of the New Testament was cus-
tomarily used by the lecturer.

Sam, from his knowledge of the Divinity School, was able to
tell John that entries in the first year for the Irish and Hebrew
prizes would not be many and that his chances of success were good.[2]
Aunt Jane would have encouraged him to study both languages

---

[1] T.C.D. MS. 4382; cf. *C.W.* II. 13.

[2] Synge won a junior prize in both languages in the following autumn. Nine
students received prizes in the Hebrew examination, and Synge—who seems to
have been placed last of the seven winners in his class—was given £3 of the £40
awarded. In Irish, he was the only representative of his class—though there were
three senior prize winners—and received £4 of the £20 prize money. (T.C.D.
Calendar for 1893, pp. 125–7; cf. GS, p. 27.)

for she remembered how much her brother Alexander had needed a knowledge of Irish during his ministry in the Aran Islands and she remembered how, in her childhood at Glanmore, her father had taught his children Hebrew from the books he printed with the type that she still preserved in one of the old trunks in the lumber room.

John never carried his study of Hebrew further than was necessary for the prize examination, but his introduction to the Irish language was to prove of the first importance to his literary career. It was when he was studying Irish in Trinity College that he first began to read the epic tales of ancient Ireland. They caught his folk imagination as the Greek tales had done,[1] but for him they had a new quality that seemed akin to the mode of expression used by his friends among the country people, a wild, fantastic exaggeration which had no counterpart in the classics of Greece. He had delighted in Homeric realism which gave power equally to stories of fabulous monsters and unhappy mortals. In the Irish tales he found the lives of human heroes as fantastic as the lives of the gods themselves, yet full of natural emotion. These tales were local and belonged to a people among whom their imagery was still living. For him they had the same force in their references to Tara Hill and other places he knew as the Homeric stories might have had for a Greek in their references to the blue water, the shores and islands of the eastern Mediterranean. The heroic tales of both races, illuminated by his imagination, mingled in his mind which had never been damaged or confined by ordinary schooling. . . . When he left college, he abandoned the study of Greek; but he continued to read the Irish tales and to find in them the power that was inspiring the national literary movement. . . .

⟨John's⟩ feelings about Ireland were acquiring a new force; referring to his patriotic emotions at this period, he afterwards wrote . . .: 'Patriotism gratifies man's need for adoration and has, therefore, a peculiar power upon the imaginative sceptic.'[2] He was gradually extending to the whole of Ireland the love he had for the part of the country that he knew best. One of his chief inspirations in doing this he had found in reading the Irish ballads that had

---

[1] In an analysis of Synge's reading during his first year at Trinity, Stephens had stressed the important effect which the discovery of Greek drama had upon his development (TS. 372–4).

[2] T.C.D. MS. 4382; cf. *C.W.* II. 14.

been first published by *The Nation* newspaper nearly fifty years before. The youthful enthusiasm they evoked led him to overesti-mate their literary value and he seems afterwards to have been so mortified by this mistake that he forgot their real influence, for he wrote: 'The Irish ballad poetry of *The Spirit of the Nation* school engrossed me for a while; I thought it excellent for a considerable time and then repented bitterly....'[1] [Even though it was obviously a political rather than a literary influence that worked on John's imagination when he was engrossed with these ballads,] it is impossible to believe that the new way in which he was regarding his country was other than the result of their subtle force; for looking back to this time, he wrote:

The Irish country rains, mists, pale insular skies, the old churches, manuscripts, jewels, everything in fact that was Irish had a charm neither human nor divine, rather perhaps as if I had fallen in love with a goddess.[2]

In search of books that would influence his love, he read ancient Irish lore and works on archaeology and history, but did not at this time seek to interpret his imaginative nationalism by a political theory. The Society for the Preservation of the Irish Language was making the ancient epic tales available for everyone to read in cheap well-printed volumes containing both the Irish text and an English translation. On 18 March, John noted in his diary that he began reading *The Children of Lir*, a story published in one of these volumes just ten years before. He continued reading it slowly, studying the Irish text and noting from time to time in his diary incidents from the narrative as if they were happenings in the lives of real people. Besides *The Children of Lir* he began Wakeman's *Handbook of Irish Antiquities*, a book which helped him to construct in his mind a realistic background for the lore of ancient Ireland....

[This discovery of another side of Ireland obviously gave John great pleasure, for he concluded one of the entries in his diary with the following comment in Latin:] '*Homo, qui per orbem totam erravit, Hiberniam optimam faciliter vivendo putat*' (A man who has wandered through the whole world thinks Ireland easily the best country to live in)....

[1] T.C.D. MS. 4382; cf. *C.W.* II. 13.

[2] T.C.D. MS. 4382, f. 51v. The passage has been struck out forcefully by Synge, in ink.

[John's diary for 1892 contains notes of memorable passages from books he was reading and shows how very wide his interests had become.] These notes were in English but among them, on Saturday 26 March, he made an entry in Latin on a different subject in which he was to find increasing interest. He had had a dream which, although unimportant in itself, seemed to him a psychic experience and he wrote: '*Edmundus T. junior in superiore nocte mihi in somno venit; hodie epistola ejus ex Argentina venit.*'[1] By this he meant that his cousin, Ned Traill, had appeared to him in a dream the night before and that a letter from him had arrived from Argentina that day.

The reality of psychic phenomena was tacitly assumed by the members of the family group at Crosthwaite Park to an extent not usual among the supporters of the evangelical revival. Their assumption was founded chiefly on my father's claim to remarkable powers of second sight, powers which were claimed, to some degree, also by his sisters. He was a busy lawyer who did nothing to develop his unusual faculties. Spiritualism and occult lore he hated, and denounced mystics as untidy and unwashed. From time to time he described having seen apparitions, assuming that his observation was not open to doubt. Many of them were of people at a distance doing ordinary things—a family sitting round a fire, a friend making purchases in a shop. About matters of this kind, he was never known to have been mistaken. A story was told of how at one time he had risen to greet an old school-fellow as if he were coming into the room and of how it was afterwards learnt that at the same time his old school-fellow had died.

Mrs. Synge, without denying their truth, did not allow herself to be greatly moved by my father's stories. She said that it might not be possible to avoid seeing apparitions, but that calling them up was clearly forbidden by the Bible. She quoted the command: 'Thou shalt not suffer a witch to live,' the prophet Isaiah's words against wizards 'That peep and that mutter', and the story of the witch of Endor calling up the spirit of the prophet Samuel. . . . She said that the knowledge necessary for securing salvation was very simple, that we had been taught it clearly and that, if we made undirected investigations of the unseen world, we were laying ourselves open to the deceits of evil spirits. John's divergence from the members of the family group at Crosthwaite Park on questions of

[1] T.C.D. MS. 4413.

religion had not led him to reject their belief in apparitions. He remained always primarily concerned with his impressions of the substantial world but sometimes, particularly when his mind was tense and overstrained, he seemed to find in himself a capacity for psychic experience. His growing interest in dreams, premonitions, and visions helped him to understand the lore of the country people and was to prove an important link between him and the more mystically-minded Irish writers after he met Yeats in Paris some years later. It was not inconsistent with his general theories which had been gradually growing less dogmatic. . . .

9

At this time, Mrs. Synge made in her summer plans an apparently insignificant change which proved to have peculiarly important consequences for John. He was now of age and, just as the neighbourhood of Greystones had been associated with the experiences of his childhood and youth, the Wicklow plateau was to be associated with the experiences that most impressed his mind in later life. Since his great-grandfather, Francis Synge, had gone to live at Roundwood . . . , a decline in the population had given an added sense of desolation to the surrounding district. The lives of the people who remained had continued as unaffected by outside influences as the lives of the people of the promontories and islands of the western coast. John had been through most of east Wicklow on foot or on his bicycle, but it was not until this year that he had an opportunity of acquiring any great familiarity with the plateau and the hills to its south and west.

The day before his Irish examination, Mrs. Synge had returned from ⟨a visit to⟩ Greystones to make holiday arrangements for the members of the family at Crosthwaite Park. Because she believed that change of air was important to their health, she had arranged, when they lived at Orwell Park, that they should go annually to the seaside and now that they lived near the sea, she was planning that their summer removals should be to the mountains. For information as to where a suitable house might be found she relied, as usual, on a member of the family clan. Since 1850, Roundwood Park had remained in the possession of strangers, but Cousin Emily[1]

---

[1] Cousin Emily Synge, a first cousin of Synge's father, had been brought up in England; after the death of her mother in 1881, she returned to Ireland to live in the Wicklow hills. (See TS. 214–15.)

was living nearby at 'Uplands', the small house she had built over-looking the river. From her Mrs. Synge heard that Castle Kevin, an old house belonging to the Frizelle family, was unoccupied and was to be let furnished for the summer months. Mrs. Synge had planned to share it with my father and to bring a family party together under one roof, as she had done at Dromont[1] and Rath-down in her mother's lifetime. The matter had been discussed before she had gone to Greystones, but nothing had been settled. It was always difficult to conclude any arrangement with my father and there was one very strong reason against going to Castle Kevin —the house was boycotted.[2] There was difficulty in deciding whether it would be safe to take children there, and whether a summer holiday would be spoiled by hostility from the neighbours. On the other hand, the rent of a boycotted house was low and, as time passed, the danger of disturbance grew less. The worst of the evictions which had given rise to the boycott had taken place ten years before. The house had not been damaged since Mr. Frizelle had left it in the care of Harry Harding, a local farmer. The members of the family group staying in the house as summer visitors would be in no way connected with the dispute, and they had many friends in the district. After long deliberation, Mrs. Synge's plan was adopted and, on 14 July, she wrote in her diary: 'Harry and Annie came in this evening, all settled about Castle Kevin. . . .' Mrs. Synge's decision to move on less than a week's notice threw her household into a great commotion. John laid aside most of his reading and helped his mother to pack and to arrange the house. His own preparations were quickly made. He bought a new fishing line, a road map, and a copy of the Irish epic tale, *The Flight of Diarmuid and Grania*, and packed his books and clothes. The move was organized on Mrs. Synge's established system. The luggage was to be carted and John was to travel on his bicycle the twenty-five miles by road; Mrs. Synge, leaving her house in the care of Miss McCutcheon, one of her old Protestant retainers, was to go

[1] Dromont was another large house at Greystones.

[2] During the period of the so-called 'Land War' in Ireland (1879–82)—when the evictions had taken place on the Frizelles' estate—the Land League, headed by Parnell and Davitt, had organized resistance to the landlords to prevent evictions, to secure a reduction in rents and—in the long run—to bring about a change in land ownership in Ireland. The ultimate weapon used by the Land League was social ostracism, the boycott, named after a Mayo land agent against whom it was first employed.

with her party by train to Greystones and drive the fifteen miles from there to Castle Kevin.

Wednesday, 20 July, was a beautifully sunny day and Mrs. Synge was up early to finish her packing. After breakfast there was an hour of great bustle when everyone available carried out bundles of bedding, portmanteaux, cooking utensils, and parcels. At half past ten, the cart moved off slowly with its heavy load securely roped. The rest of the morning she devoted to putting the house in order before handing it over to the care of Miss McCutcheon. After Mrs. Synge and her party had lunched with my mother, two cabs arrived to carry her, Aunt Lizzie,[1] Florence,[2] Sam, and the two maids to Sandycove station for the Greystones train and John, when he had seen the cabs off, set out alone on his bicycle for Castle Kevin.[3]

He was glad to travel slowly because the day was warm and much of his way was through the country that he most enjoyed. It was well that he went to Castle Kevin by road and alone, for the journey helped him to incorporate his impressions of the part of Wicklow that he had known from childhood with his impressions of the district which was to be one of his chief sources of inspiration for the rest of his life. For the first twelve miles he went south towards the town of Wicklow, but at Kilmacanogue village turned up a road that, winding round Great Sugarloaf, climbed to the plateau. At once he had left the fields and demesnes of the Golden Belt and was among the foothills of the retaining wall going through the Rocky Valley, a small ravine across the foot of the mountain. On his left Sugarloaf rose from the edge of the road and on his right a small jagged hill called Carrig Una. Where their

[1] Aunt Lizzie was Elizabeth Synge, another sister of Synge's father. Stephens says that she was interested in oil painting but 'was better endowed with dexterity than with any artistic powers' (TS. 527). He also remarks that 'her manner to children, though perhaps too effusive, was affectionate and made such a pleasant contrast with the repression of all feeling customary in our house that I, when a very young child, called her "the beloved Aunt Lizzie" ' (TS. 528).

[2] Florence Ross, Synge's childhood friend, had come to make her home with Mrs. Synge in December 1891 after the death of her mother, Mrs. Synge's sister Agnes (TS. 468, 476, 482).

[3] The passage which follows (pp. 71–6) is typical of Stephens's method of imaginative recreation of incidents in Synge's life. Certain details—weather, train-times etc.—are taken from diaries, but the descriptive details are Stephens's own. He often rode to Annamoe, sometimes with Synge, and his recreation of the sights, sounds, and smells of the journey is based on his memories of such occasions.

sides were not of naked rock or barren scree, sheep grazed among the bracken and heather. For about a mile, parts only of the road were too steep for riding, but at the upper end of the valley he dismounted for a half-hour's walk up the Long Hill.

A cloud of flies over his head rose and fell at every step, but as he climbed the air grew fresher and, when from time to time he stopped for a few minutes' rest, he had a widening view looking back to the country between him and Dublin. Well-known landmarks came into sight—the Scalp, the Smelting Chimney, and Powerscourt House.[1] Above the road was the rough side of the mountain, and below, reclaimed fields running down to a sheltered water course. Beyond its opposite bank and the trees of Powerscourt demesne, he was looking straight up the wide valley of Glencree to the distant heather-covered barrier of mountain that closed its upper end above Lough Bray.

After he had been walking with his bicycle for nearly half an hour, he came to a place where the road, bending round a gully, brought him over the top of the hill on to the broad expanse of Calary Bog. Besides the natural pleasure in reaching the top of a long hill, he felt a sort of fresh surprise whenever he climbed one of the hills to the plateau and suddenly came out, as if he were Jack at the top of the beanstalk, into a country of a character quite different from that of the country below.

The edge of the plateau had cut off his view of the Golden Belt; the fragrance of moorland was in the air. The road, here turned to a bright purple by the local sandstone, lay unfenced straight across a waste. Beside it there was a lonely schoolhouse to which, in term time, parties of children converged each morning from the scattered farms. Beyond the open moor he passed a two-storied public house set back from the road so that carts might stop in the open space before the door. It was always known as 'Elijah Sutton's' although the name MOUNTAIN SIDE TAVERN was printed in black letters across the whitewash of its front wall. The public house marked the beginning of the fenced farms, many of them prosperous. They stretched on his right for a mile or two towards the

---

[1] These landmarks are mentioned frequently in the TS.; the Scalp (Ir. *scealp*, a cleft or chasm) is a rift in a ridge of hills north of Enniskerry, the smelting chimney of Ballycorus is on a hill near the Scalp, and Powerscourt House and demesne lie to the south of Enniskerry. Glencree runs from Enniskerry west up into the Dublin Mountains.

west until they were stopped by the rounded purple mass of Djouce
Mountain, and on his left, for two or three miles, to the low hills
fringing the eastern edge of the plateau. Riding was easy, for the
general fall of the ground was towards the south, but occasionally
he got off his bicycle to walk up a short hill. As he went along,
yellow-hammers were singing and his attention was caught from
time to time by a passing bird—it might be a curlew whistling high
overhead or a plover rising to stagger in the air crying over one of
the patches of bog scattered among the fields.

After travelling about six miles from the top of the Long Hill,
he rode into the village of Roundwood.... He had passed through
⟨the district⟩ from time to time on excursions from Greystones and
had no need to ask his way. Above him, on the hill beyond the
village, were the trees of Roundwood Park. More than a century
had passed since the fine day in June when his great-grandfather,
Francis Synge, had arrived there in his four-in-hand with his young
wife.[1] Without either the wealth or the prejudices that might have
separated him from the people, John had come to stay in the district
with which his family had ever since been associated. He passed the
fair-green and went up the village street as far as the Roman Catholic
church. There he turned, not up towards the old house, but to his
right, along under the hill on which it stood: ...⟨soon⟩ John was
among hills where land, not so fertile as that of the more level parts
of the plateau, had not provided wealth enough to pay for the
introduction of change in the people's mode of life. Rushes grew
beside the road and below it, on the right, lay the rocky townlands[2]
of Raheen and Baltinannima, where the boulders, some of which
bore the incised markings of pagan times, were too many to remove
for reclamation. It was the edge of a district where archaic words
were specially noticeable in the current speech of the people, a
district where a few of the women still spun wool from their own
sheep.

Along the hillside to his left, above the fields, John could see the
fence of the old road . . . [near which] was the square-towered
Protestant parish church of Derrylossery, in its walled graveyard;
. . . it was the church in which Cousin Emily had her pew. John's
family and the local Protestant people, who had never heard of

---

[1] Stephens had earlier (TS. 29) described how Francis Synge had brought his
young wife to Roundwood in 1787.

[2] A townland is the smallest administrative division of land in Ireland.

agnosticism, would go there on Sundays. Here were new problems
for John: was he to refrain from going to church in a place where
every member of the congregation would notice his absence, but
nobody could explain it rightly? Was he to embarrass his mother
by appearing to be careless about religion? Should he, on the other
hand, join in simple worship as Wordsworth[1] had done when he
returned to Cumberland with his mind full of enthusiasm for the
French Revolution? Wordsworth had not allowed theories to
prevent him from attending church with the country people; so
far at least his example was clear, but the emotions he described,
as separating him from the congregation, were different from the
feelings that made John wish to continue his lonely walks on
Sunday instead of taking his place in the Castle Kevin pew.
Wordsworth had written:

> It was a grief,
> Grief call it not, 'twas anything but that,
> A conflict of sensations without name,
> Of which he only who may love the sight
> Of a Village Steeple as I do can judge
> When in the Congregation, bending all
> To their great Father, prayers were offer'd up,
> Or praises for our Country's Victories,
> And 'mid the simple worshippers, perchance,
> I only, like an uninvited Guest
> Whom no one own'd sate silent. . . .[2]

In thinking about going to church John was not troubled by the
question whether he could take part in the prayers and thanks-
givings of the congregation, but whether he ought to express by a
public act a belief in doctrines that he did not accept. In the early
days of his unbelief it is probable that he would not have hesitated
to demonstrate his opinions, but now that, under Wordsworth's
influence, his mind had turned again towards religion, the path
of duty was not clear. He might go to church regarding himself as
a sophisticated person willing to accept the simplicity of a peasant
congregation, yet in many ways the conditions in Cumberland
differed greatly from those in Wicklow. . . . [In the end, he]
decided to adopt the kindly course of attending service often

[1] Wordsworth exercised a powerful influence over Synge at this time; GS, pp.
29, 33, 40.
[2] *The Prelude* (text of 1805), x. 263–73.

enough to avoid giving scandal and, when he again stayed in the
district, continued this conformity until after the events of the next
few years had made it possible for him to consider with detachment
the opinions of his family on social and religious questions.

A short twisted hill from ⟨Derrylossery⟩ church met the new
road at a place where it ran down a gradual slope which John could
coast, his feet over the handlebars of his bicycle. After nearly a
mile the road met the brown, turf-stained river from Lough Dan
and turned east beside it through Brady's Glen. On the hill above,
looking up the river, was Cousin Emily's house Uplands, ... hidden
from the road by a coppice of oaks. Beyond the little glen, in a
more open part of the valley, under the steep, furzy sheep pasture
of Ballinacorbeg, he passed the mill of Annamoe, built for his
great-great-grandfather, John Hatch, in 1765.[1] There was no stir
about the place, for the small local mills were being deserted and
falling into decay. The sluice was shut and no current in the full
mill pool shook the reflection of the grey gable and its motionless
wheel. Just below the mill the road from Annamoe crossed an old
bridge and, with a single line of telegraph wire, joined his on the
right. A short climb from the river, up a steep bend in the road,
enabled him to see the rectory on the far bank and the village. Then,
on a hill in front of him, at some distance, he caught sight of a grey
stone house surrounded by trees. It was Castle Kevin. . . .

Soon after passing the mill, John came to 'the red bank', a
waste bit of land in the angle between the main road, bending
round Tomriland Hill, and a by-road, dropping away on the right
to Castle Kevin. Across the bog he could see the square green mound
where the old manorial castle of the archbishops of Dublin had
stood, and near him, on his left, the great circular mound where,
the people said, Cromwell's cannon had been placed for the attack
by which the castle had been finally destroyed. After crossing the
sudden hump of a small stone bridge, his road joined the road round
the town[2] opposite the gate of Castle Kevin.

The house faced north and was approached by a long avenue

---

[1] It was at this mill that Laurence Sterne had a miraculous escape when a child;
he fell through the mill race while the mill was going and was 'taken up unhurt'
(*The Works of Laurence Sterne*, ed. James P. Brown (London, 1885), I. 35). See TS.
10.

[2] A local name for the largely disused road which circled the townland of Castle
Kevin.

from each side of the hill. It was so far from the road that few
tinkers and tramps came to the door begging, although many
slept under carts or in the shelter of bushes beside the road round the
town where, passing the remains of the old castle, it ran from one
avenue gate to the other. There was no lodge by the gate at which
John arrived because, although the west avenue ran directly up to
the front door, it was so steep that it could not be used as the
principal approach. The chief entrance was at the other side of the
hill where the east avenue climbed with easier gradient to the stable
yard and, before reaching it, branched to the front gravel sweep.

John pushed open the gate which squealed on its hinges and
clanged behind him, and began to climb the steepest part of the
unkept avenue running unfenced across a boggy hillside. In places
rushes were beginning to grow in its surface and naked outcrops of
rock were appearing here and there. He came to a second gate and
passed through it into a grove from which the avenue, in this part
grass-grown, curved up under a line of lime trees across a wide
lawn. Above the lawn was the last gate by which he passed into the
pleasure grounds before the house, and a final steep climb of fifty
yards brought him to the hall door.

His mother had arrived first and had kept a boiling kettle ready
for his tea. She was delighted by the place and had enjoyed her long
drive from Greystones. Her son, Edward, and Aunt Jane, who were
staying there, had been at the station to welcome her party and to
see them off on John Evans's outside car.[1] They had been a heavy
load, but the young people had eased the horse by walking all the
hills. The way they had chosen for their climb to the plateau was by
Colla hill, whence they had driven along a road which passed
through the Synge estate about a mile above the waterfall. Coming
from the direction of the Devil's Glen they had arrived at the
principal entrance to Castle Kevin, two graceful old iron gates
hanging from high stone piers, which were moss-grown in the
shade of overhanging beeches. They had admired the lodge, standing in a sunny space to the right of the gate, a long low cottage
facing across a small flower garden towards the road. The edges of
its thatched roof were ornamented with a wicker border, and the
thickness of the thatch made eaves above the irregular whitewashed
walls. Old Douglas, the tailor, and his wife lived in the gate lodge.

[1] John Evans and Willie Belton were two carters often employed by Mrs.
Synge.

He used to sit on a table cross-legged at his work before a window which looked out on the garden where Mrs. Douglas grew pansies and mignonette in small beds protected with wire netting from the rabbits.

On Mrs. Synge's arrival, Mrs. Douglas had come out to open the gate and curtsey as the car drove in. Some of the party had got off the car and walked up the avenue. At first it was a green tunnel formed at the sides by high banks and above by the thick foliage of beeches which had been topped when they were young, and spread their branches like the groins of a gothic aisle. Passing from under them, where the avenue turned abruptly to the right, the party had come to another thatched gate lodge by a walled ring made for turning carriages. It was a place which created a strange impression of decay, for the thatch of the lodge had partly fallen in and the gates of the ring were rotting off their hinges.

After turning up the hill again, the party had passed under tall trees meeting overhead until at the garden wall the avenue branched and, by a short level drive, they had emerged from the trees at the hall door from where the mountains were in full view. When John had arrived he had walked up from the gate pushing his bicycle, his back to the view until he reached the door.

Large trees near the house hid the eastern edge of the plateau but to the north and west, over the sloping lawn and the treetops of the grove below, there was a wide view of the valley, of hills covered with fields and woods and, behind them, of heather-topped mountains. Opposite Castle Kevin to the north was Tomriland hill ending steeply at its western end in Ballinacorbeg, where Cousin Emily lived. Beyond the river was Mrs. Barton's demesne of Drumin, its green lands interspersed with trees, and its oak woods stretching across the hills towards Lough Dan. The higher mountains were four or five miles away. Seen from Castle Kevin, their outlines formed naturally a beautiful composition and the colours of their rocks and heather were bright on clear days. It was this view that John described, in a veiled way, when he wrote some years later of a curious experience in which the landscape before him seemed to melt into a world of visionary splendour for which there was no natural counterpart.[1] The view influenced everyone who lived at Castle Kevin, but it became stamped on John's memory as one of the deep impressions of his life.

[1] *C.W.* II. 10.

The house was three-storied, of grey stone, square, and so strongly built that the local people used to say it was cannon-proof at the time of the rebellion. Its roof projected on all sides in wide eaves, under which house-martins dived and twittered. The sombre appearance given to the front of the house by grey stone and a northern aspect was accentuated by contrast with the dazzling whiteness of the carriage sweep, which was covered with crushed quartz drawn from the disused mines at Glendalough. This quartz sand was sufficiently poisoned with lead to prevent weeds from growing and it did not require as much care as gravel because the rain smoothed wheel marks from its surface. Eight granite steps led up to the porch, a grey timber structure built on a stone platform bridging a deep area that surrounded the house. Into this area the heavily barred windows of the basement opened. The sitting rooms were on the hall floor. Of the bedrooms above them those in front were allotted to Mrs. Synge and her party and those at the back were reserved for our family. Mrs. Synge chose the west bedroom over the drawing-room and John had the next room over the hall. The windows of both rooms shared the view of the mountains.

John's arrival was soon followed by that of the luggage cart, which he had passed on the road. The ropes were untied and everything unloaded quickly, but the members of the party were too tired to arrange the house more than was necessary for going to bed. The evening was fine and, when the sound of the cart died away, an unbroken silence settled on Castle Kevin. . . .

[The holiday was a peaceful, restful one.] Mrs. Synge's way of enjoying her visit to Castle Kevin helped to ensure the tranquillity of her party. Being in a beautiful place gave her contentment and she did not feel bored if, after attending to her household duties, her only recreation was walking on the avenues or in nearby fields. . . . On fine afternoons, when she could stop to rest by the road, Mrs. Synge sometimes walked to places three or four miles distant. She always took with her at least one of the young people to bear her company, to carry her camp stool or her air cushion and to protect her from tramps, dogs, and farm animals. They did not grudge the time they spent in going for these quiet walks for there was no organized programme of amusement at Castle Kevin; . . . Sam had to devote a considerable amount of his time to reading for his medical course, but part of this work he could do while sitting

with his mother in the fields. Any day when he had finished his
allotted reading, he was willing to help her to pick fruit in the
garden or go with her for a walk. Aunt Lizzie and Florence were
occupied chiefly in painting, and John soon fell into his usual
habits of reading and ranging over the country alone.

Coming to Castle Kevin at twenty-one years of age with his
mind stirred by *The Nation* ballads was an event of real importance
in his life. The surrounding district was for him a particularly rich
source of the experience that his mind was at that time most ready
to receive. [John and his brothers] looked on themselves as Wicklow
men ⟨and⟩ he felt stirred by coming to his native district. It was a
wild and sparsely-populated place where villages were small, and
the cottages that were scattered in the open spaces and valleys
thinned near the heather to a few isolated cabins reached by
unfrequented tracks. Above them the purple hills were an unfenced
pasture for mountain sheep. Throughout the district, remains of
graves, fortifications and buildings furnished material for recon-
structing in imagination the history of its people. Many of the
remains belonged to the period of the early Celtic church, some
were more ancient and a few belonged to medieval times. . . .

Although, as days passed, no threat was made to the members of
the party at Castle Kevin, they were not allowed to forget that they
were staying in a boycotted house. In the evenings sometimes two
constables came up the avenue and walked round the outbuildings
to see that all was well. On the door-post of the porch John discovered, scribbled in pencil, a few lines of verse [expressing
exultation at the departure of Mr. Frizelle,] which afterwards he
published, tactfully misdescribing the place where they were
found.[1] . . . The only direct attempt to boycott our party came from
the blacksmith and it proved to be of a formal character. The
first time that the stable man took Joey to the forge, he returned to
say that D'Arcy, the smith, refused to shoe a horse from the boycotted house. It seemed as if serious trouble was beginning; but
D'Arcy soon sent, through a Protestant neighbour, a message that
he could not deal with the stable man who had been concerned
in the evictions but that the horse would be shod if brought to the
forge by a member of Mrs. Synge's family. My father rode over to
the forge and formed a lasting friendship with the smith. The
remainder of the holidays were perfectly tranquil. . . .

[1] The poem is printed in *C.W.* II. 212.

[We all travelled back to Crosthwaite Park in the middle of September after the first of many holidays spent at Castle Kevin. John's stay there] had been memorable mostly for what he had felt and thought alone, but it had brought also a few opportunities, rare in his home life, of talking with girls of his own age. Those whom he met in the students' orchestra were working companions with whom he talked about music. In ordinary life, except for the company of Florence⟨Ross⟩, ... he was without female society. ... [But this summer, his two English cousins, Maude Synge and Alice Owen, had been visiting Cousin Emily at Uplands, close to Castle Kevin.] On the few occasions when he had met them, he had found them delightful companions and had been greatly attracted by Alice, who had been occupying a special place in his thoughts. ⟨On the last Sunday evening of the holiday,⟩ he had written in his diary: 'I saw Alice';[1] but he wrote in Irish so that nobody who might chance to see the page could understand. ...

Among a holiday party at Castle Kevin, John had found musical composition impossible, but no sooner was he home than he began to work again. On the day after his return, although he had to devote time to laying carpets with Sam and Florence, he entered in his diary: 'Wrote airs in E♭ & G.' He had come home in very good health and refreshed by his stay in Wicklow. ... [He took a lot of exercise, wrote several musical compositions, and also continued reading as much as he could.]

On 28 September, his work was pleasantly interrupted by the coming of his cousins from Uplands on their way to England. As usual, without any opportunity of being alone with either, he met them and talked with them in the family circle. ... In the evening John saw them off at the pier and when the mailboat cast off, ⟨he⟩ waited to listen and watch as the paddle-wheels thumped the still water into foam and the outline of the ship grew dim in the darkness of the harbour. He walked home to Crosthwaite Park and wrote in his diary in the Irish language: 'Alice went away alas! alas!' and added in English: 'Read Tennyson's Maud.' Alice had vanished leaving his emotions stirred by an imaginative picture, the validity of which it was impossible to test by closer acquaintance. This was not the beginning of a love affair, but of a way of being in love with objects remote and idealized, a feeling which, as it developed, was to determine his way of writing about women. ...

[1] T.C.D. MS. 4413.

PART TWO

1893-1900

[Early in December 1892, John sat for his final examination at Trinity College and soon afterwards he heard that he had been granted a second class degree in the pass school.] On Thursday 15 December, my mother and Florence went to 'Commencements' to see the conferring of his degree. Although ambitious for scholarship and intensely industrious, he had never attempted to gain a degree with honours; and yet, during the years of his college course, he had reached a higher standard of education than many who devoted themselves to winning academic distinctions. He did not regard becoming a graduate as in any sense the end of his education but as so slight an incident that it did not even seem to him to warrant a holiday. . . .

[Now that he had the degree, John was obviously in a position to start earning his living. But still he would only consider a career as a musician. Three months after his degree ceremony, the one member of Mrs. Synge's clan who was a professional musician, Cousin Mary Synge,[1] came to stay with my mother for some weeks. She immediately took an interest in John and his musical aspirations. After he had helped her to organize a successful concert in Dublin, she suggested that he should go to Germany, as she herself had done, to study music.]

John recognized the wisdom of her advice, but he had no means of going to Germany unless his mother paid his expenses, for his own income at this time did not exceed ten pounds a year. If he had himself proposed a plan for studying music abroad, she would have regarded it as another of his impractical ideas, but Cousin Mary was convincing. . . . [Also, though Cousin Mary was poor,] she at least earned her living by music. She sometimes stayed on the river island of Oberwerth near Coblenz in a boarding-house kept by four sisters, her friends Hedwig, Emma, Claire, and Valeska von Eiken. Her plan was that when she next went to Oberwerth, John

---

[1] Stephens describes Cousin Mary Synge as follows: 'Small and full of violence, she used to jerk her body round instead of turning her head. She had thick, white hair which seemed almost to stand on end, and she used to set her teeth rather aggressively when she laughed. If anyone spoke when she was playing, she used to hit the notes and wrench herself round from the keyboard . . .' (TS. 593–4). A photograph of Cousin Mary, probably taken by Synge, may be found in *My Wallet of Photographs: The Collected Photographs of J. M. Synge,* arranged and introduced by Lilo Stephens (Dublin, 1971), plate 53.

should accompany her and try whether the neighbourhood of Coblenz provided the environment in which he could develop his musical talents.

After talking the matter over, Mrs. Synge thought Cousin Mary's suggestion the most practical that had been made for giving John a profession or, if he were overestimating his musical gifts, of showing him that it was foolish to adopt music as his calling. The plan for his going to Oberwerth insured him against the danger of going alone to a foreign country among godless strangers. Cousin Mary promised to make all necessary arrangements for a visit to her friends in Germany in the coming summer. . . .

[When John left for Germany at the end of July 1893, he was aware that] a new stage in his life was opening. The next seven years he afterwards regarded as a specially defined period in his evolution. He dated its beginning by his first meeting with people who shared his opinions and its termination by the commencement of his literary career. Of its beginning, he wrote . . .: 'Till I was twenty-three I never met or at least knew a man or woman who shared my opinions.'[1] Its termination did not seem to him quite so clearly marked, but when he was between twenty-eight and thirty, he wrote in one of his autobiographical notes:

A young man is not able to compose, and an old man, a man who is thirty, is not able to experience. When we have learned expression we go among the fields and mountains, and kiss the lips of girls with wild efforts to remember.[2]

His judgement he partly revised, but he never ceased to regard the seven years after he was twenty-two as a special epoch in his development. . . .

[Germany was certainly a revelation to him; he found the von Eiken sisters—particularly the youngest, Valeska—delightful companions and enjoyed his visit to Oberwerth so much that he stayed longer than he had planned.] In the von Eikens' boarding-house he found a new companionship; he was among people who regarded the stage as an important art and accepted his ambition to become a musician as perfectly natural. He enjoyed their society. On warm evenings he sat with them drinking coffee under the

[1] *C.W.* II. 11.   [2] T.C.D. MS. 4350; cf. *C.W.* II. 23.

trees in the garden that ran down to the river's edge. In the mornings, when he practised on the violin, he had the help of Cousin Mary or one of his new friends playing his accompaniments. Sometimes, in the afternoons, he joined them for picnic parties to the forest. . . . His intimate knowledge of his own country and his love of its traditions and antiquities had prepared him to appreciate the Rhineland. He had come to a country which provided, in the strictly historical sense, the scenery of romance and he missed none of its significance. With his new friends he walked through the forests and among the vineyards and cherry orchards. . . .

[John's stay in Germany was also instilling in him a new sense of independence. In particular, Christmas in Germany impressed him:] among the German people there was a primitive feeling of real festivity. . . . The idea that he had lost immeasurably through his early isolation from society was becoming his settled conviction. He did not believe that he had been the victim of any intentional wrong, but he felt that parental authority and the narrow routine of his home had restricted his life. His going to Germany seemed to have brought him unexpected liberation and, with it, regret that he had grown up ill-adapted to the company of other people. He was passing through an experience which he afterwards regarded as a crisis in his life, a crisis which he dramatized with peculiar force in *The Playboy of the Western World*. In a letter to his mother he told her a little of what was passing in his mind, but she found his doubts about the wisdom of his upbringing as difficult to understand as his doubts about religion. . . .[1]

[In the new year, John regretfully left the von Eikens, to whom he had become very attached, and set out to fend for himself in the town of Würzburg where he felt he could further his musical career more advantageously. It was at this time that he first became aware of the work of Goethe which was to exercise a] direct and powerful influence over his method of synthesizing his experiences and marshalling them for productive purposes. . . . [In particular, John was impressed by Goethe's autobiography *Truth and Poetry: from my own life*.] From boyhood, John had been entangled in doctrinal controversy and had read philosophic arguments without reaching satisfying conclusions. He found that Goethe, in his

[1] Mrs. Synge described the letter as a curious one, 'attributing his unsociableness to his narrow upbringing and warning me . . .' (Diary entry 29 December 1893). GS, p. 37.

autobiography, answered intellectual perplexity out of the rich
experience of his life. As John read, his own experience became
illuminated by a new light. Some of the events of their lives seemed
comparable: their environments had differed greatly in detail but in
basic pattern showed similar features.

Goethe as a boy had, like John, been greatly influenced by his
mother. He had been brought up a Protestant on scriptural teaching
and, as a student, had learnt enough Hebrew to give him a deep
interest in the Old Testament. The study of nature and the beauty
of the country had, from his earliest days, been his constant inspiration. In his time, the power of Greek tradition had flowed into
German literature just as the power of Celtic tradition was
beginning to flow in the literature of John's home country. . . .
⟨Goethe's⟩ works had inspired Scott to write romances of the north
English border and John, when he read Scott at Castle Kevin, had
found the antiquities and lore of his own country freshly illuminated. On long solitary walks ⟨he⟩ thought over and digested all the
emotional experiences of his secluded life: Goethe had thought in
a similar way, and had taken a further step in giving the results of
his reflections poetic form. From his example John was to learn a
way of dramatizing his own life in any story which happened to
provide appropriate symbols. At the close of his career he could have
said—like Goethe—that all his writings had been fragments of one
long confession. Merck, if he had been alive, might have said to
him, as he said to Goethe: 'Thy unswerving effort is to give a
poetic form to the real. . . .'[1]

[John's stay in Würzburg provided him with the isolation necessary for creative work and it was during the spring of 1894 that he
drafted his first idea for a play:[2] in one way, his initial idea was to
remain of considerable importance to him, for the hero of the play
—a young Irish landlord—learns to value 'the higher things' in
life from his experiences with two brothers in the play, a poet and
a good-for-nothing.] The idea of associating and contrasting the
character of the good-for-nothing and the poet persisted in John's
work: it represented one of the principal conflicts of his life. His
relations regarded him as misguided and wasteful, but for him his
mode of life was determined by his belief in his destiny as an artist.

[1] *The Autobiography of Goethe: Truth and Poetry: from my own life*, tr. John
Oxenford (London, 1881–4), II. III.

[2] *C.W.* III. 181–2.

. . . To develop his gifts he had to diverge from the mode of life that his relations sought to prescribe. He knew that if he were to be successful, events would prove him to have been right but that if he were to fail, nobody would believe him. He wondered whether the good-for-nothing was not often the talented person who had failed to bring his gifts to fruition. In 'The Vagrants of Wicklow' he afterwards wrote:

In the middle classes the gifted son of a family is always the poorest— usually a writer or artist with no sense for speculation—and in a family of peasants, where the average comfort is just over penury, the gifted son sinks also, and is soon a tramp on the roadside.[1]

John's plan for a play was as boyish as his verses,[2] but it was based on a conception which was to manifest itself in his finished work. It was dependent on the idea that events may have a dramatic rela- tion to each other in their effect on the life of an individual and reach a climax in his full realization of the possibilities of his own life. To this conception he afterwards gave peculiarly clear expres- sion in Christy Mahon's closing speech:

Ten thousand blessings upon all that's here, for you've turned me a likely gaffer in the end of all, the way I'll go romancing through a romping lifetime from this hour to the dawning of the judgment day.[3]

In the preface to his poems, that were going through the press at the time of his death, he wrote:

Many of the older poets, such as Villon and Herrick and Burns, used the whole of their personal life as their material, and the verse written in this way was read by strong men, and thieves, and deacons, not by little cliques only.[4]

It was his ambition to do on the stage what they had done in poetry, and to use the whole of his personal life in his dramatic work. He ultimately achieved this by retaining the conception of drama

---

[1] *C.W.* II. 202.
[2] Earlier in the TS., Stephens quotes many of Synge's early verses, not included in *C.W.* I.
[3] *C.W.* IV. 173.   [4] *C.W.* I. xxxvi.

underlying his plan for a play and by dramatizing himself, disguised as the central character or, in different capacities, as several of the leading characters, in some story from country lore or heroic tradition. It is in this sense that his dramatic work was autobiographical and that the outwardly dull story of his life became transmuted into the gold of literature. . . .

[In June, he left Germany and returned to Ireland. Early in July, Mrs. Synge's household and our family all moved to Castle Kevin where we settled into our usual routine; John, who enjoyed talking to children, often sat with us and told us about birds and butterflies or about his travels.] Sometimes he used to come with us when our mother took us to pick fruit. Passing through the doorway in the high wall of the garden on a sunny day always brought a feeling of surprise. The northern side of the wall under the trees by the avenue was in deep shadow, moist, cold and green with moss and ferns. Two mossy steps led up to the door which, when it opened, made a stir among the insects basking inside. When it closed, it shut in warm air filled with fragrance drawn by the sun from an unkept box hedge, masses of 'Rose of Sharon', festoons of creeper and overhanging limes.[1]

Since the Frizelles had left, the garden had been allowed to grow into a wilderness, but old apple trees covered with lichen still bore fruit and large quantities of raspberries and gooseberries grew tangled with thistles and convolvulus. Through paths cut in this thicket, we helped the grown-up people to gather fruit for cooking and ate as much as we could hold. John told us that we would burst and, as a warning against gluttony, composed a rhyme on the sad fate of three children who ate too much. It was avowedly comic, but I always suspected that it had a serious intent. I have forgotten all but the last two lines:

> When the church clock struck eleven
> Three little froginettes went up to Heaven.

The tragic ending always called up in my mind a picture of the bell tower and the weather cock standing motionless over the yard ⟨at Castle Kevin⟩ at night. . . .

The family party was large enough to fill the house but Mrs. Synge, knowing that Florence would want a sketching companion,

---

[1] cf. *C.W.* II. 230.

suggested that she should ask ⟨a friend⟩ to share her room during part of⟨the⟩ stay at Castle Kevin. [This friend was Cherrie Matheson, a girl of John's age who lived only three doors from Mrs. Synge and John in Crosthwaite Park. John had first met Cherrie] at Greystones, for her parents used to take their family there for summer holidays. Since moving to Crosthwaite Park he had seen her often and, as she had begun to develop a friendship with Florence, he had found opportunities for talking with her occasionally. Gradually she had taken possession of his imagination and he had begun to worship her from a distance. It was a distance which, to him, it seemed impossible to bridge, . . . for her father was a leader of the Plymouth Brethren and expected his family to conform with his religious practices and to obey his directions. . . . ⟨Cherrie, who was a cheerful girl,⟩ was not oppressed by her father's strict discipline and ascetic creed, but accepted them with unquestioning faith. John felt certain that she would form no intimacy with a man who could neither assure her that he was 'saved', nor claim any wiser ambition than artistic success. It seemed to him that . . . he was condemned to strain his gaze on one completely remote. . . .

[It was at the end of July that Cherrie Matheson came to stay at Castle Kevin. If John had been looking forward to the day,] he gave none of the party at Castle Kevin the slightest indication that for him it had any importance. He did not wait about the house for her arrival, but set off after breakfast with Sam for one of their very long walks. . . . That evening when they reached home, Cherrie had arrived. . . .

The greater part of each day Cherrie spent with Florence, while John occupied his time as he would have if she had not come, reading, practising, walking, and fishing. As the summer was fine, he often read in the wood near the house and he sometimes played the violin there, perhaps with the intention of serenading Cherrie when he thought she was near by. His opportunities for talking to her came in the evenings. Sometimes she, Florence, and he strolled under the avenue trees, sometimes they walked up to the tower field at sunset; there they used to sit in the shelter of the cairn and watch the sun go down and the afterglow, beginning faintly over the sea in the east and creeping round the sky until it blazed over the place where the sun had set. They watched the stars coming out and sometimes saw nightjars flying silently among the furze. John talked of music and literature, of his life in Germany and his ambitions, but he avoided any question of religious controversy which Florence and Cherrie might have thought a temptation to the sin of doubt. Cherrie's slight knowledge of poetry and painting enabled her to take some part in the conversation and John did not know how little she understood of all he sought to convey.[1] His devotion to her deepened, but none of the family party noticed it because he and Cherrie were never alone together and never made themselves remarkable in any way. So my mother told me years afterwards. . . .

[Among my recollections of Cherrie's visit, one seems particularly important; one day] I went into the drawing-room where Cherrie was sitting by the window and John was playing his fiddle. I knew that I was not allowed to interrupt a conversation, but the thought that I should not interrupt anyone who was playing never entered my mind. I said something to John and he soon stopped playing and went away, leaving me feeling that I had been in the wrong—but I do not remember any reproof.[2]

Within the next few days, John drove Cherrie in the phaeton to the railway station and Aunt Lizzie came to Castle Kevin in her stead. . . . [On 3 September, the family returned to Kingstown and John spent September and October preparing to leave for the Continent again.] He had decided to make languages, not music, his principal study and began to revive his knowledge of Greek and Irish grammar. In conjunction with all other studies, for general guidance, he continued to read the works of Goethe. His plan was to return for a short visit to Oberwerth and to move to Paris, where he hoped to make a little money teaching languages and to attend lectures at the Sorbonne. . . .

[He finally left Kingstown on 30 October and arrived in Oberwerth four days later. Once there, he was able to tell the von Eikens of his change of plans;] it was arranged that he should take regular lessons in German from Valeska and in French from one of her friends, Mlle Mansaca. Next day he hired a grand piano, bought a German dictionary and the complete works of Heine, and was ready to begin work.

He had come to Oberwerth intending to make a very short stay, but once there he felt reluctant to leave. The company of the von

---

[1] Stephens's opinion is based on his reading of Cherrie Matheson's recollections of Synge, published in the *Irish Statesman* on 5 July 1924.
[2] See *C.W.* II. 16 for Synge's reference to the incident.

Eiken sisters and their friends he found as delightful as ever and he wanted to have some conversational knowledge of French before he went to Paris. . . . [The Christmas festivities in Oberwerth were very elaborate and John took part in everything, even appearing in a tableau of a gipsy camp. But on the first of January 1895, having resolutely set the date for leaving his friends, he set out by train for Paris, where he made arrangements to lodge with a family named Arbeau.

[M. Arbeau's apartment was a great contrast with the house at Oberwerth; it was sordid and ill-kept and John's attic room was comfortless. M. Arbeau was a cook who] used to make a little extra money by selling tooth-powder and by teaching French to lodgers. He cooked and mixed tooth-powder in the sitting-room where his wife, with one assistant, made ladies' hats. John's early practice in putting up fishing tackle, setting moths and butterflies, and stuffing and mounting birds had given him a dexterity that was useful when he helped sometimes in the tooth-powder mixing or in bending wire for hat-frames. He wanted to improve his knowledge of French by joining almost unnoticed in the activities of the household, but in this he was unsuccessful. M. Arbeau was friendly and gave him the lessons for which they had agreed, but the women looked on him as an unsophisticated and uninteresting boy and assisted him but little in conversation.

In the evenings he had a fire in his attic and, sitting alone, listened to the sounds of a strange city. In one of his boyish verses he wrote of hearing 'the murmur in the street' and 'the Paris laughter rising from below'. He was lonely and, as he sat and watched his small fire dying, he dreamed that he was back in Wicklow.[1] . . . Sometimes his mind was filled with longing to be with his idealized love; he wrote of ⟨Cherrie⟩ in his verses without mentioning her name, treating her as something holy and remote, full of 'deep devotion rare'. Then his own perplexities about matter, time, and space swept over his mind and he resolved to keep aloof from his 'Holy One' for fear that his lack of faith should steal her comfort or her joy, or even for half a noon-tide destroy her rest. . . .

[However, John's depression and loneliness did not last long. His knowledge of French improved rapidly; he began to give lessons in English, to attend lectures at the Sorbonne, and to spend

[1] A poem he wrote at this time is in GS, p. 48.

much of his free time in the Louvre, the Luxembourg, and Notre Dame. In general, he was much enjoying his stay in Paris. He even succeeded in changing his lodgings and he soon had many friends.] He loved the spring in the parks and boulevards where he walked and talked with men of his own age. Intellectual problems and the criticism of art and literature he discussed with animation and enthusiasm. He was interested in his companions and encouraged them to talk of their love adventures and dissipations, but in these phases of their lives he took no share. They tolerantly accepted his settled habits and laughed good-humouredly at his asceticism. . . .

As May passed, he worked steadily at the courses on which he was attending lectures, took part (as either teacher or pupil) in language lessons, sometimes in as many as three in a day, practised his violin, for exercise walked in the great parks of Paris and, on Sundays, went to the Louvre. His friend, Edward Denny,[1] who had been untiring in his efforts on John's behalf, in June introduced him to a new pupil with whose sister he was himself exchanging English lessons for French. On Monday 3 June, John entered in his diary: 'First lesson with Miss B.' He was to return to Ireland before the end of the month, but during the lessons that they gave each other in the meantime, he formed with her one of the most valued friendships of his life.

The new pupil was Mlle Beydon, a teacher of drawing at a girls' school. She was a devout Protestant but had none of the insular prejudices of the Irish evangelicals. Besides art, with which her occupation was concerned, she was interested in politics. She sympathized generally with the feminist movement which was then taking shape and, in particular, with the efforts that were being made to organize the nursing profession. . . . She was to be one of John's wisest counsellors in the next three or four years, which proved to be an emotionally distressing period of his life.

John was interested in every phase of political thought and wanted to understand not only liberal opinions, of the sort held by Mlle Beydon, but also the theories held by the extreme revolutionaries among his student friends. On the evening of Saturday 18 June, one of them took him to a lecture by Sébastien Faure[2] on anarchy. Contrary to his usual custom, he noted in his diary a

[1] Nothing definite is known of Edward Denny; Stephens describes him (TS. 705) as 'probably a fellow Irishman'.

[2] Sébastien Faure (1858–1942), author of *La Douleur universelle* (1892).

criticism of what he had heard. It was short and dynamic: '*Très intéressant, mais fou*';—and the word '*fou*' was underlined three times. . . .

[At the end of June, John returned to Ireland filled with the excitement of his experiences abroad. He spent several weeks with his family at a farmhouse near Castle Kevin which Mrs. Synge had taken for the summer, and as usual, passed most of the time out of doors, reading or walking. When the family returned to Crosthwaite Park in September,] John often saw Cherrie Matheson passing on the road or sitting reading in the bow window of No. 25. Sometimes he met her by chance on his way from the railway station and stopped to exchange a few words. These glimpses of his 'Holy One' inspired his imagination to beautify her image, but he had no opportunities for long or intimate conversations.[1] . . . As autumn gave way to winter, his resolution about going to Paris had weakened. It was difficult for him to leave the place where his 'Holy One' lived and he was afraid that, alone in Paris, he might suffer from colds which would affect his chest. He had begun to think that his next step should be to follow Goethe's example by going to Italy, and for that it would be necessary to stay at home long enough to save a little money and to begin learning Italian. . . .

As the days passed, he was continually tantalized by seeing his 'Holy One' in the distance only and had been trying to devise some way of meeting her regularly. The opening of the Sketching Club exhibition at last afforded the opportunity for making a beginning. The interest he had taken in her painting when she was at Castle Kevin enabled him to suggest that they should go to the exhibition together. His invitation was gladly accepted and on Saturday 16 November he wrote in his diary: 'To the Sketching Club with C.M.' He had established the precedent of going out with her alone, but it was not easy to follow it up by arranging another meeting quickly. . . . [However, ten days later] he suggested their going together to the National Gallery, where they went on Saturday 30 November.

Seeing works of art with her was for him a delightful but disturbing experience; restless in the evening, he walked alone

[1] Cherrie no longer visited Mrs. Synge's house as Florence Ross had left Ireland to keep house for her brother who had been appointed the doctor on Tonga. Stephens explains that 'by her going, ⟨Synge lost⟩ not only the greatest friend of his childhood, but his chief link with Cherrie Matheson' (TS. 698).

after dark to the end of the East Pier.[1] He knew that she was willing to make him her friend; her parents, who had known his family for many years, seemed to raise no obstacle to his meeting their daughter. . . . An intimacy between them seemed to be developing in the way of which he had dreamed. His mind went back to the plan he had devised, more than a year before in Würzburg, for writing a play based on an imaginary version of their love affair. He gave her the fictitious name of 'Scherma' and on 10 December, after mentioning a meeting with her, entered in his diary: 'Continued writing Sir John and Scherma.' No manuscript of what he wrote has been preserved, but it seems certain that the note in his diary referred to another dramatization of himself in love.

In the next four days, he contrived to meet her three times and on one occasion at least took her for a walk. As they walked, they discussed questions of faith. The ideas that perplexed his mind were quite beyond the range of her conceptions or knowledge, but she felt sure that his failure to share her beliefs was wrong, and told him of the comfort she found in assured salvation. She lent him religious books in the hope that they might convey what she could ill express. They added nothing to the teaching he had known from childhood and, on 22 December, he noted in his diary: 'Wrote to Scherma with her books, which I have read. . . .'

The Christmas season interrupted his meetings with Cherrie but on the Sunday after Christmas, he met her again. They went for a short walk before it was time for her to go with her father to the Plymouth Brethren's meeting house, and then he set out alone for the Smelting Chimney on the hill above Ballycorus. As he walked, his mind was filled with conflicting feelings, for he had arranged to leave for Paris ⟨and Rome⟩ in a few days. On 31 December he went to Dublin and had his photograph taken so that she might have it when he was away. It was of this photograph that she wrote in her recollections:

It is exactly like him as I remember him. He is sitting, his head thrown rather back, his hand firmly holding a stick, and there is that far-away look in his eyes. . . .[2]

2

On 1 January 1896, John packed his old portmanteau and said

[1] The east pier of Dún Laoghaire (Kingstown) harbour.
[2] *Irish Statesman*, 5 July 1924, p. 534. The photograph forms the frontispiece to *C.W.* II.

The Synge family. (Seated, from left) *Samuel, Mrs. Synge, John;* (standing) *Annie (later Mrs. Harry Stephens), Robert, Edward.*

Glanmore Castle, Co. Wicklow, late in the nineteenth century

Roundwood Park

Castle Kevin

Tomriland House

At Castle Kevin: Claire and Edward Stephens with their dogs, the
Wicklow Mountains beyond; (below) Synge with his mother, Rosie
Calthrop (centre), and Annie Harmar, in the summer of 1900.

*Florence Ross,
Synge's cousin and
childhood friend*

Cherrie Matheson

Crosthwaite Park: Nos. 31 and 29 (from left, nearest to camera),
with one of the sitting rooms on the ground floor.

good-bye to Cherrie Matheson. Next morning, long before it was light, . . . he set out on his way to Paris. . . . He had left the woman he idealized and had refused to engage in any money-making occupation which might have enabled him to offer her a home. He was going to Paris and to Rome with a general plan for studying languages and literature, inspired by the hope of developing his own productive powers in a way which, as yet, he could picture but dimly. . . .

[He spent a month in Paris, continuing his exchange of English and French lessons with Mlle Beydon and also with George Roder, one of the young men he had met towards the end of his last visit. At the beginning of February, in accord with his plans, he left Paris for Italy. Although the weather was cold, he was immediately thrilled with Rome and wrote to Mlle Beydon that it was even more enchanting than he had expected. He found himself lodgings in an Italian household and set about perfecting his Italian and seeing the city.] He had arranged to spend nearly three months in Rome as a definite step in his artistic education and he planned his work as methodically as he had planned it in Paris. His host gave him lessons in Italian and read Italian, French, and German literature. Each day he walked through the city . . . ⟨using Goethe's *Letters from Italy*⟩ as a running commentary on his own experiences in Rome. . . .

Occasionally he went out into the country, but his studies left him so little time for excursions that he usually took his exercise in the neighbourhood where he was staying. Walking often along the Pincio, he fixed in his memory a view of Rome as a whole dominated by the dome of St. Peter's. In the quiet avenues of the Borghese Gardens, among dark ilex trees and conifers, he collected his thoughts and gave some kind of synthesis to his impressions of the city. As he walked in the gardens, he passed finely-dressed ladies in carriages, mounted officers in splendid uniforms, and an occasional troop of clerical students in their long cassocks. At a little distance from the main avenue a fountain, beginning to lean slightly with age, threw—a little sideways—into the air the waters that fell dribbling and splashing from its overflowing basins. Round the fountain there was a wide gravel path edged by a stone seat where he could sit in the sun sheltered from the wind.[1]

[1] Stephens himself visited Italy when in his twenties, partly, it seems, in order to experience for himself some of the phases of Synge's early life. These descriptions, and others later in the TS., are based on his recollections of that visit.

His visit to Rome had not dimmed in his mind the idealized image of his 'Holy One'... and he wrote to her of Rome and told her about the sculptures of the Vatican and the paintings of the Sistine Chapel; then he waited longingly for a reply. On 26 February he entered in his diary, 'I bought the poems of Petrarca (Ed. 1740) for two soldi.' ⟨Although⟩ it was long afterwards that he published his fragments of translation from Petrarch in Irish dialect, . . . the emotions they expressed seemed to belong to this period.[1] ⟨For⟩ though Cherrie Matheson was alive and well, he felt as if she had been removed from him to the company of Heaven, ⟨and⟩ it was on this feeling that he seems to have been dwelling when he translated from Petrarch:

What is it you're thinking lonesome heart? For what is it you're turning back ever and always to times that are gone away from you? For what is it you're throwing sticks on the fire where it is your own self that is burning?

The little looks and sweet words you've taken one by one and written down among your songs, are gone up into the Heavens and it's late you know well, to go seeking them on the face of the earth.

Let you not be giving new life every day to your own destruction, and following a fool's thoughts forever. Let you seek Heaven when there is nothing left pleasing on the earth, and it a poor thing if a great beauty, the like of her, would be destroying your peace and she living or dead.[2]

. . . He longed to talk with someone about all that was passing in his mind and gradually made friends with Miss Capps, an American lady, who was one of the paying guests in the house where he was staying. She was conventional but friendly, and had a much wider knowledge of the world than the members of the family group at Crosthwaite Park. Though naturally reserved, he felt free—in foreign countries—to discuss his life with friends who would never meet the people of his home circle. Miss Capps and he discussed art, religion, and the ways of life of the people they knew. He talked to her about the questions of faith that had overshadowed his mind from boyhood and of the way in which his unbelief separated him from the object of his devotion. . . .

[1] These translations, which have been reprinted several times, first appeared in *Poems and Translations* (1909). See *C.W.* I. 86–102.
[2] *C.W.* I. 87.

On 3 March[1] he entered in his diary: 'Saw the Pope in the Vatican.' During the two months since his arrival in Rome he had been quickly increasing his knowledge of the great monuments and treasures of the Church. His fleeting view of the ⟨Pope⟩ was the climax of a series of impressions that had made his early ideas of Catholicism seem fantastic and had widened the gap that separated him from his relations and friends. His beliefs on dogma remained unchanged but he had a new understanding of the antiquity, power, and learning of the Church. He knew that his mother, praying for 'the poor dark Roman Catholics', and Cherrie, listening to her father expounding the Bible in the little meeting house ⟨in Glenageary⟩, could never comprehend the Church of Rome.

On 15 April he entered in his diary: 'Letter from Scherma', and followed the entry with five exclamation marks. Cherrie's letter had given him hope. Next day he was twenty-five years old. He received a card from Valeska von Eiken bringing good wishes from all his friends at Oberwerth. His mood of romantic melancholy vanished, and he felt freer to enjoy Rome just when spring had come. . . .

On 30 April, the day before he left Rome, he went out to Tivoli where numberless spouted rivulets poured down through the gardens of the Villa d'Este to still pools edged with cut stone. From there he walked through the olive groves to the villa of Hadrian. Two or three years later, reflecting on his impressions of the Rhine and of Rome, they seemed most clearly symbolized for him in the medium that he had early learnt to understand, for he wrote: . . .

There are even natures who have no firm consciousness of an intellectual movement unless registered by some definite sound or melody, and for them the memory of voyages is but a medley of musical suggestion. I remember the Rhine country, not by the colour and contours, but by the singing of peasants in the woods near Coblence, and by the quaint rhythm sung by the cabin boy as the steamer I travelled in neared each station from Bonn to Mayence. At another time, as I sat at an albergo near the edge of the Roman campagna and ate bread and cheese and drank the cheapest wine of the country, an old man and a girl came with

[1] Stephens's TS. and GS give the date as 6 March; T.C.D. MS. 4417 shows that it should be 3 March.

a guitar and sang among the guests, forming for me a synthetic excitement of all my experience in Italy.[1]

On the first of May, John travelled to Florence. . . . He had been enchanted by the antiquity, continuity, and grandeur of Rome, the city that preserved in its architecture the monuments of many ages. Gradually its grey stone pillars and wide paved spaces had acquired for him a settled meaning. His appreciation of Florence required a complete readjustment of mind. In the Tuscan capital, built on a beautiful river site and surrounded by hilly country stretching to the mountains, he saw a city of the Middle Ages, a flower of a particular period. . . . The colouring of Florence seemed to him amazingly rich after looking for three months on the grey austerity of Rome. He saw the red and brown of the roof tiles, the green of the river, and the coloured marbles of churches, the Cathedral, and the Campanile blended endlessly in the summer light. At sunset the red of the sky turned the white marble of the Campanile to pink, and in the darkness, when he walked out of the town breathing the scent of flowers in the air, he saw fireflies moving among the fruit trees. . . .

[He continued with his reading, finding particular sympathy with stories of idealized love in the poetry of Dante and Petrarch.] These poets were the masters from whom John learned his mode of approach to women, ⟨and⟩ at the time it seemed to him that they were instructing him in the way to receive illumination from his 'Holy One'. . . . Solitary reflections on his isolation from her might have enveloped his mind in melancholy had he not made friends with two ladies among the guests in the pension where he was staying. They contrasted strangely with each other and seem to have suggested to him the two imaginary characters in the *Étude Morbide*, ⟨the⟩ Chouska and ⟨the⟩ Celliniani, round whom he wove greatly disguised stories of Florence Ross and Cherrie Matheson.[2] One was a Polish student of sculpture, Maria Antonina Zdowska, a devout Roman Catholic; the other was an Englishwoman, Hope Rea, a student of Tuscan art, who was rationalistic in her beliefs and interested in literature and social work.[3]

[1] T.C.D. MS. 4382, f. 11v. The MS. is very difficult to decipher, and Stephens's edited text is reproduced here.

[2] See also p. 125. Stephens's conjectures on the identity of the models for characters in both *Étude Morbide* and *Vita Vecchia* should be treated with caution.

[3] Among Hope Rea's publications was *Tuscan Artists: their Thought and Work*

John used to discuss religion with Maria Zdowska, who recommended theological books which she hoped would resolve his doubts. Hope Rea nicknamed her '*Figliuola*' and John '*Figliuolo*', and joined in their religious discussions with a sort of maternal detachment. When John was alone with Maria Zdowska he talked freely, not only of his unbeliefs but of the barrier that it interposed between him and his 'Holy One'. He had developed brilliant powers of conversation but could employ them fully only with women who accepted his strict standards of propriety. Unconventional women would have embarrassed him, and his conversation with his men friends, although often interesting, was limited in its scope by the failure of most of them to understand his asceticism.

Gradually he grew accustomed to the rattle of old cabs over the paving stones along the quays by the Arno, the shouting of the cab drivers and the cracking of their whips, and to all the other sounds of Florence. . . . Much of his time was spent before the endless array of masterpieces in the Pitti and Uffizi galleries. As his daily walks made him familiar with the streets, he took increasing pleasure in the beauty of the Campanile, the Cathedral, the Palazzo Vecchio, and the other great buildings of Florence. Sometimes he went out alone, at other times with one or both of his new friends. He walked in the Cascine Gardens with Maria Zdowska, in the Boboli Gardens with Hope Rea, and spent an afternoon with both of them at Fiesole. . . .

[Despite the pleasures of his stay in Italy, John did not alter his plans and, at the beginning of June, he left Florence to return to Paris. Once there,] he felt he had an opportunity for collecting his thoughts and digesting, in familiar surroundings, the overwhelming impressions of the three months he had spent in Italy. . . . He did not attempt to form any regular plan of work, but chose for his reading works of different authors according to his mood. By dwelling continually on the image of his 'Holy One' he had convinced himself that on the successful development of his relations with her all his future happiness must depend. He had not decided upon any definite method of earning his living, but mixing

(London, 1898). It has not proved possible to establish the correct name for Synge's Polish friend: Stephens refers to her as Maria Antonina Zdowska on her first appearance, but later calls her Marie Zdanowska. GS and later books give her as Marie Antoinette Zdanowska.

with strangers and making new friends in Rome and Florence had given him confidence in himself. Soon he was to return to Ireland and he was sure that he would see Cherrie again. His hopes rose until he pictured himself returning as the recognized lover of his 'Holy One', and, on 9 June, he wrote her a proposal of marriage.

The week that followed was pervaded by a sense of anxious waiting. In the mornings he read or wandered through the Louvre or round Notre Dame. The evenings he spent with his friends. On 17 June Cherrie's answer came. He wrote in his diary: 'Answer from Scherma—Refusal.' To him it seemed as if he had been left suddenly in the dark. All the delight that he had drawn from his stay in Italy was quenched. In great distress he wrote at once to his mother.

Mrs. Synge entered in her diary for Friday 19 June: 'I got a *sad sad* letter from my poor Johnnie from Paris.' It filled her mind with conflicting emotions for it came at a time when her joy and pride in Sam had been raised to great heights by the approach of his ordination. Next day when Sam, in preparation for taking holy orders, left her to stay a night with the Regius Professor of Divinity, she wrote sadly to John. As usual he had brought her anxiety and perplexity while Sam brought her contentment and happiness. She closed her letter and turned her thoughts again to Sam's ordination. On Sunday, 21 May, she wrote in her diary:

Annie and I went in by the 9 train to dearest Sam's ordination—Bishop of Meath and Dr. Kennedy in our carriage. We drove up—very nice service. Sam so mild and gentle looking in his white surplice and red hood. My heart went up to God for him as he knelt before the Bishop to be admitted into the Ministry of the Gospel. Sermon on 'I am the Light of the World'. Sam and I went to church in the evening. . . .

After . . . the day on which he received Cherrie's letter refusing his proposal of marriage, John made no entry in his diary, until on 29 June he wrote: 'Left Paris.' He was in misery but he did not abandon the idealization of his 'Holy One'. The thought of attempting to see her seemed to him useless and distressing. He did not delay at Crosthwaite Park, where he arrived on the morning after his mother had left for the country, but ⟨left at once to join her⟩.

Next day he had a long talk with his mother. She believed that a marriage with Cherrie would draw him back towards the faith that he had abandoned, and thought that in directing his affections he had shown good feeling. Yet, although the marriage he longed for was what she wished for him, she did not allow her anxiety for his happiness to bias her judgement. She could understand Cherrie's difficulties perfectly. In spite of all his study he had not become self-supporting and there seemed no likelihood of his being able to support a wife. His mother knew that if John married he would not bring up children 'in the nurture and admonition of the Lord' and she asked herself: 'How can two walk together unless they be agreed?' She could sympathize with him and continue to pray for his conversion, but she did not think that any solution of his troubles was possible so long as he continued in unbelief.

His cousin Alec, when arranging to marry Daisy Graves, had feigned the religious devotion necessary for obtaining her mother's consent,[1] but John hated deceit of any kind. His reading and discussions with his friends had, in the last year, increased his scepticism, and he had found that religion was the principal barrier between him and his beloved. She had told him that, when staying at Castle Kevin, she had been misled as to his beliefs by his attending church. He determined that his conformity with his family's worship, even in the country, must cease. This conclusion he arrived at sadly for, especially at the beginning of Sam's ministry, people would be surprised by seeing his mother sitting in church unaccompanied by any member of her family. On Sunday 5 July Mrs. Synge wrote in her diary: 'We drove to church. Sam took part of the service, read 2 lessons very nicely, also helped at communion. I felt very thankful at the beginning of his ministry.' John was interested in Sam's first public acts as a clergyman, but he could not share the happiness they brought his mother. Two days later she wrote to Robert:

Oh! my dear Johnnie is a great sorrow to my heart—his belief or misbelief has no joy in it and his residence abroad has been no help to him—he is wonderfully separate from us. I show him all the love I can. I pity

[1] Stephens refers to a story told earlier in the TS.; Daisy Graves's mother feared that Alec, who was a London company promoter, was 'careless about matters of faith'. When Alec went to stay with his prospective mother-in-law, he 'adopted the practice of retiring early each evening in order that he might pray before going to sleep. His room was over the drawing-room and he used to bump down by his bed on his knees with a violence sufficient to convince of his devotion anyone who might be in the room beneath.' (TS. 297.)

him so much and I love him so deeply—and I believe God is hearing my
cry to Him, but the answer is delayed long. If we are all taken up to meet
the Lord and he is left behind—how sad a thought, but I won't think
that—God can do all things—so I say to my doubts, 'be gone'. . . .

On Saturday 18 July Mrs. Synge wrote in her diary: 'John at
home all day poor boy.' In the solitude of Avonmore[1] where there
was no relief from the overwhelming sense of loneliness left by
Cherrie's refusal, he read again the *Vita Nuova*. The record of his
childhood love affairs with Florence⟨Ross⟩[2] and ⟨the⟩ *Vita Vecchia*
convey a clear impression of the effect which the story of Dante's
love for Beatrice had on the development of his imagination. They
leave no doubt that Dante's influence increased his tendency to
dramatize his own life and gave a clear literary quality to his
thoughts, which had been confused by grief.

It seemed to him that he was like Dante in giving his devotion to
a beautiful but inaccessible woman who was a source of pure and
boundless inspiration. John had not met Cherrie—as Dante had
met Beatrice—at the age of nine, but he had fallen in love with
Florence at that age, and later, when childish love had settled into
maturer friendship, had fixed his devotion on her friend. He had
spent glorious evenings with them both, two years before, watching the sunset from the cairn on Castle Kevin hill. Now Florence
was in Tonga and Cherrie had refused his offer of marriage. For the
purpose of his story,[3] as he reviewed it in imagination, they seemed
like one person who had vanished from his life leaving him to draw
inspiration from memory.

On Sunday 19 July, John's absence from church was particularly
trying for his mother because it was the day on which Sam preached
his first sermon. That evening she wrote in her diary:

Very fine and very hot day. Sam and I drove to Laragh. Miss Power and
Miss Hipwell sat in the seat with me. Sam read and preached very nice
sermon. Matt. 28:3 last verses—spoke on 'Son give me thine heart'.
Very earnest and solemn. Very still and attentive congregation. We
had the Communion. Sam crossed the river on our way home and

---

1 The farmhouse near Castle Kevin where Mrs. Synge and her party had stayed
also in 1895.

2 i.e. in the autobiography, *C.W.* II. 6-9.

3 i.e. *Vita Vecchia, C.W.* II. 16-24.

started for Derrylossery. John and I sat on the hill, very silent when I am. . . .

On Wednesday 29 July Mrs. Synge, Sam, and John moved up from Avonmore to Castle Kevin where the remainder of the party arrived on Saturday 1 August. . . . John seemed to us a little like a stranger, but we soon found him as entertaining as ever. He told us stories of Paris, Rome, and Florence, occasionally walked with us in the fields or in the wood behind the house, and, when our father went to town on business, took us out driving with our mother in the new trap.

Once, as I was walking with John through the great beech trees beside the avenue, he asked me if I knew who sowed the beech nuts. I had heard of his dreadful unbelief and knew that he did not go to church. The situation was very embarrassing but I felt I must not deny the faith and said: 'God sows them.' John relieved my mind by accepting my answer as a matter of course, but said he had been thinking of the squirrels which stored the nuts in hiding places in the ground ⟨where⟩ some were often forgotten and grew into trees. . . .

[A holiday at Castle Kevin was probably one of the best cures for melancholy which could have been devised, and certainly John had little opportunity for solitary reflection.] With my father as his companion, he began going again on fishing expeditions to Kelly's Lake and other places in the hills. My father was not interested in John's problems nor in Sam's ministry. He wanted to enjoy the country in an athletic way, to walk and fish and to forget for a time the worries of his work. There was no danger that his conversation would recall distressing subjects to John's mind. . . .

On fine days, when he was at leisure, ⟨John⟩ sometimes sat talking on the steps and sometimes strolled into the wood to sit in the twisted boughs of a laurel reading the works of Browning, Thoreau, or Virgil, or the *Little Flowers* of St. Francis of which... he thought of publishing an English translation.[1]. . . [For him, as for the whole party, the time passed peacefully and, on the whole, without excitement, until the middle of September when we all went home to Dublin.]

At the time of his return to Crosthwaite Park, John's ideas were

[1] See Maurice Bourgeois, *John Millington Synge and the Irish Theatre* (London, 1913), p. 25.

in a state of revolution. In Paris he had listened to advocates of socialism, and wondered whether a new and scientifically organized society would make peaceful life possible for sane men. He turned from reading Thoreau, Browning, and Virgil to reading Marx's *Das Kapital*. Its conclusions were not of a kind that he would have been likely to accept quickly, but its history of feudalism, and of the rise from it of industrialism, at once threw a new light on many of his problems. The effect of the book on his mind was an important preparation for his hearing, a few months later in Paris, the advocates of the Irish agrarian and national movements.

John knew that a meeting between him and Cherrie was inevitable as soon as they were both again living in the same terrace. He had thought of writing her a letter in preparation for it, but without having done so he met her by chance on 25 September. As Mlle Beydon had foreseen ⟨in a letter to John⟩, the meeting was tense with emotion, but Cherrie greeted him so pleasantly that she gave him new hope. He thought that her decision had been based on her doctrinal beliefs rather than on personal feelings and that it might be changed if he could but interpret himself fully to her.

On 30 September he wrote in his diary: 'Scherma here to tea', and his mother made a similar entry in hers, adding, 'Poor John showed all his photographs.' Her visit was a new beginning to his courtship. On Thursday 8 October she went with him to St. Patrick's Cathedral. Taking her there was to him like taking her to the cairn on Castle Kevin hill—one step in his attempt to introduce her to everything on which he set a value. . . . ⟨But⟩ John was mistaken in hoping that Cherrie would understand the power of the Cathedral in a way which would draw her mind nearer to his. . . . In her recollections of this time she afterwards wrote:

Sometimes we went to the National Gallery or some picture exhibition, sometimes to sit for an hour in St. Patrick's Cathedral and just drink in the beauty of the dear old place. I remember so well the light from the stained glass streaming in on the tattered banners of the old knights of St. Patrick. He liked that part of Dublin more than the modern part and especially Patrick's Street which runs between the two Cathedrals, and was then more like some queer continental street with little booths all down the centre of it.[1]

John was altogether absorbed in his efforts to ensure that his

---

[1] *Irish Statesman*, loc. cit.

'Holy One' should understand the values that determined his way of life and thought. For days he made no entry in his diary except to note that he was reading Morris, Marx, and Dante. On Tuesday 20 October he took Cherrie to Christ Church Cathedral and afterwards to the museum, where it was possible to talk undisturbed. His attempt to reach understanding was a terrible experience. The more he tried to explain himself the more she relied on evangelical doctrine. He ended the note in his diary for that day with the Irish lament: '*ochone, ochone*'. . . .

The outcome of the struggle that ⟨John⟩ had to face was not to be easily decided, for he might have wasted himself in the barren depression of a disappointed lover. His imaginative picture of his 'Holy One' was very closely knit with his dramatic conceptions. . . . As the image of his love disintegrated in his mind, he was in danger of believing that his opportunities were dead. It was through his finding in his love affair not merely personal misfortunes, but symbols of universal experience, that he emerged from this period of distress with developed dramatic powers, and equipped to take his part in the Irish literary movement.

3

[John spent the winter of 1896-7 in Paris; the circle of his acquaintance was widening and he made some important new friends. He was now able to mix freely with the Irish in Paris and found several writers and artists whose company he enjoyed. Among these was one of the most influential of his life-long friends, the writer and translator Stephen MacKenna.[1] He also met W. B. Yeats and Maud Gonne who were both in Paris working for the Irish national movement.[2] With Yeats, John had many common interests in literary matters, but he was also impressed by the fervour of the Irish nationalism he saw in Paris and by the principles of international socialism which he heard advocated around him. He wrote to his mother telling her of his leanings towards socialism, but Mrs. Synge considered his political notions 'utter folly', and her distress was all the greater because she thought that anarchists and socialists were 'much the same'.

[1] Stephen MacKenna (1872–1934). See 'Synge to MacKenna; The Mature Years', ed. Ann Saddlemyer, *Massachusetts Review*, v (Winter 1964), 279–96.
[2] Yeats gave his account of the meeting with Synge in his introduction to the 1905 edition of *The Well of the Saints*, *C.W.* III. 63–8.

[Initially, John joined with enthusiasm in the activities of Maud Gonne's Irish League and became a member of the committee; but his interests were more in the cultural aspects of Celtic nationalism than in the political ones, and he resigned from the committee after a few months.[1] In April, he attended a lecture by the Breton scholar and philologist, Anatole Le Braz,[2] whose enthusiasm for Celtic communities and Celtic culture he found contagious. He read several of Le Braz's books and sought out other works on Brittany; it was not difficult to see similarities between the problems of Brittany and those of the west of Ireland.]

In the month of April, feeling in Paris was running very high about the issues of the war that had broken out between the Greeks and the Turks, and extreme Irish nationalists were passionate in their support of the Greeks. John, who was drawn into the public excitement by his friends in the Irish League, was nearly knocked unconscious in a chance fray outside the Café Harcourt. . . . He was sitting with ⟨some friends⟩ at a table outside the Café Harcourt joining in the cry '*Conspuez les Turcs*'. Suddenly a number of students, shouting it wildly, rushed past followed by the police who were laying about them with their batons. The Irish party scrambled for safety and all escaped except John, who got a heavy blow on the head. He turned very white, but said nothing, and none of the party knew that he had been hit until Stephen Mac-Kenna, when seeing him home, discovered that he was bleeding from the baton wound.

MacKenna was living in a room on the top floor at 90 Rue d'Assas, not far from John's lodgings. . . . Another room on the top floor of the same house was occupied by a young Irishman who, like MacKenna, later proved a most useful friend to John. This was Richard Best, afterwards Librarian of the National Library.[3] He and MacKenna had met in Dublin at the Irish Literary Society and, living under one roof, had become friends. Best . . . was studying literature and was interested in the Irish Literary Revival, but had no acquaintance with political nationalism. As MacKenna soon left Paris he had no opportunity of introducing his friend to John, who did not meet Best until January 1898. . . .

---

[1] His letter of resignation is printed in GS, pp. 62–3.

[2] Anatole Le Braz (1859–1926). Synge wrote an article in praise of him, *C.W.* II. 394.

[3] Richard Best (1872–1959), a noted Celtic scholar and bibliographer.

John . . . returned⟨to Dublin in mid-May 1897⟩ with his way of
regarding Ireland revolutionized, for ideas long developed in his
mind had acquired definition and synthesis. Through his connection with the Irish League, he had learned to understand Irish
political feeling. Yeats had given him a new conception of the aims
and power of the literary revival. Anatole Le Braz, by his description of the Celtic people of Brittany, had intensified his interest in
the people of his own country, and particularly in the Celtic fringe
of the population living along the western coast. In addition to his
usual roving through the classics, he began anew to study Irish
grammar and *The Fate of the Children of Lir,* and to read again
Goethe's works which had early indicated to him a way of reviving
ancient lore in modern literature. . . .

[For the summer of 1897, Mrs. Synge and John could not take
Castle Kevin, but moved instead for July to Avonmore; for August,
they joined our family at 'Casino', a dower house on the Parnell
estate near Rathdrum. At this time,] Charles Stewart Parnell had
been dead six years . . . and his mansion house was empty. When I
asked my mother who had lived there, she told me that the owner
had been a Protestant who had joined the nationalists and had come
to a bad end. Her voice deprecated further questions. . . .

Near the garden gate of Casino ran a path over which there was
a right-of-way from the Avoca road to the avenue of Avondale.
My sister and I used to watch women walking home that way from
Rathdrum wrapped in black shawls and carrying large baskets.
One day a big merry-looking woman put down her basket and,
shaking us by the hands, said, 'Welcome to Casino.' We were very
shy but she, not seeming to notice it, gave us smooth sugar sweets
of which she had a little bag in her basket. Just then our mother came
out and said 'Good evening' rather stiffly. The woman walked on,
and our mother told us that we must never eat sweets given to us
by strangers: this was a very hard saying because we were very
rarely given any by people whom we knew.

Our mother had a piece of green silk which she used to crimp
with her fingers as a centre-piece in the middle of the dining-room
table, and about this time she gave it to us as a plaything because our
father had splashed it with gravy. Somehow we had heard that the
following year was to be the centenary of the rebellion of 1798.
We thought it would be fun to honour the centenary by waving a
green flag, so we mounted the silk on a long stick and ran with it

round the little garden in front of the house shouting, 'Who fears to speak of '98.' Our mother stopped us and said that we must be more quiet for fear that people passing the gate might hear what we were shouting and think that we meant it. I replied: 'But we do mean it,' and she said: 'If I thought you did mean it, I should not allow you to play that game at all.' We crept quietly away without pushing the matter further. . . .

My father did not like staying at the steward's house instead of the mansion house of Avondale and his visits, which created a sense of unrest in the family party, were not long. In his absence, the days passed as tranquilly for its members as was usual when they stayed in Co. Wicklow for the summer. My brother and I spent much of our time fishing and on fine days, if we were tired, lay in the grass among innumerable grasshoppers trembling their legs in the sun on a steep bank above the river. On wet days we listened to our grandmother reading *King Solomon's Mines* aloud.

Once, when I had just come up to tea from the river, I unexpectedly threw John into one of those sudden passions which occasionally seized him and then left him amused by his own indignation. I had sat down next him and he had cut himself an outside slice from the loaf. At that time I did not know that he hotly resented remarks about anything he was eating. Just as I began my tea he accused me, whether justly or not I cannot remember, of having come to the table without washing my hands after baiting hooks with worms. I retorted: 'You are eating the microbe parade off the loaf.' He jumped round furiously on his chair and hit me a slap on the head. Partly from surprise and partly, I suspect, to stop myself crying, I put out my tongue at him with the reflex action of a jack-in-the-box, and his temper vanished in a roar of laughter. . . .

[At the end of August, the family returned to Kingstown, but] as autumn closed in, ⟨John⟩ did not allow the weather to restrict his outdoor exercise. He continued to ride my father's horse,[1] walked often to Carrickmines, sometimes taking me with him, walked great distances on Sundays, and rode up to pay Cousin Emily a . . . visit at Uplands. In spite of his strength and energy, he began to suffer from distressing symptoms which made him anxious about

[1] Harry Stephens used to buy young horses—sometimes insufficiently trained—to pull the pony trap in the summer holidays. The TS. contains several stories of these horses misbehaving. Carrickmines is a village to the south of Dublin.

his health. His hair fell out, and a large lump developed on his neck. He consulted Dr. Wallace Beatty who prescribed ointments for his hair but said that the swelling on his neck was one for surgical treatment. His symptoms made him uncertain as to whether he could return soon to Paris. Some members of his family attributed them to distress of mind about his sad love affair. The swelling on his neck was spoken of as an 'enlarged gland', but . . . ⟨nobody either knew, or⟩ pretended to know, its significance. It was in reality the first manifestation of Hodgkin's disease or lymphatic sarcoma, from which he ultimately died. . . . [1]

While he was under medical observation, John continued reading widely, choosing many books from ⟨a⟩ list given him by Stephen MacKenna. His mother complained of his procrastination in making an appointment with his doctor for the purpose of deciding whether he was to undergo the suggested operation, but by 10 December a decision had been reached, and she wrote to Robert:

Johnnie is at home still. He has to get those large glands taken out of his neck, poor fellow. It is very unpleasant. He will have to go into the nursing home in Lower Mount Street to have it done. Since his hair fell out he got cold in the glands, and they became so large they were, or rather are, quite disfiguring to him. He has been very anxious to go away to Paris. He had been advised by his friend Yeats, the Irish poet, to go in for reviewing French literature so John is working away with that end in view. His general health is very good and he is strong and able to walk, so I trust he may get over this time well, please God, and Oh I do ask Him to reveal Himself to my dear boy.

The Mount Street Nursing Home, where John had decided to go for the operation, was perhaps the earliest private hospital to be established in Dublin. Its proprietors were three partners, Miss Margaret Huxley, matron of Sir Patrick Dun's Hospital, one of her friends who acted as superintendent of the home, and my father. It had been formed by uniting two large adjoining houses without greatly changing their structure, and as it was not at first equipped with an operating theatre or a lift, operations were performed in the patients' rooms.

[1] For some indication of Synge's symptoms, see *Letters to Molly,* ed. Ann Saddlemyer (Cambridge, Mass., 1971), pp. xvi and xvii.

For Friday 10 December 1897, John entered in his diary: 'Spinoza, 20.19; Lower Mount Street,' and for the following day: 'Spinoza; Operation on neck by C. B. Ball.[1]. . .' [The experience of going under ether was an extraordinarily vivid one and John later wrote a short essay describing it and showing how his love affair and his enquiries into mysticism[2] dominated his mind at the time of the operation.]

The next period I remember but vaguely. I seemed to traverse whole epochs of desolation and bliss. All secrets were open before me, and simple as the universe to its God. Now and then something recalled my physical life, and I smiled at what seemed a moment of sickly infancy. At other times I felt I might return to earth, and laughed aloud to think what a god I should be among men. For there could be no more terror in my life. I was a light, a joy.

These earthly recollections were few and faint, for the rest I was in raptures I have no power to translate. At last clouds came over me again. My joy seemed slipping from my grasp, and at times I touched the memory of the operation as one gropes for a forgotten dream. I heard noises and grew conscious of weight. The weight took shape; it was my body lying motionless in a bed. The clouds broke, and I saw a gaselier over my head. I realized with intense horror that my visions were fleeing away, leaving scarcely a trace. . . . The impression was very strong on me that I had died . . . and come to life again, and this impression has never changed. . . .[3]

[Ten days after the operation, John was well enough to return home and he grew stronger every day.] Operations were not spoken of to children in our household, and I had been told that John was staying in town. I was surprised when he appeared for Christmas dinner looking rather ill, with a silk scarf tied loosely round his neck, and after watching him for a few minutes said: 'Where have you been, Uncle John?' He laughed off the question and gave no satisfactory answer. My suspicions were more than ever aroused. I had heard that he had joined the nationalists. His

[1] C. B. Ball, later Sir Charles Ball, performed all the operations that Synge underwent. He was Regius Professor of Surgery at Dublin University from 1895 until his death in 1916.

[2] In Paris, Synge had been fascinated by the subject and discussed it often with Yeats and Stephen MacKenna. He noted in his diary for 19 February 1897 'Saw manifestations'. (TS. 830.)

[3] *C.W.* II. 42, 43.

appearance corresponded with my idea of a released prisoner. 'I know,' I shouted, 'you've been in gaol.' This was met with such a general laugh that I began to doubt the accuracy of my guess, and the problem seemed as obscure as ever. It was forgotten for the moment as the housemaid came in with the turkey. . . .

John was reassured by all the doctors told him about the success of the operation and believed that, if the swelling did not develop again in the neck while he was recovering his strength, he would prove to have been completely cured. Although the operation had been successful, the doctors must have known the nature of the disease and that its symptoms might recur. My father, as one of the owners of the Mount Street Nursing Home, may have been aware of their anxiety, but John and the other members of Mrs. Synge's family remained in ignorance of his danger. As it was not until nearly ten years later that another operation became necessary, he was to be free of serious anxiety about his health during the period in which he established his reputation as a writer.

4

In the two years that had passed since the making of the 'cross-door'[1] my sister and I had become accustomed to spend much of our time with our grandmother. Although I can remember her in earlier years, it is from this period that my clearest recollections of her begin.

Being the mother of a family was her vocation, and the instinct for securing the immediate well-being of her children and grand-children inspired her nearly as much as her faith. She might at times be anxious about their future, she might disapprove of their plans or ways of life, but nothing they said or did could deter her from seeking to supply their needs. She always wanted to feel assured that they were warmed and fed, and when they were ill to know that they were properly attended, dosed with the appropriate medicines and, if she thought necessary, poulticed with hot linseed.

As her family feelings did not extend to pet animals, she had no dog, and only for a short period kept a cat. She used to employ my brother to trap the mice, paying him 2d each, or 1d when they were very plentiful. If he were busy, she sometimes employed me at the same rates and used to buy from me, for 1d each, heads of lettuce

[1] The door connecting Nos. 29 and 31 Crosthwaite Park.

that I grew in the back garden. As my brother's pocket money was only 2*d* per week and mine 1*d*, we could not have taken photographs[1] had it not been for the business we did with Mrs. Synge. At that time, quarter-plates for our camera cost 1/– per dozen, printing paper cost 1/– for a packet of 36 sheets and there were chemicals to be paid for as well.

Our mother, when she went out or had visitors, was glad to leave my sister and me in our grandmother's care, and we often ran in of our own accord to spend an hour with her when we were tired of sitting in our dining-room. She allowed us to make scrap-books and paint with water-colours at her round table when she was writing letters or adding up her accounts. At other times she talked or read aloud, or gave us Bible lessons. Her choice of books was judicious and, although they were mostly of the kind that she called 'improving books', we enjoyed listening.

By the beginning of 1898, she had set apart the hour after breakfast on Sundays for teaching my brother and me about religion. Our sister sometimes joined us for these lessons, but sometimes she preferred to stay with our mother. Mrs. Synge told us that the Bible, though composed of many books, was to be accepted from beginning to end as the inspired word of God, infallible in each of its parts. On its authority she taught us that the human race had begun perfect in a garden situated on the river Euphrates and that our first parents had fallen into sin which made eternal damnation the just reward of all succeeding generations. From retribution the atonement had, she explained, provided a way of escape, but only for those who made the free gift of salvation their own by an act of acceptance through faith. In her belief those who had little opportunity for understanding the gospel and the heathen who had never heard it, might rely on the uncovenanted mercies of God, but it was the duty of Christians to go into all the world and preach the gospel to every creature. . . . Though she preferred to dwell on the means of gaining salvation, she felt it her duty to emphasize the horror of eternal damnation. 'There shall be weeping and gnashing of teeth,' she read and, folding her steel spectacles on the open page, she added: 'It will be terrible for some people. We don't know who will be lost, but some people will reject Christ's offer of salvation

---

[1] Stephens's elder brother, Frank, had been given a camera several years earlier. The two boys enjoyed developing and printing their photographs, and Synge's own interest in photography was stimulated by the boys' hobby.

and will be lost for ever.' At every pause her black marble clock seemed to tick with unusual distinctness, and through her lesson I watched its quick little pendulum catch the gilt cog wheel first at one side and then at the other.

We received the same teaching as she had given to John, for it was her pride that she never wavered in her faith. She explained to us that he was self-willed and had turned away from God, but that he would be brought to a knowledge of the light as an answer to prayer, in God's good time, and asked us never to forget him in our prayers. Sometimes our lessons were interrupted by his entering the room. I remember particularly his coming in once when we were having a Bible reading. He was twirling his pocket scissors on his finger chanting softly to himself, 'Holy, Holy, Holy Moses.' We greeted him and he sat in the window for a few minutes and then, feeling that he had caused an interruption, went quietly out again. Our grandmother said: 'Don't put down your Bibles when Uncle John comes in,' and resumed her reading.

When I was very young, people who were grandparents seemed immeasurably old. My idea of age changed so slowly that Mrs. Synge's appearance seemed to alter but little as years passed and consequently my recollection of her is static, like a portrait. She was tall and had grey, direct eyes and had a high forehead, finely marked features, a thin, firm mouth and straight nose. Her carriage was erect and her step firm and self-assured. She wore a full black dress almost sweeping the ground, a white lace cap, and a black case for her spectacles dangling by chains from her belt. While about the house, she often wore a shawl wrapped round her shoulders and always carried a curious little basket filled with keys. She had a ready smile that was calm and reassuring, but she never laughed loudly.

At the opening of 1898, Mrs. Synge was watching John's health with great care. On 3 January she noted at the end of her diary for the old year: 'John not well—made me anxious,' and two days later she wrote to Robert:

Johnnie looks much better, but he is not strong, and I am anxious lest he should go to Paris too soon and be laid up again in some way, as the Hotel life is anything but comfortable or healthy. He is very impatient to be off. He is very silent, poor fellow, and spends all his time over his books except when he goes out for a walk. . . .

[By the middle of January, Dr. Beatty considered John sufficiently well to go to Paris and he left as soon as possible. Once there, he soon made the acquaintance of Richard Best and also renewed contact with several old friends. In Paris, John was better able to devote himself to study than he was at home where the criticism of his relations, though usually unspoken, tended to interrupt his application. He noted in his diary reading many books in French and in English and each day he entered the word '*écrit*'.]

He was working at a novel of which he preserved only a few draft fragments in his black notebook.[1] They suggest that he was trying to embody in fiction the emotions and theories on which his mind continually dwelt, and seem to indicate the kind of artistic synthesis that he sought to give to his experience of love thwarted by a young woman's sense of duty, his indignation against everything that tended to make human life and feeling abortive, and his theories of revolt. Some years had to pass before he could write, as he did in the preface to *The Tinker's Wedding*: 'Analysts with their problems, and teachers with their systems, are soon as old-fashioned as the pharmacopœia of Galen.'[2] His story, besides being intended as a medium for artistic writing, was clearly de-signed to illustrate social conditions that required reform. It was about hospital nurses whose dangerous work was under-paid, under-praised, and continued night and day without time for necessary rest. . . .

Again in the society of his nationalist friends, John returned to Irish studies and, on Friday 18 February, began attending lectures delivered by M. d'Arbois de Jubainville,[3] Professor of Celtic at the Collège de France. . . . The subject of the lectures . . . was a comparison between the ancient Irish and ancient Greek civiliza-tions; it formed no part of the critical studies to which he had planned to devote himself during his stay in Paris but, once again in his life, an event apparently trivial was to prove of determining importance to his career. Up to this time he had never visited an Irish-speaking district, but his study of the Gaelic language in Trinity College and of some Irish epic literature had prepared his mind for ⟨de Jubainville's⟩ lectures. His nationalist emotions had

[1] T.C.D. MS. 4382.

[2] *C.W.* IV. 3. The preface was written in 1907.

[3] Professor d'Arbois de Jubainville (1827–1910) was one of the French supporters of the Irish cause, and a friend of Maud Gonne.

been quickened so that he listened with enthusiasm to any authoritative teaching that added to the prestige of his country. ⟨De
Jubainville⟩ had found in ancient Irish literature a source of learning
important to European culture. As John listened to his exposition,
he understood for the first time the place of Irish heroic literature
in the mythology of Europe. Learning to compare the Irish and
Homeric heroes enabled him to relate with new force to the Irish
sagas Goethe's familiar teaching about ancient Greek literature. . . .

On Saturday 2 April, John met Miss Margaret Hardon ⟨an
American student of art criticism,⟩ who soon became one of his
best friends in Paris. . . . Before long she discovered John's power
of argument and invited him to meet . . . her friends who enjoyed
philosophic disputations. . . . John was interested in his work and
was enjoying the society of his friends; he was even seeing a little
of Parisian amusements, for on 25 March he wrote in his diary:
'*Au cabaret des Noctambules*', and on 9 April: '*Dîner chez les Beydons,
après au Moulin Rouge.*' There was much in Paris that he was loath
to leave; yet on the other hand, he always revolted against city
life in the spring. Besides a craving to be in the country, he had
definite reasons for returning home—his lodgings were so uncomfortable that on 4 April his mother wrote in her diary: 'I heard
from Johnnie; troubled by bugs.' He had decided to make himself
as familiar with the life of the Gaelic-speaking people of the Aran
Islands as he was with that of the people of Dublin and Wicklow.
Cherrie Matheson was at home and he knew that he would have an
opportunity for renewing his proposal of marriage to her if he
stopped at Crosthwaite Park on his way to the West. . . .

[When John arrived home on 23 April,] his mother was in
Greystones . . . ⟨where⟩ she had gone for change of air after an
attack of influenza, and had taken with her my brother, who had
been suffering from a sore throat. As she had sent away her servants,
John slept at the top of an empty house and came in through the
cross-door for meals with us. . . .

[John had decided to spend part of the summer in the Aran
Islands, but before he left for the west, he had two interviews with
Cherrie Matheson. They met at the Museum one afternoon, and
Cherrie obviously told him again that their differences were irreconcilable. Two days later, he called at her home and had an
interview with her and her mother.] Mrs. Matheson, with Cherrie's
approval, rated him soundly for pressing a rejected proposal of

marriage when he was not earning enough money to support himself. He left in despair. . . . His mind was still distraught with anguish when, on the morning of Monday 9 May, he left by the morning train for Galway.

It is a remarkable experience for any native of the eastern counties to cross Ireland and, after a journey of only 130 miles, to stand for the first time on the western shore. There the sun, instead of setting behind the hills or the straight edge of the midland plain, drops at evening into the ocean. The rocky western coast, indented and broken by the Atlantic waves, is altogether different from the sloping strands of Dublin and Wicklow, washed by a paler sea. The people, descending from a mixture of races, the fusion of whose blood took place long ago, have more common characteristics than have their fellow countrymen of the districts where lineage has been confused by constant immigration. Galway could be likened to Dublin in little except its central position on the coast. . . . The port had decayed, partly through the decline in the Irish population and partly through an increase in the size of ships, until there was little shipping in the harbour; many of the warehouses were ruinous, and the townspeople conducted their business with a peculiar indifference to time.

John arrived there in the afternoon, but could not go to Aran until the following day, because the sailings of the small steamer that plied between Galway and the islands were dependent on the tide, and she was not due to leave until ⟨six o'clock on Tuesday morning.⟩ He engaged a room for the night and after a meal, strolled about the town. . . .

The narrative of the book that John afterwards wrote about the Aran Islands begins . . . when from the deck of *The City of the Tribes*, he watched the sailors cast off in a fog from Galway pier. After three hours steaming through the mist, without seeing the wide bay between the coast of Connemara and the Cliffs of Moher or the islands lying across its mouth, he landed on the pier at Kilronan, the chief fishing village of Aranmore,[1] as if he had been brought there blindfold. On his arrival as a stranger, he did not attempt to take lodgings in a cottage, but engaged a room in the small two-storied public house that was called 'the hotel'. . . .

On the day of his arrival, John asked his landlady to find some-

_____

[1] Aranmore (or Inishmore) is the largest and the most northerly of the Aran Islands. Inishmaan, the middle island and Inisheer, to the south, are smaller.

one who would teach him Irish, and she in the afternoon brought in an old, blind man who was delighted to undertake the tuition of a stranger. He acted so constantly as John's instructor and guide that he likened John and himself to a cuckoo and its pipit. In his notebook John wrote:

I have found a professor, an old man who walked with and guided Petrie, Sir William Wilde, Sir William Stokes and many others. He is one of the Aran Islanders I read of in Petrie's notes when first touched with antiquarian passion I used to wander many miles to seek the vestige of some tiny church gloating on its few fragments with more joy than I have felt since at Rouen or Amiens. . . .

His first walk ⟨the next⟩ morning was by the poor village of Killeany to the sand hills at the southern end of the island where he had a view of Inishmaan, the middle island. . . . In a fortnight, he was able to make arrangements to move there and share for a month a life that he described as 'perhaps the most primitive that is left in Europe'. Meanwhile, he spent his days watching from the cliffs the birds and the sea, learning Irish, reading books of the kind that he had been reading in Paris, and walking over Aranmore to see every holy place and the ruins of every fort, church, or hut about which he had read or chanced to learn from the local tradition. . . .

⟨Most of the time,⟩ the weather was broken, so he saw the island in rain and storm and in bright intervals when scraps of rainbow formed in the clouds that drifted across the sea. . . . ⟨He found that⟩ in Aran, his anxiety to learn overcame his usual shyness; he called on the Revd. William Kilbride, the Protestant clergyman . . . and on Father Farragher, the priest who was to serve the islands for more than twenty years—a man who could steer a *curragh* as well as any islander. At the inn, he talked with his one fellow-visitor, ⟨a schoolteacher named Redmond,⟩ who had known the island for some years.

Early in their acquaintance, John chanced to say that he wished he had brought a camera. Redmond replied that he would have his Lancaster hand camera sent out by the next boat and would sell it to John if he thought it suitable. John was glad of the offer, and the camera was his in a few days. It was an ingeniously designed instrument, beautifully made of polished mahogany and carried in a black leather jacket in which eye-holes were cut . . . for the lens and view-finders.[1] When fully loaded, it held twelve quarter-plates, which were moved from one compartment into another—and when exposed, into another—by different mechanisms. It was heavy and conspicuous and had one serious defect: a trigger operated the shutter which had to be set before a plate was dropped into the magazine; ... if the trigger were pulled the wrong way by a hair's breadth, the shutter opened enough to fog the plate without taking any photograph.

John loaded his camera at night in his bedroom without any light, changing the plates in their metal holders and placing them one by one in the magazine. He had no means of testing his results, but wrapped the exposed plates carefully and packed them in card plate boxes to be developed by my brother at Castle Kevin. . . .

For part of almost every day, when the weather allowed him, John used to sit alone on the cliff watching the sea and the birds, and listening to the sound of the waves, to the cry of the gulls and to the chatter of the choughs. Sometimes he was content to remain for hours without attempting to write or formulate anything, absorbing impressions that nothing in his life afterwards could efface. At other times, as he sat on the edge of the cliff, he wrote descriptions of the sea and the birds and jotted passing thoughts in his pocket notebook.[2] Although he had abandoned the study of music, at times of emotion he continued to seek in his musical experience for similes and aesthetic standards. While sitting one day on the cliff, he wrote in his notebook:

When the sun is covered, six distinct and beautiful shades still blend in one another—the limestone, the sea, leaden at my feet, and with a steel tinge far away, the mountains on the coast of Clare and then the clouds, transparent and opaque. There is not any affectation in borrowing a term from music, ⟨for⟩ no pictorial wording can express these movements peculiar to our humid insularity, unknown in the more radiant south. Today three delicious movements differ only from a symphony in that the finale is always the opening of a new design. There are these: the dim *adagio* in six tones, the *presto* of the quick colourless rain, followed by a glorious *allegro con brio* where sun and clouds unite in brilliant joy.

[1] This is an earlier camera than the one reproduced as 'Synge's camera' (plate 1) in *My Wallet of Photographs*.

[2] T.C.D. MS. 4385. Notes on Synge's first visit to Aran are also found in MS. 4382.

⟨John⟩ had gone to Aran at one of the critical times in his development, and had found an environment which was to have a determining effect on its direction. There he was inspired to use his literary powers in the interpretation of fundamental feeling and to turn gradually from the exposition of theories. For some years, he had been learning the importance of the life that he had known from childhood in Dublin and Wicklow; it had been difficult to criticize because of its familiarity, but it had prepared him for understanding the life of the islands. In Aran he was to find not only a new balance for his appreciation, but a society which provided a medium for its use.

The growth of education had tended to make folk-lore inaccessible in Dublin and Wicklow, but it was part of ordinary talk among the island people. Not only did they continue to tell ancient stories, but their narratives of current happenings were marked by the qualities that make lore eternal. The stories that John heard in Aran provided him with plots for his plays because they were free from disputations and rich in symbols for the truths that are apprehended through emotional experience. . . .

⟨On Tuesday 24 May, John left Aranmore for Inishmaan.⟩ In the morning a *curragh* of the largest kind used in the islands came into Kilronan harbour. It was about twenty feet in length and had a uniform width of about four feet, except where the bow was bent up and tapered to turn the sea. Pat MacDonagh, in whose cottage John had arranged to stay, and three other men were rowing, each pulling a pair of oars. They showed John where to sit in the stern on the wooden framework that supported the tarred canvas of which the canoe was made, and stowed near him his portmanteau heavy with books and his camera. Hardly had the *curragh* left the shelter of the pier before she began to ride buoyantly on the waves. The day was not wild, but in Gregory Sound—where the Atlantic tide runs between Aranmore and Inishmaan—the sea is never still.

The party landed at a little pier used for shipping horses to the mainland in summer, when water and grass are scarce, and for mooring hookers to unload the turf without which life on the treeless, rocky island would be impossible. There were no wheeled vehicles on Inishmaan because there were no roads on which they could have been used. . . . Everything was carried either on the backs of the men or women or in panniers on horses or donkeys. There was no priest, doctor, or policeman resident on the island ⟨and⟩ the post office was Pat MacDonagh's cottage. . . .

At the first opportunity, he sent his mother his new address and she, passing on his news in her next letter to Sam, wrote:

I had a very interesting letter from Johnnie last week. . . . The islanders of Aran found out that he was related to Uncle Aleck[1] and came to see him and were quite pleased. He is now on Inishmaan island—went there in a *curragh* and is much pleased with his abode, a room in a cottage inside the kitchen of a house, . . . and he lives on mackerel and eggs and learns Irish; how wonderfully he accommodates himself to his various surroundings. . . .

The day after his arrival on Inishmaan, John made a tour of the whole island with ⟨Martin⟩ MacDonagh.[2] They visited a dolmen of druidic times, the fort, the cliffs, and the ruin of a small church built in the early Christian period by anchorite monks who had found seclusion in the islands of the western coast as they had in the Wicklow plateau and the adjoining hills. On his return from his survey of the island, John found Pat Dirane, the greatest story-teller of Inishmaan, sitting by the kitchen fire. Pat Dirane had occasionally left Inishmaan as a harvester when he was young, but not for long enough to be affected by vulgarity, the great temptation of gifted entertainers. He held a position among the people like that of an actor in a more sophisticated community and was famous even in Aranmore. He was able to tell stories well in English, although his natural medium was Irish, and ⟨he⟩ was particularly valuable as a teacher of lore to John who did not then know enough Irish to understand narrative. . . .

John's time was spent learning Irish, listening to stories from Pat Dirane, wandering on wet days through driving rain along by the sea and on fine days lying in the sun on the walk of the great fort or sitting on the cliffs watching the waves. . . . After his interview with Cherrie and her mother, John had arrived in Aran exhausted and despairing, and he had found that life there stilled his nerves. At times he dwelt on his melancholy romance, . . . but gradually the quiet life of the islands made unhappy incidents seem remote. In his notebook he wrote:

It is a great gain to have learned to wander. If trouble overtakes me, I set

---

[1] Synge's uncle, the Revd. Alexander Synge, who had spent several years in the islands as a missionary. See *C.W.* II. 53 and GS, pp. 75–6.

[2] He is called Michael in *The Aran Islands*. See *C.W.* II. 112n.

out, and in new scenes becoming always a new soul, I am not any more the man who was suffering. I do not forget my grief, but ponder it continually with the tamed sympathy one may feel for a bereaved brother or sister till it grows powerless to wound. . . .

Quiet as was John's life on the island, it yielded him memories that were peculiarly rich in primitive feeling. One was of the funeral of an old woman who was buried on Sunday 12 June. Every detail long remained clear in his mind from the making of the coffin until the last sounds of the women keening died away across the rocks. He listened to the men hammering the nails and watched them opening the grave in ground so shallow that often at funerals the people of the island recognized, and keened over, the remains of long dead relatives disinterred in the making of a new grave.

About fourteen years later, when I was ⟨in Aran⟩ walking by the sea near the graveyard, I met Father Farragher who was staying on Inishmaan for a mission. He said: 'I'm feeling an old man today, for I was conducting a funeral here lately and they dug up the skull of a man I buried twenty years ago; we knew it by the black mark where it was broken with a stick.' Next day, I saw Father Farragher, dressed in oilskins, sitting in the stern of a *curragh* steering with an oar for Inisheer. A terrible sea was running through the sounds, and for long periods the *curragh*, carrying a tiny sail to steady her, used to disappear between the waves and then reappear on a mountain-top of moving water.

It was crossing the sound that John had his first experience of a *curragh* in a bad sea. He crouched in the bow, . . . little more separated from the waters of the ocean by the tarred canvas of the canoe than the swimming gulls were by their oily feathers. In the Aran book, he wrote:

The men seemed excited and uneasy, and I thought for a moment that we were likely to be swamped. In a little while, however, I realised the capacity of the curagh to raise its head among the waves, and the motion became strangely exhilarating.[1]

He closed the paragraph with a reflection on how much better death by drowning in the Atlantic would be than most other

[1] *C.W.* II. 97.

deaths that one is likely to meet, but he did not transcribe fully the entry that he made in his notebook. In it he wrote:

I thought almost enviously what fatiguing care I would escape if the canoe turned a few inches nearer to those waves and dropped me helpless into the blue bosom of the sea. No death were so delightful. What a difference to die here with the fresh sea saltness in my hair than to struggle in soiled sheets and thick stifling blankets with a smell of my own illness in my nostril and a half paid death tender at my side till my long death battle will be fought out. . . .

[As John's visit to the islands drew to a close, he tried to take stock of the knowledge he had gained in Inishmaan, and also to express the profound impression that the primitive life of Aran had had on him.] On his last Sunday on the island, he wrote in his notebook: 'Am I not leaving in Inishmaan spiritual treasure unexplored whose presence is a great magnet to my soul? In this ocean alone is not every symbol of the cosmos?'

It is not possible to fix exact dates for the beginning or ending of stages in the development of a person but, in a general way, John's first visit to Aran may be regarded as marking the end of his apprenticeship. He had gone there at the end of his long, melancholy love affair. Sometimes he was to meet Cherrie again on friendly terms, but she was no longer to be the goal of his imaginings. For a time he was to be involved in a strange struggle to create in his own mind a clear image of himself as he had lived and as he had emerged from his fixed devotion. Not until that struggle was over did he know fully what he wanted to say in literature. When he had created a picture of himself, he did not want to argue that his picture was justified by facts. He sought to interpret the experience of the person he conceived as himself, and for doing this found the medium ready to his hand. Its development in a definite form seems to date from his first visit to Aran. It was a use of symbols, not to state, illustrate or explain theories, but to interpret his most profound feelings in the different stages of his life. The sophisticated mysticism that he had studied with the assistance of Stephen MacKenna helped him to sympathize with the islander's acceptance of a wonderful spirit world intermingling with the substantial universe, but he had the wit to understand the difference. The close contact with nature that had influenced his life from childhood prevented him from filling his mind with the mystical metaphor of introspective poets. In Aran he found, in pure type, primitive feeling that he had always appreciated. His mind had begun to clear. . . .

5

[Before he left Aran, John received a letter from W. B. Yeats, who had encouraged him in his project of visiting the islands and who was, at this time, deeply interested in all aspects of Irish mythology. Yeats asked him to try and unearth any memories of stories of the Irish heroes among the people, and also passed on an invitation from Lady Gregory for John to visit her home, Coole Park—where Yeats himself was staying—on his way back to Dublin. John was delighted to accept and was present at Coole at the end of June when Yeats, Lady Gregory, and Edward Martyn were taking the first practical steps towards the establishment of a literary theatre in Dublin.[1] Though he seems to have taken very little part in the actual discussions, John was thus aware, from its earliest inception, of the theatre which was to dominate his artistic life.

[When he returned to Dublin, he slipped back at once into the usual family routine. On 1 July, he bicycled to Castle Kevin to join his mother and her party for the summer and we all spent July and August at Annamoe. As always, John passed the time walking and bicycling through the Wicklow countryside, joining the family for various excursions—picnics and fishing trips particularly—or reading by himself. He was also taking notes of conversations he had with country people such as 'Honest Jack Tar', a tramp famous around Annamoe for his great age and Mary Kavanagh, the knitting woman. Both used to talk with John, and he later used snatches of the conversations he had with them in his articles on Wicklow. Honest Jack Tar claimed to be over a hundred years old and to have known Roundwood Park when Francis Synge lived there: John told us that he had said: 'I never went there but Mrs. Synge offered me a glass of whisky.' One evening, when I was strolling with my grandmother on the avenue, I said something about the wonderful age of the Honest Tar, and she said: 'I wish Uncle Johnnie would not encourage tramps; I don't know why he wants to talk to queer people. I'm quite sure that Mrs. Synge never offered a tramp whisky.'. . .

[1] A forerunner of the Irish National Theatre Society. See below p. 158 and n.

[In the autumn, John returned to Paris and rented for himself an unfurnished room in the Rue d'Assas. He was still upset about Cherrie's refusal to marry him and it was during this winter in Paris that he dramatized his experience of the affair in the *Étude Morbide* or *Imaginary Portrait*.[1] He later referred to this work as 'a morbid thing about a mad fiddler in Paris', and exhorted Yeats not to have it printed rashly; but it has considerable biographical interest and helps to explain the emotional and intellectual crisis through which John was passing at this time.]

Cherrie, perhaps from natural vanity, had found difficulty in cutting off the approaches of a lover to whom she knew not how to respond. . . . She had promised to pray for his conversion which, she hoped, would lead to their union; but she had taken very little part in his experiences, which belonged mostly to the life of his imagination. At first, as John began to realize that his devotion to her could never find any fulfilment, he tended to idealize her refusal as much as he had idealized her friendship. Instead of recognizing the real lack of accord between them, he preferred to imagine her refusal to be the result of a mistaken but profound sense of religious duty. It was not until some time later, when this last delusion had been shattered, that he was able to complete his readjustment to the world.

To John, the mental conflict in which he was plunged brought a longing to give it literary interpretation in a way for which his critical writing afforded no opportunity. He was reading *Imaginary Portraits* by Walter Pater and thought of writing an imaginary portrait of himself. It is probable that he began work shortly before Christmas and there can be no doubt that the first winter months mentioned in it are the winter months of 1898. . . . The work took the form of letters mingled with a fragmentary journal . . . ⟨which⟩ appears to have been put together in a period of about fourteen months. . . . For the purpose of writing it, ⟨John⟩ made an analysis of his experience, an analysis that afterwards moulded the plots of his plays. As he did not write the *Étude Morbide* as history, he completely disguised all references to people and places, but through it can be traced an account of the greatest crisis of his life. . . .

[1] Dr. Price (*C.W.* II. 16 n., 25 n.), agreed with Stephens that the *Étude Morbide* was started during this winter. Professor Greene (GS, pp. 58–60) suggests that it may date from 1896.

[It is impossible to be certain to what extent the two women in the *Étude Morbide*—the Celliniani and the Chouska—represent women whom John actually knew. Each contains characteristics of many of the women in his life, but the figure of the Celliniani seems to be based to a great extent on Cherrie Matheson and the Chouska to contain traits of Florence Ross, perhaps of Hope Rea and also of John's American friend, Margaret Hardon.[1] He certainly thought of all these friends from time to time and the two figures in the *Étude Morbide* are composite ones made up of impressions from many sources.]

Margaret Hardon was John's constant companion during the spring of 1899 when he was in Paris working at the *Étude Morbide*. He enjoyed her company not only for her personal attraction but also because her interest in Celtic lore and mysticism encouraged him to talk of his studies. She took a place of growing importance in his thoughts and he began to weave round her a new romance. When, on 14 March, he noted in his diary that they had met for *déjeuner*, he referred to her not, as had been his custom by her initials, but as '*La Robe Verte*', a name which had for him some special significance; for both the women of the *Étude Morbide* dressed in green. . . .

The companionship of Miss Hardon began to dissolve his romantic picture of Cherrie, a picture that he had created by years of lonely reflection. He began to understand that the attributes he had attached to her were the product of his own mind and wrote:

'You are my God and my Heaven
Take me and my pearls and gold,
Yet give me a franc for my supper,
The kitchen is bare and cold.'

She gathered my gold and jewels
Spangled her breast and head
Yet when I sought my veau-piqué,
She had left me a franc of lead.[2]

A revised form of this poem was among the collection of his verse

[1] Again, this is conjecture on Stephens's part.
[2] cf. the version in *C.W.* I. 22.

that John afterwards submitted to Yeats for advice as to its publication. The typed copy is marked in Yeats's handwriting with the word 'obscure'; but Yeats did not know John's story. . . .

[John paid a fortnight's visit to Brittany in April, then went back to Paris for a short time before returning to Ireland.] Sometimes he . . . spent an evening at Miss Hardon's room in Montparnasse talking with her either alone or with one or two fellow students, sometimes he . . . talked with her over tea in his attic, and sometimes he . . . met her at the Louvre; . . . on Friday 28 April, they went out together to St. Cloud to spend the whole day in the country. Their relationship seemed to be deepening as his dreams had predicted. . . .[1]

On his return to Crosthwaite Park ⟨on 9 May⟩, John had found his mother greatly concerned about her summer plans. . . . [For a number of reasons, she decided to leave home early and to rent Castle Kevin from the first of June.] As none of her family party, except John, could join her in the early part of the summer, Mrs. Synge had invited Sam's sister-in-law, Edie Harmar,[2] to come and bring a friend of her own age for company. Edie Harmar wrote to say that she would bring a friend called Madeline Kerr, a neighbour in Norwood, who was her colleague in mission work, and it was arranged that the two visitors should arrive at Castle Kevin on 6 June when the house would have been opened and aired for a few days. . . .

Edie Harmar who . . . was at once accepted by Mrs. Synge as a member of her family circle, was a person of interesting gifts and qualities; but her life had been limited by her evangelical religion.[3] Her hair was tightly drawn back and fastened in a bun behind her head. She wore a shirt-blouse, high-necked and stiff, and, pinned to the front of it, her glasses hanging from a light chain which was attached to a spring roller in a chain-case like the back of a gunmetal watch. A slightly undershot jaw gave her face a look of peculiar determination, but her grey eyes were generally ready to

[1] Synge was most strongly influenced by dreams during the period 1897–1900 and in his relationship with Margaret Hardon.

[2] The Stephens TS. (835–41) contains a full account of the way in which Samuel Synge, who was at this time a medical missionary in China, had met and married a fellow medical missionary named Mary Harmar. She was one of four sisters, and came from Norwood, near London.

[3] Stephens's unfavourable attitude towards Irish evangelicalism is obvious in this passage.

laugh. Her figure was neat and her step quick and decided. Although her religion was evangelical it provided a wider scope for sympathy than Irish Protestantism and allowed her to discuss faith without feeling that everyone who differed from her was blaspheming the revelation of Almighty God. By studying art she had broadened her understanding and her oil painting manifested talent, though it never developed beyond the stage of clever sketching.

In both mind and appearance Madeline Kerr contrasted strangely with Edie Harmar. She had accepted Ireland's stage reputation and was prepared to find every detail of life amusing. Her large face was almost always smiling and her usual mood was one of buoyant good humour. Although high-spirited she was serious-minded and did not indulge in worldly excitements. Mrs. Synge liked her and was soon convinced that Edie Harmar had chosen her companion wisely.

The two visitors were to be John's chief companions for more than a month, but he did not make friends with them quickly. For the first week of their stay, although he talked with them entertainingly at meals, he left them mostly in Mrs. Synge's company, and went out walking and fishing alone. His thoughts lingered, not on either of the strangers, but on Miss Hardon. . . .

Soon after his return to Ireland he had written her a letter filled with his romantic imaginings and dreams that had begun to find a focus in her. To this letter he had received no reply so he wrote her another on 8 June. She had not needed this reminder as before receiving it she had written to him. On 12 June he entered in his diary: 'Letter from the Green One.' She explained that she had been overworked and had interrupted her studies in Paris to rest for a fortnight in England, but had returned to Montparnasse, and after giving some account of her plans wrote . . .: 'When I was in London I went to a palmist and she told me I was to marry a military man and go across the sea to live. I am still looking for him. . . .' [She went on to urge John not to pay attention to any romantic dreams he might have of her. Marriage with him was out of the question and] 'If you let this come so definitely into your life you will make yourself and me very unhappy and the end will be that I cannot see you any more. . . .' She was quite right. John wrote in reply the day after he received her letter and seems to have accepted fully the wisdom of her view. . . .

⟨After Edie Harmar and Madeline Kerr⟩ had been at Castle Kevin for a week, John was beginning to feel that they were no longer strangers and was spending more time in the porch or on the steps with them after meals. Mrs. Synge had been introducing them to the people in the cottages and, as she liked to engage in religious conversations, he did not go visiting with her. On Saturday 17 June, they all went together to tea with Cousin Emily and in the evening after supper John took both visitors for a walk over the top of Castle Kevin hill and across the bog towards Trooperstown and Laragh. They were pleasant company together, but Edie Harmar interested him more than her friend. He planned to take her to the top of Trooperstown hill so that he might have an opportunity for undisturbed conversation and might know her feeling towards country of the kind he loved best.

On the following Tuesday, in a long letter to Sam, Mrs. Synge described how her party had been spending their days. She wrote:

On Sunday we went to the afternoon service at Derrylossery. . . . After a good tea at 6, Johnnie and Edie set off for a walk. They went over our hill and crossed the bog and then up Trooperstown Hill. Miss Kerr and I went out about 7 and walked up past Mavourneen's[1] and sat on the hill side. We saw two figures on the top of Trooperstown, walking about. They saw the sun set, as we did, at 8.10—it got chilly then and we came home.

Edie told me afterwards she had had some very serious conversation with poor John. She is very wise and does not argue, but when opportunity occurs speaks of God and His works. John seems to have spoken very freely to her and told her what he believes. It is so sad and made her feel so sorry for him. We have been and are praying much for him. They think he has such a very sad face. He has a sort of belief in a state hereafter —he does not now think we come to an end when we die.

Both the girls are very lively and there is a great deal of joking and fun goes on between them and John. I have not seen him laugh so much for years. . . .

---

[1] 'Mavourneen' was the name given by Mrs. Synge and her party to an old farmer's wife, Mrs. Rochford, who lived in a long low thatched cottage not far from Castle Kevin. Although she did not speak Irish, she retained a few words of the language in her ordinary speech. Stephens recounts that she remembered the famine; of her cottage on the top of the hill, she used to say: 'If it's a lonesome place and a wild place, it's a wholesome place where no one is ever a day ill, thank God, unless it is death itself that comes, and that is the will of God and who can complain?' (TS. 555.)

John had learnt to enjoy their company so much that he never withdrew to read in his room when he had an opportunity of sitting with them on the steps looking at the view or, on wet days, on camp stools in the porch looking into the mist that hid everything but the tops of the trees below the house. . . .

Every fine day successive phases of loveliness passed over the face of the country on which Castle Kevin looked down, until at sunset films of white mist from the marshes and rivers filled the valleys. If an evening was warm, John and the visitors used to remain out to see the stars appearing in the deepening blue and to watch for a night-jar that sometimes wheeled silently over the white-sanded carriage sweep before the door. Talking with Edie Harmar about religion had heightened mystical imagery in John's mind and sitting at sunset gazing from the door of Castle Kevin brought the opportunity for vision.

Years afterwards, Edie Harmar told me that one evening, when she was in the house with Mrs. Synge, Madeline Kerr had come in and beckoned to her and as they passed through the hall had whispered: 'Look at Mr. Synge.' He was sitting in the porch with a fixed expression on his face and had not noticed that Miss Kerr had left him. Edie Harmar, when she saw his ghastly appearance, gave an exclamation which recalled him to consciousness. He explained that he had been looking down into the valley at two fields which had taken on the appearance of great eyes because in the distance they formed oval spaces of equal size and in each, similar clumps of dark trees surrounded by white mist formed eyeballs. He said that by gazing at these he had become entranced, and it was some time before he regained his normal composure.

He afterwards wrote an account of his experience, but he gave his story an imaginary setting, and told it as if it belonged to the time when he used to go out in the evenings collecting insects. . . .

One night I was collecting on the brow of a valley near Annamoe. The day had been unusually warm and wreaths of white fog were rising from the bogs by the river. A little before dark I ran my eyes round the horizon and saw two luminous colossal eyes looking at me from the base of the valley at my feet. I knew instantly how they were caused—two low lozenge-shaped fields covered in the fog with clumps of trees, which formed eye-balls, standing out about the centre. Still I was fascinated. I dropped my net and caught hold of a gate that was before me. A band of heavy woodland behind the fields formed a sinister forehead and as I

looked the eyes seemed to eat into and consume my personality. Then
the whole valley grew full of light and movement and the opposite
hillside was covered with a pageant of castles and spires. I do not know
how long I stood. Then someone spoke to me—a man going home in the
lane nearby. I woke. It was quite dark and the eyes were no more visible.
For many days I could not look on those lozenge-shaped fields, even in
sunshine without shuddering.[1]

Whatever may have produced in John at this time the aptitude
for mystical experience seems also to have affected Edie Harmar,
for a few hours later she saw a vision that made a lasting impression
on her mind. It was she herself who described it to me long afterwards as vividly as if it were still before her eyes. She had not long
fallen asleep when she thought that she awoke to find a hand
mirror lying on her bed. A voice said in the dark: 'Do you wish to
know? Do you want to see?' Then she lifted the mirror and in it
she saw a girl friend standing by the dead body of her brother lying
in an open coffin. She laid down the mirror; but the voice repeated
the same words and she looked again, this time to see John leaning
on his bicycle, as she was accustomed to see him, and talking
eagerly. Then the vision changed and she saw him sitting outside a
cottage smoking his pipe. Again she laid down the mirror, and once
more the voice said: 'Do you wish to know? Do you want to see?'
She lifted the mirror and saw in it a vision of John praying in a
church.

Next morning when she came down to breakfast she looked as
if she had been without sleep. John, noticing her fatigued appearance, inquired anxiously about her health and when they were
alone she told him the whole story. He questioned her closely about
the vision. She described it in detail and drew in outline a picture of
him as she had seen him sitting smoking outside a cottage. He
recognized the cottage where he had been staying in Aran ⟨the
summer before⟩ and was able to identify a curious German pipe
that he had been smoking there. When she told him of how she had
seen him praying, he said fervently: 'If you believe in prayer, pray
that this may never happen'; but some years later he said to her:
'I think your vision is coming true, but never in a church. . . .'

Mrs. Synge had arranged that on Tuesday 4 July, she and her

---

[1] This version, Stephens's edited text of T.C.D. MS. 4353, ff. 61-2, differs
slightly from the text in *C.W.* II. 10, based on ff. 18-19.

visitors should go on ⟨Willie⟩ Belton's car[1] to call on Aunt Editha who was living at Tiglin so that she might let Glanmore. John joined the party because he loved the Devil's Glen and the woods and enjoyed showing the family home to friends. Aunt Editha received them with her peculiar cordiality which, to the time of her death, almost led her relations to forget the harm that she had done to the Wicklow estate. After tea she took Mrs. Synge, her visitors, and John walking up the path to the hill behind the house, and out on the View Rock. As the party looked down on the tree-tops, five hawks flew out over the fox caves and showed the neat brown plumage of their backs and stretched wings. After sitting for a while in the heather the party returned to the path and followed it into the wood and down to Glanmore. How the large plastered castellated house may have appeared to strangers is impossible to know, but for John and his mother old associations were too strong to allow them to criticize its architecture. The party walked round the house and up the gradual slope of the Upper Glen path, first through the laurel bushes and beech trees, then through the scrub oak woods above the river along the craggy part of the hill, through the archway that John's grandfather had cut in the rock, and back to Tiglin.

Walking in the glen along the paths made by his grandfather and great-grandfather, and at Tiglin between the lines of cut stone buildings that Uncle Francis had designed for the hill farm, gave John a sense of belonging to the land. The party sat waiting in Aunt Editha's little sitting-room while Belton yoked the car and ⟨then they⟩ drove slowly back to Castle Kevin across the open ground of the plateau towards the whole range of hill lit by the evening light. . . .

[Edie Harmar only stayed at Castle Kevin for five weeks. When she left, Mrs. Synge wrote to Sam telling him in more detail about the friendship which had built up between Edie and John:]

She and Johnnie set off for Lough Nahanigan one evening late, about 5.30, but did not tell me where they were going. I guessed it. It had been raining heavily all the afternoon but cleared. They were not home until 10.20. . . .

Johnnie likes these late walks and has spoken very earnestly to Edie

[1] Probably a jaunting-car, a light two-wheeled vehicle which carries four people and is still used in parts of Ireland.

about his views and thoughts. When it is dark he talks more freely. Poor fellow all is still dark with him—he told her not to speak of what he said to her, so she could not do it: it is just the old thing wanting to have his intellect convinced by reasoning and proofs; it is sad and he looks so very sad when not laughing and joking. He will miss his lively companions very much now. He is gone to town today about his bicycle. The screw of the pedal is loose. It is an expensive luxury always getting wrong. He is to show Edie the College library.'

It had been arranged that my parents should come to Castle Kevin ten days later, but until then Mrs. Synge, John, and I were each other's only companions. As I had no bicycle and was too small for walking great distances, I rarely went out with him except in the evenings to fish. My grandmother used often to take me with her into the fields where she used to sit under sheltering banks and talk or read aloud or, if we went to a field where hay was in the making, watch me riding up and down on the horse that drew the rake. When she was busy I went out alone. She would not have allowed me to wander about the roads where I might have got into trouble with tinkers or made friends with people she did not know, but she used to send me across the hill to make hay with the Edge children who lived in Lizzie Belton's cottage.[1] The sort of experience that she thought good for me she had thought good for John seventeen years before, when he was ten years old, and, as the last of her family, left without young companions. . . .

[When John and I went out for an evening's fishing,] we usually went to Annamoe bridge and each fished alternate pools as we went down the river past the rectory. John carried his old brown rod, which used to lie against the chimney-piece in the back drawing-room as he did not trouble to take it down unless he were going to fish at a distance. He had an old leather fly book in his pocket, a spare cast round his hat, and a fish basket on his back, but he used no other equipment. The trout in the Annamoe river were not so large as to make a landing net necessary and John never thought of waders. He wore his usual knickerbockers, home-knit stockings, and strong shoes and was quite indifferent as to whether he walked on the bank or in the water. I often watched him excited and intent, standing with his feet firmly set apart among slippery stones and

---

[1] The Edge and Belton families were among the Protestant cottagers with whom Mrs. Synge maintained contact.

crouching slightly while he watched cast after cast on the end of a rapid as it slid in decreasing waves to calm in a deep pool.

When it was too dark to see our tackle we walked home, often in silence except for the measured squelch of water from John's shoes. It was pleasant to slide fish out of his basket when we reached home and lay them evenly on a plate under the lamp. I caught very few, but John said that the gift for catching fish would come to me with practice and would seem to come quite suddenly. . . .

6

[Early in September, we all returned to Dublin and John, who had decided on a second visit to the Aran Islands, left for Galway soon afterwards.] When he had first visited the islands, ⟨John's⟩ mind had been in the tumult produced by his most trying interview with Cherrie and her mother. At the time of his second visit, though he still idealized his devotion to Cherrie, he regarded his suit as a lost cause. The mental struggle that found expression in the *Étude Morbide* had not reached a conclusion. His powers of observation and appreciation were keen and realistic, but in the reflections that appear in Part II of the Aran book, and perhaps in the choice of its subject-matter, there are indications that his mind was oppressed by a sense of desolation and an unrewarded search for sympathy and understanding. When he used in his later writing the impressions formed during his visit to Aran in 1899, they retained the significance that they acquired from his mood at that time. . . .

John had gone to Aran for his second visit at the end of the summer when the evenings were closing in and the equinoctial gales were beginning. 'This year', he wrote, 'I see a darker side of life in the islands.'[1] He may have been predisposed by his own frame of mind to write of the life of the people as if lived against a background of wild waves surging and breaking themselves with incredible fury. There were, however, some calm days when he was staying in Inishmaan, for he saw the horses brought home from their summer grazing in Connemara and they could not have been shipped in rough weather. . . .

He had decided to spend a few days on Aranmore before returning home and when he inquired about crossing the sound, was offered a place in a *curragh* that was going for the priest. When a crew had the duty of bringing the priest to serve Inishmaan, they

[1] *C.W.* II. 107.

felt under a special obligation to go out in any weather because if
they failed the whole island would suffer. It was not the first time
that John had been in a *curragh* when the sea was rough, but on the
day he left Inishmaan, the crew were doubtful as to whether they
should take the risk of putting out. Of the struggle between the
curragh and the waves he wrote a vivid description which concluded with the words: 'Our lives depended upon the skill and
courage of the men, as the life of the rider or swimmer is often in
his own hands, and the excitement of the struggle was too great
to allow time for fear.'[1] This description explains his giving his
drama of island life the title *Riders to the Sea*. . . .

[Early in November, John returned to Paris. Again he immersed
himself in mystical reflections and continued writing the *Étude
Morbide*. He was also working on the first two parts of his book on
the Aran Islands and spending time with his many friends.] ⟨When
spring came,⟩ Cherrie Matheson, who had spent the winter in the
south of France, set out for home. Her father met her in Paris and
on the first of May she drove with him to the opening of the Salon.
On her way, she chanced to catch sight of John, but he remained
quite unaware of her presence. In her recollections she wrote: 'I
remember the glimpse I had of him so well in his Capuchin cloak,
with his head turned towards the man he was with speaking rapidly
all the time.'[2]

One Sunday after Cherrie came home . . ., I was sitting with my
mother in the bow window of our drawing-room and looking
down the terrace. Suddenly a door slammed and Kenneth Houghton, the second-form mathematics master ⟨at Corrig school,⟩[3] . . .
ran down the steps of No. 25 ⟨with Cherrie Matheson;⟩ they
started at a brisk walk towards the country. Her step was light and
she was laughing as I had seen her laughing at Castle Kevin. 'There
go Houghton and Cherrie Matheson,' I said. My mother started as
if I had fired a shot. I asked her what was the matter. She said quietly
but with noticeable intensity: 'It seems so soon after she was
thinking of marrying Uncle John.'

[Mrs. Synge had secured the letting of Castle Kevin for the
summer of 1900 and encouraged John to come home from Paris
to accompany her. He arrived in Dublin at the end of May and on 1
June they moved to Annamoe. Mrs. Synge's companions were to be

---

[1] *C.W.* II. 120.   [2] *Irish Statesman*, loc. cit.
[3] Corrig School, Dún Laoghaire, where Stephens was a pupil.

Edie Harmar's sister Annie and a cousin named Rosie Calthrop. They were to arrive by train on 6 June and John left Castle Kevin early in the morning to meet them at the station.]

Years afterwards Rosie Calthrop told me that her recollections of her first journey to Castle Kevin and her arrival there would never fade from her memory.[1] She described how she had come in the early morning with Annie Harmar to Rathdrum Station and found John, in very homely cycling clothes and thick stockings, waiting for them on the platform, and how he had arranged for the luggage to travel by cart and had taken them with their bicycles, walking and riding by turns, along the narrow, hilly road between hedges of dewy gorse that filled the air with fragrance. They came at last, she said, to the old iron gates of Castle Kevin, climbed the steep avenue through the trees and, just as they came out in full view of the hills, were greeted by Mrs. Synge wearing a lace cap over her grey hair and standing erect on the steps in front of the square grey house.

John was glad to meet Annie Harmar as an old friend, but as a woman Rosie Calthrop interested him much more. . . . Rosie was thirty-six, seven years older than John. In a letter to Sam, Mrs. Synge wrote of her: 'She has fair hair which hangs very loosely about her face and she is small and wears very short skirts—here at least—so has a youthful appearance.' From the time of her arrival at Castle Kevin, John and she began a lasting friendship, but in it he again encountered a strange barrier which prevented the final accord that he hoped to find with some woman. It was different from the barrier that had separated him from Cherrie, but for him as insurmountable. Rosie was the daughter of a scholarly and devout clergyman and had grown up in the Anglican communion without hearing the controversial theology in which Irish Protestants were trained. She had musical gifts and a fine, clear voice; but since the man she had been engaged to had died, she had not sung except with the congregation in church. He had been an organist who, when he was practising in the evening, had been accustomed to play for her as she sat alone among the darkened pews. Outwardly she was as Mrs. Synge described her: 'A cheerful, bright little person

---

[1] Stephens presents Rosie Calthrop very sympathetically; the reasons for his affection are fully explained in his account of her visit in 1901 (pp. 145–6). But she and Annie Harmar were probably the two 'missionary ladies' about whom Synge complained to MacKenna in July 1900 (GS, pp. 111–12).

very kind and unselfish'; but she confronted with an old sorrow
any new person who might seek to elicit her love. John's friendship
with her was happy, but its limitations increased his tendency to
dramatize himself as seeking to liberate some woman by enabling
her to understand that purity of affirmation is greater than purity of
negation. . . .

[Almost every day of Rosie Calthrop's stay at Castle Kevin, she
went out for a long walk or bicycle ride with John, sometimes in
the company of Annie Harmar and sometimes alone with him.
Both girls seem to have taken much pleasure in John's company
and they were certainly sorry when the time came for them to leave.
Mrs. Synge, who had found their company a mixed blessing,
reported to Sam, on the night before their departure, the impression that the visit had had on Rosie's mind:]

She said to me last evening as we were going up through the wood
that she could not have had a happier time, though the weather was so
wet! She seemed to appreciate Johnnie's thoughtfulness and kindness
very much! It is a pity he does not show it to me and not only to strangers.
He was most attentive to both in little matters I could see, and he was
always at their beck and call to walk or ride or escort them anywhere!
So no wonder they like him, but it was rather aggravating to me; he
wanted to put me aside entirely. But I told Rosie and then she did not fall
in with his plans, though she loved to be out walking with him I know. . . .

Not long afterwards my grandmother was speaking—as she
often spoke—of her trouble concerning John's lack of faith; ⟨she⟩
told me that she had received a strange assurance of his belief in a
life after death [from Cousin Emily whom John used to visit
fairly regularly at this time]. She said that once Cousin Emily had
broken her usual silence about all that John discussed at Uplands,
and had recounted a story she had heard from him of how he had
been on the verge of abandoning all belief in the spirit world when
Yeats was sent to him by the spirits to show him his mistake. What
Yeats had shown him, Mrs. Synge did not know, but she said it had
been enough to remove from his mind all doubt about our survival
after death. On hearing the story of this unorthodox revelation I
hesitated, not knowing what to say; but my grandmother told me
that any belief in the spirit world naturally carried with it a sense
that some way of salvation is necessary. . . .

[We returned to Dublin in September; John had decided to

visit the Aran Islands again, but before he set out, he spent nearly a week at Crosthwaite Park. The term had started at Corrig School, and every day Kenneth Houghton came to No. 25 to see Cherrie Matheson,] to whom he was at this time formally engaged. The result of John's seeing them together was to disintegrate his dream image of her—an image which she herself had never comprehended. He had mistaken it for a reflection of all that was essential in her, mirrored in a lover's mind. . . . Someone told me that when John accidentally met Cherrie and Kenneth Houghton, she stopped with complete composure to introduce the two men, but that John had cut the interview as short as possible. . . .

On Thursday 13 September, John set out for his third visit to the Aran Islands and next day made his passage in the steamer from Galway to Inishmaan. . . . At the times of his earlier visits, John had gone to the Aran Islands with Cherrie's refusals fresh in his mind; but this time he had gone knowing that her acceptance of another man had closed his love affair with a finality like that of death itself. *Riders to the Sea* sprang from the identification of his loss with the loss suffered by the Aran mothers whose sons were drowned, but his creative powers had yet to pass through their final stage of development before the play could take definite form. In the meantime, he sought in ancient lore for a medium in which he could use the symbol that had taken possession of his imagination, the symbol of the overwhelming sea. He had been reading *The History of Ireland* by Geoffrey Keating and had found in it a story which seemed to harmonize fantastically with his experiences of Aran. It was the story of the first invasion of Ireland before the Flood by settlers who were all washed from the world soon after their landing . . ., [the story of Capa, Laine, and Luasnad.]

It was on this story of Capa and his companions that John seized.[1] It associated his impressions of the sea, against which the Aran fishermen fought for their lives, and of the Flood which had been a terrible reality in his mind from the times of his earliest recollections; for his mother made it a most important part of her teaching. She used to describe Noah building the Ark in fine weather, and the foolish people of the world laughing at his work. Then, with realistic detail, she called up to the minds of her listeners a terrible picture of those who had sneered at the offer of security facing the relentless water after the ark was closed. . . .

[1] The fragmentary play Synge wrote on this theme is in *C.W.* III. 194–205.

[John spent about a fortnight on Inishmaan and then] crossed Gregory Sound in a *curragh* to stay for a few days on Inisheer. For some unexplained reason, he never felt the same accord with the people of that island as he did with ⟨those⟩ of Inishmaan ⟨and⟩ his stories of Inisheer chiefly concern people from whom he recoiled. . . . [Soon he returned to Inishmaan and the MacDonaghs' cottage where he stayed for the rest of his visit. On 17 October, Mrs. Synge wrote to Sam:]

Johnnie came home last night from the Aran Islands. He has one very large gland on his neck just above his collar; he looks well and the time on the islands agreed with him. I am glad to have him safe back. The sea has been very rough and great gales lately and it was hard for him to get away. He had a very rough passage to Galway and a miserable little steamer. The engines stopped several times and went on again. . . .

In the fortnight for which John was at home, there were beautiful autumn days when he rode to Enniskerry and other places at the foot of the hills to see the colours that were spreading over the trees of the Golden Belt, but he was occupied mostly with preparations for his ⟨return to⟩ Paris and spent much of his time in town shopping and seeing his friends. . . . Richard Best, who had been interested in his work in Paris, ⟨was in Dublin⟩ and was glad to give him advice about the writing of the Aran books. Best advised him not only on the general literary problems of his work but on practical steps necessary to its production. From his experience in helping John to revise several articles, Best knew John's way of scribbling on his manuscripts, his bad spelling and his grammar that often needed revision, and told him that if he wanted to publish good prose, he must first produce a clear script to criticize and correct and then a fair copy for publishers to read. For these purposes, Best advised John to buy a portable typewriter and, as John knew nothing about typewriters, selected one for him. It was a Blickensdorfer, a curious little machine in a varnished, wooden case. Its keyboard, which was not of the standard kind, operated type on an indiarubber roller which turned and dipped to the paper as each key was struck. John said, when he brought it home, that it spelt worse than he did; but he soon taught himself to use it and to the end of his life, though he wrote personal letters and preliminary notes by hand, he wrote literary compositions on the machine without making drafts for copying.

On 22 October, Mrs. Synge wrote to Sam:

Robert[1] and John are gone into town together to do some shopping. . . .
I am very glad he is kind to Johnnie and likes to be with him and they
have a great deal in common that they can talk about. . . . Poor Johnnie,
I feel so sorry for him. No light as yet, but the promise is sure. . . .

[A few days later, John left for Paris again and she wrote:]

My poor Johnnie went off this morning; it is very calm, I am thankful
to say, but it is raining and thick at sea. . . . I miss Johnnie. As usual I have
been very busy stitching and mending his clothes and getting him some
new ones. The gland on his neck is very large, but back pretty far. He is
getting rather anxious about it. I think he is improved; he has been more
pleasant and chatty than usual of late, and I think his queer time in Paris
always injures him, and he is so queer when he comes home and so out
of all our ways, and then it wears off by degrees. I am trying to persuade
him to give up his room in Paris in spring and make a fresh start nearer
home. . . .

In Paris, John found his usual recreation and inspiration in the
company of Stephen MacKenna and other literary friends and . . .
settled to a more regular programme of writing than he ever had
adopted before. He was working on the first three parts of the Aran
book and on his unpublished play.[2] In the opening words ⟨of an
early draft of the play,⟩ he outlined his aims as a dramatist. . . .

Every life is a symphony and the translation of this sequence into music
and from music again, for those who are not musicians into literature or
painting or sculpture, is the real effort of the artist. The emotions which
pass through us have neither end nor beginning, are part of eternal
sensations, and it is this almost cosmic element in the person which gives
all personal art a share in the dignity of the world. Biography, even autobiography, cannot give this revelation, for the deeds of a man's lifetime
are impersonal and concrete and might have been done by anyone, while
art is the expression of the abstract beauty of the person. . . .[3]

[1] Robert Synge returned with his family from the Argentine in 1900; he settled
in Ireland.

[2] *When the Moon Has Set*, which remained unpublished until its appearance in
C.W. III. 155–77.

[3] cf. *C.W.* III. 279 and II. I.

PART THREE

1901-1909

When John was in Paris, the family party at Crosthwaite Park heard only such news of him as came in his letters to his mother and, at the beginning of 1901, it was very scanty. On Sunday mornings, when my brother and I were with her for Bible instruction, she used to sigh over John's perversity and the long delay there seemed to be in the answering of her prayers. . . . [For John, however, life in Paris was, as always, stimulating and enjoyable; it was also productive for him as a writer. During the winter, he finished the first three parts of his book on Aran, wrote two articles, and completed much of the dialogue of an early two-act version of *When the Moon Has Set*. Such concentrated work tired him, but when he returned from Paris to Ireland for the summer, he seemed in reasonably good health, except for the gland in his neck. Mrs. Synge told Sam that John had 'grown stout and looks well, only for the very large gland which is terribly disfiguring to him'. When he consulted his Dublin doctor, he was given an ointment and a different medicine; gradually, the swelling seemed to be going down and it was decided that he would not have to undergo another operation, for the time being at any rate.

[Mrs. Synge had taken Castle Kevin from 1 June, and for the month of May, John stayed at Crosthwaite Park. In the evenings, my sister and I—who had been allowed to take over a portion of Mrs. Synge's garden to grow flowers and vegetables—used to water our borders.] Sometimes we could hear the click of John's typewriter from his open window, and sometimes he used to stroll out . . . to nibble lettuce leaves and comment on our gardening. One day, when my brother and I were on our way to Mrs. Synge's drawing-room, we met John on the stairs with a paper in his hand. He showed us in great triumph the April number of *The Gael* which he had just received from New York, containing his article 'The Last Fortress of the Celt'.[1] We were excited by his success but . . . said that he had chosen a sentimental title; he replied that . . . it exactly described the western islands and that we had not enough sense to understand it; ⟨he went on⟩ downstairs in the best of humour. . . .

[For the summer of 1901, Mrs. Synge again invited Rosie Calthrop to spend some time at Castle Kevin. John and Rosie were

---

[1] Not included in *C.W.* II; see *The Gael*, April 1901, p. 109.

pleased to renew their friendship and took many long bicycle rides together. Mrs. Synge wrote to Sam:]

Rosie Calthrop and John had a great ride yesterday of 46 miles. . . . They rode to Arklow via Rathdrum. There they went to the Hotel and ordered dinner—bacon and eggs was all they could get—and they had to wait nearly an hour for it and were charged 2/– each. They rode back by Rathdrum and had a very nice tea there, 1/– each, and 6d John gave in tips, so it was pretty costly 6/6d for food alone—John does not mind at all, of course it is my money and he has no scruples about that. However, I don't mind now and then, but I would not like it often.

By ⟨the end of June⟩ the weather had become warm and sunny, so ⟨on the last Saturday of the month,⟩ John and Rosie went for another long ride and Mrs. Synge enjoyed sitting out in front of the house to write her letters. . . . Next day she and her two visitors[1] drove to church. When they returned they found John in a state of great excitement about the adventure that he afterwards described in his article 'A Landlord's Garden in County Wicklow'.[2] In a letter to Sam begun on Monday, Mrs. Synge told a version of the story which . . . shows how closely John adhered to the account he gave at that time. She wrote:

The garden is visited by thieves more than formerly and they leave us very little. There were a number of cherries nearly ripe on the cherry trees. John and Rosie were watching them daily waiting for them to be ripe, but three youths got in yesterday while we were at Church and stole them all. John was in the garden at the time, lying down under a tree reading, and never heard them until one, a man of about 17 or 18, came strolling along the path where John was. He jumped up and gave chase and the man ran for his life. John had only on his slippers so he fell as he ran among the raspberry bushes, he got entangled (I am afraid he damaged them more than himself!) but he jumped up and ran on; two younger boys made off over the wall, and the other was half over when John got up and caught him by the leg and shook and shook till he got him down! Then they were so breathless they could only whisper to each other! John sent us into fits of laughter telling us. He was highly indignant. I don't know what he said, but he managed to frighten the man—or lad rather—very much. He thought John would prosecute him. He gave his name as McClean, and said he came from the Vale of Clara and was only passing through on his way to Mass, and

---

[1] Rosie Calthrop and a missionary named Miss Barry.   [2] *C.W.* II. 231–3.

the others he says were Walshes, but John does not believe he gave the right names. He promised he would never come again! John is not a good watchman or he would have heard them at work at the cherries, but they were very quiet. I am sure I am glad they got a fright.

On Friday 5 July my brother and I arrived on our bicycles ⟨from Dublin while⟩ Kate, Mrs. Synge's cook, ⟨came⟩ on an outside car with the luggage and our little dog, Bruno. We found the party at Castle Kevin in very good humour, and John eager to tell us about his adventure with the thieves on the previous Sunday. He said that after they had gone he found on a shelf in the dining-room an old book containing a list of the punishments to which they were liable, and that he wished he had brought them in and read it to them.

Rosie Calthrop was almost a stranger to us as we had met her only once when she came to dinner at Crosthwaite Park on her way to England, but we made friends with her quickly. She and John seemed to know each other very well. One day soon after we arrived, when we were walking with John and Rosie from the garden to the house, there was a slight shower. John sat on his waterproof cape under a shrub for shelter and made a sign to her to sit next him. She drew back a step laughing and shook her head. Both his gesture and hers were so slight that either might have passed unnoticed; but there was something in his look and in the way she shook the gold waves of her hair that suggested intimacy. My brother asked me afterwards if I would like Rosie for an aunt. . . .

During Rosie's stay at Castle Kevin, John was spending most of his spare time with her, but ⟨one⟩ Thursday evening he came to fish with my brother and me. We began at Annamoe bridge and fished along the bank opposite the rectory grounds; then we crossed the stepping stones and fished down the other bank under Avonmore. At sunset the trout began to rise. Gradually the water grew black except where it reflected the sky and our tackle became difficult to see. My brother in landing his sixth trout fell into a shallow pool and soaked his clothes. John told him to keep warm by walking quickly home, and fished on with me.

After some time, when we had passed Avonmore, the fish stopped rising, so we recrossed the river on some boulders and set out for home up the lane by Lizzie Belton's cottage and crossed the top of the hill. It was dark in the wood but, when we came out on the open hillside, we could see the lane before us. As we passed the pool where Mavourneen's cows used to water, the wind-bent larch trees beside it stood out black and haggard against the sky. A short distance above it a dark bird fell soundlessly, but as if hurt, on the lane before us. It fell with the uncertain movement of a blown leaf and fluttered along the ground. We walked about thirty or forty yards without reaching it and then it vanished like a ghost over the gorse hedge. 'That was a night-jar,' John said. 'It does that to draw people away from its young.' We did not see the bird again that night, but several times on still evenings we heard the humming sound of night-jars in the pleasure ground before the house and saw them fly in the dusk over the white gravel sweep. . . .

Rosie Calthrop arranged to leave Castle Kevin on 8 August. . . . [The evening before she left,] I happened to be sitting on the bead-embroidered hearth stool by a newly lighted fire. Rosie was sitting behind me on the sofa. Very quietly she leant forward and ran her hand over my hair—a moment's gesture of natural affection towards a child of twelve. Perhaps it was that I was totally unaccustomed to demonstrativeness ⟨but⟩ it seemed to me that I had been enveloped in sheet lightning. I did not try to move. It would have been impossible. That night I cried in the dark because she was leaving. I should have been covered with shame if anyone in the hall, when she said good-bye next morning, had suspected the truth. . . .

On Friday 6 September, we all returned to Crosthwaite Park. We were up early and after breakfast loaded two carts with luggage. When they had gone and Mrs. Synge and my mother were free to sit in front of the house waiting for Evans's car to take them to Greystones, my father, John, my brother, and I set out on our bicycles to ride the twenty-five miles to Crosthwaite Park, and brought with us the two red setters.

I was exuberant, for this was the first time that I had been allowed to ride the whole way home from Castle Kevin. We travelled very slowly to avoid tiring the dogs, but they tried to range along the road and would not come to heel behind the bicycles. John rode quietly, indifferent to their misbehaviour, but my father shouted at them to come to heel and near Ballinastow stopped to cut an ash stick which he brandished at them as he rode along.

At Bray we stopped for lunch at a restaurant that my father seemed to know very well. Beside it there was a big door into a yard where we put our bicycles and left the dogs to rest. We took

our lunch in a leisurely way in an upstairs room and in the afternoon went quietly on by the Ballybrack road. At length, with the
dogs panting behind us, we rode slowly along by the broken wire
fence of the butcher's field to the ugly grey terrace and the park
surrounded by its spiked railings. . . .

[John had now finished work on his two-act draft of *When the
Moon Has Set*, and he decided to ask Lady Gregory to give an
opinion on it.] Within a week after his return from Castle Kevin,
he wrote to her and she in reply telegraphed a welcome to Coole.
He packed at once and on Saturday 14 September left Dublin by
the morning train for Galway. . . .

During the week John spent at Coole, . . . Lady Gregory read his
play. . . . [It was, as she told him, not a good play, for] John had
written a dramatization of his own life under a thin disguise of
fiction, but so direct that it was devoted more to stating, illustrating,
and discussing the problems of his particular experience than to
interpreting universal emotions. . . . ⟨Lady Gregory's⟩ opinion that
it was of no literary interest must have been a bitter disappointment
to John, but he was sufficiently judicious to hide his feelings and
profit by her advice.

In a way that neither he nor she could have foreseen, the writing
of his play was to prove a decisive step towards his ultimate success.
He had done important work in formulating a drama of his life;
though he had first tried an unsuitable medium for its use, the drama
was capable of varied interpretation. To emerge as a dramatist, he
had but to find a medium rich in symbols that would give his
synthesis the universality of folk-lore. There is an old saying: 'The
help of God is nearer than the door.' The right medium was to
begin to reveal itself to John on his return to Dublin. . . .

[From Coole, John went to Aran for his fourth visit.] The people
had grown accustomed to his visits and delighted him by talking
freely of their own interests, of faction fights, of fairy music and of
magic; but he had gone to the islands at a melancholy time. An
epidemic of typhus had spread through the cottages of Inishmaan
and, though it was reaching its closing stages, new cases were still
developing. Drowning incidents too had again robbed the island
of some of its young men. . . .

Since John had first gone to the Aran Islands, he had heard so
many stories of their men being drowned that in his mind the
islands' toll to the sea became a permanent and terrible shadow

overhanging their life. During his visit in 1901 he was able to build up a narrative that was typical of the often repeated story of death. It harmonized with the philosophy of ⟨the play he had already written⟩ and with his beliefs that a human life from the mother to the grave is the only unity, and that the wave is the most adequate symbol of human personality.

The people told him of the portents that had been seen before a young man was drowned: his dog had sat next him on a rock and howled bitterly; a woman had seen her dead son riding on a horse that the man who was to die was leading to the sea. The drowning of the young islander seemed as inevitable to John as an event determined by the fates of ancient Greece. The young man was lost for a time, his battered body was cast on the shore, it was laid with the bones of other islanders many of whom had perished in the same way and, when the grave near the ancient church was filled, all was still again except for the wind and the rain, the sea and the birds. . . .

[John found his stay in the islands valuable and he was able to improve his Irish and also to take down a number of Irish songs, ballads, and stories told him by the old men on the south island, where he spent the last nine days of his visit. On Wednesday 9 October, he returned to Crosthwaite Park from Aran inspired more than ever before by what he had seen and heard in the west.

[In the mornings, he used to sit at his typewriter in his bedroom at the top of the house finishing the Aran book.] When he went to town, he used to bring the pages he had typed to Richard Best for reading and checking. In the evenings he used to sit alone in the front parlour reading by the fire. His mother in the room above knitted stockings, read the Bible and *The Life of Faith*, and wrote long letters for the foreign posts. She had felt lonely since my sister and I had been given school-work to prepare in the evenings, so sometimes I took my lesson books and read, sitting with her at the drawing-room table.

On my way back to our house by the cross-door, I used to slip quietly into the parlour to talk with John, as often as it was possible. There was an element of stealth about my visits to him for once or twice, when Mrs. Synge discovered that after having left her I had stayed talking in the ⟨parlour⟩, she seemed agitated, and said that she thought it would have been much better if I had gone straight to bed. She seemed to think that I would be more likely to learn undesirable ideas from John when we were sitting over the fire than I would if we were out walking in the country, so I closed the door gently when I went in or out of the parlour, and visited him uninterrupted.

He seemed to be glad of company, for he was always willing to put down any book he might be reading and talk. Usually I found him in his cycling knickerbockers and thick knitted stockings, sitting in a large arm chair that was covered in black horsehair, beside a pile of books most of which were in paper covers. Sometimes he had kicked off his rough slippers, and was sitting with one foot on the mantelpiece and one on the fender. The room was lighted by an oil lamp standing in the middle of an old mahogany table that had come from Glanmore long ago; . . . it had once reflected candles and cut glass, but all polish had vanished from its surface. In keeping with it there was an old unpolished sideboard across the closed folding doors, ⟨and also⟩ a modern sideboard, light brown and shining. On it was the starling that John had stuffed and mounted in a glass-fronted case made from a small box. Between the window and the fire, to the right of John's chair, there was an old bureau in which John kept his collection of bird's eggs. Over it hung another glass-fronted case containing a duck-billed platypus which Uncle Edward had brought home from Australia. . . .

I asked ⟨John⟩ one evening why his books were mostly in paper covers, and he told me that in France people bought books covered as his were so that they would not have to pay for the expensive binding of books that they did not want to keep. Then, picking up a book, he said, 'I'm sure when you hold a book open you put your thumb in the middle, and make a dirty mark. You should hold a book like this,' and he made a book rest of his open hand by propping the pages open on one side with his little finger and on the other with his thumb.

As he talked he often spun his folding scissors on his finger, or rolled a cigarette of light tobacco, and I noticed the quick action of his sensitive hands. Sometimes for my amusement, when his shoe was off, he would grip the shining steel poker with his toes and put it into the fire. He took a child-like pleasure in this feat, and in 'Under Ether' with pride described his toes as 'always agile as a monkey's'.

He asked me about what I was doing at school. I had learnt the only poem with a nationalist inspiration to be found in *The Select Poetry Book*; it was 'The Irish Brigade', by Thomas Davis ⟨and⟩ standing awkwardly on the edge of the fender, ⟨I⟩ recited ⟨it⟩ nervously in a sing-song voice. John's reception of my recitation delighted and reassured me, and I got from him some explanation of the presence of the soldiers and chiefs of the Irish Brigade in the French army, and of Davis's reference to 'George the Elector'.

I used to stay talking with John until bed-time. Then I used to go quietly out of the room and feel my way through the dark back parlour to the cross-door and, when it clicked behind me, through our dark ⟨dining-⟩ room to the hall lit by a single gas jet in the coloured glass lamp of the gaselier. . . .

2

The first nine months of 1902 are remarkable in John's history because in them he brought his dramatic writing to fruition. At the beginning of the year he had done nothing to indicate that he could write a play of more importance than ⟨*When the Moon Has Set*, which⟩ Lady Gregory had rejected: in the autumn he was to bring her *Riders to the Sea* and *The Shadow of the Glen*. . . . [Early in the year, while he was in Paris, John worked at two verse plays[1] and wrote a number of critical and topographical articles. His book on the Aran Islands—now completed—was with London publishers but he heard in February that it had been rejected by both Grant Richards and Fisher Unwin. However he continued his studies and in the middle of the month he began attending another course of Professor d'Arbois de Jubainville's lectures in Celtic studies.[2]

[In May, he received for review a copy of Lady Gregory's *Cuchulain of Muirthemne*;] it was a happy accident that John should have been asked to study Lady Gregory's book and its preface by W. B. Yeats just at the time when he was looking for a medium in which to write plays. For the translations of ancient Irish stories comprised in her book, Lady Gregory had used a rich language based on the dialect of English spoken by the country people of her district. It was a dialect which had probably borrowed a little more from the Irish language than the dialects of counties

---

[1] *A Vernal Play* (*C.W.* III. 189–93) and *Luasnad, Capa and Laine* (ibid. 194–205).
[2] In an article which appeared in *L'Européen* of 15 March 1902, Synge paid tribute to de Jubainville and described his lectures as of 'inestimable value to all those wishing to be enlightened' on the subject of Celtic literature (*C.W.* II. 354).

where Irish had been dead for two or three generations, but speech in different parts of Ireland varies more in intonation than in words. The source of Lady Gregory's language was a dialect that did not differ greatly from the one to which John had been accustomed in Wicklow from childhood. He had used a language similar to Lady Gregory's for reported speech in his Wicklow articles, and with it had harmonized his own prose. . . .

[In his review, John described the language used by Lady Gregory as 'wonderfully simple and powerful' and noted its resemblance to the 'almost Elizabethan' peasant dialect of the west of Ireland. The Elizabethan vocabulary, he noted,

has a force and colour that make it the only form of English that is quite suitable for incidents of the epic kind, and in her intercourse with the peasants of the west Lady Gregory has learned to use this vocabulary in a new way, while she carries with her plaintive Gaelic constructions that make her language, in a true sense, a language of Ireland. . . .[1]

[It was this language that John himself adopted.]

[For the summer of 1902, Mrs. Synge did not go to Castle Kevin but took instead Tomriland House, an old farmhouse near by. John, who was given the bedroom over the kitchen, often spent the afternoons writing] at a table in his bedroom. His typewriter could scarcely be heard in the front part of the house, but it made a great noise in the kitchen which was separated from John's room only by a floor of boards that had shrunk until wide chinks divided them. Neither of the maids, who were very good-humoured, complained of the noise, but once the presence of the chinks in the floor nearly led to serious trouble.

One morning, when I was washing, I opened the door to see if John were up and, as he appeared to be asleep, I threw a wet sponge at his head. He sprang into the middle of the floor, seized the spout of a garden watering can that served him as a bedroom jug, and emptied the can on my head. Two gallons of cold water poured over me and rained through every chink into the kitchen. When all the household, except John, assembled according to custom before breakfast for family prayers, the maids looked very glum: but as the day went on their good humour returned. . . .

[One of the maids, Ellen the cook,] was a stout girl with a loud

[1] *C.W.* II. 367–8.

voice; I do not know what part of the country she came from, but
her gift of phrase was rich. She used to talk and laugh with the men
working in the farm yard as they passed the open kitchen door.
Mrs. Synge said that she thought Ellen noisy, but did not like to
reprove her when they were living under holiday conditions.
John heard what his mother said and made no comment; but he
told me in private that Ellen had a great gift of talk and a ready
wit. . . . Later he wrote:

When I was writing *The Shadow of the Glen* . . ., I got more aid than any
learning could have given me, from a chink in the floor of the old Wicklow house where I was staying, that let me hear what was being said by
the servant girls in the kitchen. . . .[1]

In his leisure time ⟨at Tomriland House,⟩ John used as his sitting-
room the little glass-sided porch where geraniums straggled up
the windows. He sat on one of the benches reading, looking out
across the untidy vegetable garden to the line of hills that edged the
plateau above Glanmore, or talking to my brother and me if we
happened to join him. ⟨One day⟩ we were sitting on the opposite
bench when I chanced to mention the Boer War which had been
ended by the treaty signed in June. John, with his elbows resting
on his knees, said in a quick, tense voice: 'What were the English
doing in South Africa but driving poor farmers out of their homes?'
Afterwards I said to my brother: 'Did you hear what Uncle J. said
about the Boers?' My brother replied: 'Perhaps he was right,' and I
was silenced by the shock of a new idea. Until then I had accepted
without question all that my grandmother had said about John
being wayward and misguided. . . .
[During this summer, John was again keeping a notebook to
record his impressions of the Wicklow countryside and of the
people he met. Near some impressions of a journey to Bray,] he
made some jottings in his notebook about an old woman he had
met at Ballyduff and a tinker's camp he had passed at Derrybawn,
where the Annamoe and Glendalough Rivers meet. These descriptive jottings he ended with a few words of personal reflection about
the wandering people he met. . . :

Dusk was coming on rapidly yet no one seemed to be at the camp but
two young children that I could see through a gate sitting up with the

[1] *C.W.* IV. 53.

light of the fire full on their faces. They were singing a few bars of some droning song over and over again that I could just hear above the noise of the two rivers and the waving of the black fir trees that stood above them.

People like these, like the old woman and these two beautiful children, are a precious possession for any country. They console us, one moment at least, for the manifold and beautiful life we have all missed who have been born in modern Europe. . . .[1]

[For a few days after John's trip to Bray the weather remained cloudy but I remember when it cleared that we had a wonderful day of bright sunshine and fresh wind when the haymakers were putting the new-mown hay into large cocks in the field in front of the house.] Mrs. Synge and her two visitors[2] went out to sit in a sheltered place and watch the work in the field. Later my brother and I joined them with the camera in the hope of taking photographs; but the haymakers did not seem well posed and went to their dinner at twelve o'clock before we had taken any. When they were away, Edie Harmar and I took their pitch-forks and tried to build a haycock. We had just realized that we had begun it on too small a base when we saw the haymakers coming into the field and left the work to them. When they reached our haycock they cheered, put their forks into it, and rocked it backwards and forwards. One of them shouted: 'You've reared it up as thin as a rush.' We joined in the laugh at ourselves and I took their photographs as they began to make a haycock that would stand in the wind. When we all went in to dinner, I told John what the haymakers had said about the haycock that Edie Harmar and I had made. 'You reared it up as thin as a rush,' he said: 'that's a good phrase.' Afterwards he was to use it in *The Playboy of the Western World*. . . .

⟨Two days later,⟩ as I was alone in the morning, John asked me whether I would be able to ride with him as far as Glenmalure. I protested that I could ride a much greater distance, and he said: 'Very well, get yourself some lunch.' We cut ourselves thick slices of home-made bread and butter, rolled them in paper, stuffed them into our pockets and set out on the road through Annamoe and Laragh.

I knew the way well as far as the corner where the military road began to climb through the oak woods of Derrybawn. From there I travelled with the feeling of being on a new adventure, though I

---

[1] *C.W.* II. 199.   [2] Edie Harmar and a Miss Massey.

had been across the ridge with Willie Belton's outside car. The hill
was steep at first, but shaded by the oaks, through which the sun
lighted at random patches of moss on the grey stems, and of fraughan[1] bushes and sedge growing among the trees. We heard at
times the sound of running water.

The wood ended at a place where a rough lane turned up on our
right, by a little stream, to serve a few mountain farms reclaimed
from the southern slope of Derrybawn, and our road twisted
sharply away and up into the open heather. At the next bend John
said: 'Would you like a drink?' and showed me beside the road one
of the little springs that he was proud of knowing. We laid our
bicycles by the road and knelt on some stones to drink from the
little basin that the spring had hollowed for itself in the ground.
John said that the tinkers knew all the springs and showed me the
marks of their carts and the bits of rag they had left near by. He
pointed out every landmark that came into view above the wood:
Castle Kevin hill, marked clearly by the straight road down to the
cottage where Lizzie Belton had lived, the rounded shoulder of
Djouce mountain, the pointed top of Sugarloaf, and the jagged
edge of Carrick to the east. . . . At a corner near a small stream running among lichen-covered stones, there were some broken walls.
He said that they marked the place where an old woman had lived
alone until a night when the stream rose to a torrent and made a
ruin of her cottage. On our left there was a wall that formed the
upper boundary of farms, but on our right the open heather
stretched to the sky line. Occasionally we heard a grouse cock
high above us on the hill. The road was steep again as we passed
under Edge's Rock, and after a walk of three miles came out on
the summit of the ridge.

There we were above all walls. The thin line of road, unfenced
from the heather, wound down before us into Glenmalure. We
stopped and leaned on the handle-bars of our bicycles to cool after
our climb and John pointed out the new landmarks that had come
in sight at the other side of the ridge: the gap before us where the
road passed over the next ridge to Aughavana, the point of Fananer-
rin to our left, and Kelly's Glen and Lugnaquilla to our right. The
air was rich with the smell of honey from the heather. We were
elated by coming to the top of a long hill to see the next stretch

---

[1] Ir. *fraochóg*, a bilberry, heathberry, or windberry, often pronounced and spelt
'fraughan'.

of road running down for miles to vanish in the woods and fields of a valley below.

There was a wonderful sense of exultation in the long descent on a bicycle. The wind blew tears from my eyes and the wheels made a rushing sound on the sandy road. I watched and dodged the stones, the ruts, the hollows and the humps and every time I could look into the valley the woods below were nearer. John did not object to my riding in front because there was no dust that I could raise, and he did not want to travel so fast that he would have to give his whole attention to the road.

When we came to the foot of the hill we turned down the valley at the crossroads and passed the little hotel where my father used to stay for shooting. As we always regarded even tea in an hotel as quite beyond our means, we went on a few hundred yards and lay on a large, flat rock by the roadside while we ate our bread and butter. There was no spring near the rock so I felt very thirsty. . . .

[For our return journey, John suggested that we should ride on to Greenane and cross the ridge from there. It was a long way and] I was feeling tired and hungry. We passed on through Laragh, and were walking up Kilafin hill, when John thought I was looking weary and said, 'Is there any fear of your giving up the ghost?' I replied that I wasn't exhausted, but that I was hungry and very thirsty. He said, 'I was wondering as we passed through Laragh whether we should stop for something to eat at Cogan's and I didn't know what the family would say if I brought you into a pub. It's hardly worth while going back now, if you can hold out.' I assured him that I could easily wait for food until we reached home. . . .

⟨One afternoon,⟩ when my brother was out, John decided to try whether, if he dictated slowly, I could take down from him on the typewriter notes that would be of use in his Wicklow articles. He set me to work at a table by the washstand ⟨in his bedroom⟩, near the open window. Then, lying on his back on the bed, with his hands behind his head and his legs crossed, he dictated an account of an old man who walked with him up the hill from Newtown-mount-kennedy and complained of the price of scythe-stones and the smells of Dublin.[1] He had previously made a rough draft of it in his notebook, but I believe he dictated from memory. . . .

[1] *C.W.* II. 214–15. In the article as published, Synge changed Newtown-mount-kennedy to Kilpeddar—the next village.

[When we returned to Crosthwaite Park in the autumn,] John again adopted regular hours for writing, and sometimes worked at one of his plays and sometimes scribbled in his notebook ideas for literary criticism or impressions of people he met. He was probably revising complete drafts of *Riders to the Sea* and *The Shadow of the Glen*. In spite of Lady Gregory's advice, he had not abandoned all hope that his first play might be worth producing if it were partly rewritten and, in trying to devise improvements, ⟨he⟩ jotted a revised fragment of one of the scenes in his notebook. He was ⟨also⟩ writing *The Tinker's Wedding* carefully in type from a draft hastily scribbled in the book that he had used for making drafts of *Riders to the Sea* and *The Shadow of the Glen*. The emotions of the three plays were drawn from John's . . . life at the time when they were written: they were products of kindred moods. *Riders to the Sea* and *The Shadow of the Glen* gave permanent form to the moods from which they came but before *The Tinker's Wedding* was published, John . . . rewrote it using its material to interpret feelings wholly different from those that inspired the other two plays.

[If it was John's sense of loss at the end of his relationship with Cherrie Matheson that] inspired *Riders to the Sea*, it was his imaginative picture of the contrast between socially advantageous marriage and marriage with an artist like himself that inspired *The Shadow of the Glen*, and his vision of the struggle of independent minds against the conventions of society that inspired *The Tinker's Wedding*. He used the tramp or tinker as his symbol of the artist not because he imagined him morally admirable but because he saw an analogy between the relation of the vagrant to peasant society and that of the artist to the educated, bourgeois classes. His symbolism was adopted for interpreting emotions, stirred in all generations by recurrent experiences, not for distributing praise or blame or for proving anything.

The early version of *The Tinker's Wedding*, like *The Shadow of the Glen*, was framed round the basic contrast between the union of wandering people, swayed by every emotion that the changing seasons inspire, and the married life of the farm or the village. . . . The material of the play was derived from the lore of the country people, not from any direct association with the tinkers themselves. They were so dirty and in their mode of life so disreputable that it would have been impossible for John to mix with them at his ease.

He warned me against dropping into conversation with them on the road. Though his characters were true to the reputation of tinkers among the country people, they did not take part in a realistic drama of tinker life, but were partly idealized to suit an artistic purpose.

Some years later, I chanced to hear two tinkers discussing a problem such as John chose for the plot of his play. I was riding a horse through Laragh and drew up to a slow walk so that I might hear the altercation that was going on outside Cogan's. A man was sitting on the ground with his back against the public house working at a tin can repeating in a monotonous voice to a woman standing before him: 'You're a bloody old whore.' She was shaking with passion and screaming in reply: 'Then show me your woman.' They had not varied their phrases when I rode out of earshot. . . .

I once asked John whether he thought the tramps and tinkers were useless parasites living on the work of other people. He said that he was glad that he wasn't a policeman who might have to think of them in that way, but for himself ⟨he⟩ looked on them as picturesque and interesting and did not believe that the country people grudged them their food. . . .

[By the beginning of October, John had completed the final drafts of *Riders to the Sea* and *The Shadow of the Glen*. He set off for Aran to pay what was to be his last visit, and stopped off on the way at Coole Park in order to show the plays to Lady Gregory and to Yeats. Lady Gregory described the plays as 'both masterpieces, both perfect in their way', and wrote later of John's visit:] 'He had gathered emotion, the driving force he needed from his life among the people, and it was the working in dialect that had set free his style.'[1] ⟨But⟩ John drew with Lady Gregory and Yeats on another source of language besides dialect; in *Samhain*[2] for 1902, Yeats wrote; 'English men of letters founded themselves on the English Bible, where religious thought gets its living speech. . . .' For the people of the Irish Protestant minority, who regarded themselves as living in a permanent state of theological war, the Bible had an even greater significance than it had for their English neighbours. As a

---

[1] Lady Gregory, *Our Irish Theatre: A Chapter of Autobiography* (3rd ed., 1972), p. 76.

[2] An occasional review primarily used for the publication of plays performed by the Irish National Theatre Society.

result of his mother's early teaching, John knew large parts of the
Bible by heart; its language came to his mind quite as readily as the
vernacular of his native Wicklow. . . .

When John was on Inisheer, an ⟨important⟩ new step was
taken in Dublin towards the success of the dramatic movement—
the first presentation of plays by the Irish National Theatre Society.[1]
[This society drew together many of the enthusiastic amateur
actors and playwrights of Dublin, including the brothers Frank and
Willie Fay, who had started staging Irish plays in Dublin in 1899.
The Irish National Theatre Society included Yeats, Maud Gonne,
Douglas Hyde, and Æ and had the support also of Lady Gregory—
though not of Edward Martyn. Its aims, as spelled out in *Samhain*,
were 'good playwriting, good speaking, good acting and the scenic
art'; but it was also, in the eyes of most of its supporters, a theatre
dedicated to the national interest of Ireland as much as to dramatic
art. For John, it was to provide what seemed to be the perfect
vehicle for the presentation of his work.]

3

[At the beginning of 1903, John spent several weeks in London. He had decided that, if he wanted to get his book on the
Aran Islands published and his plays heard, he would stand a better
chance there than in Dublin—particularly as Yeats was well
known to editors and publishers in London. Although it proved
very difficult to find a publisher prepared to risk taking the Aran
book, John's plays were well received at private readings in
London, and he made some interesting friends, including John
Masefield who remembered him later with affection.[2] Lady
Gregory wrote from Dublin that she had read *The Shadow of the
Glen* to the Irish National Theatre Society and that they 'were
much taken by it. . . .' Later it was confirmed that the Society would
put on the play during the autumn.

[John had decided to give up his room in Paris and went over
from London during March for a quick visit to close it up; then

[1] A useful short introduction to the rise of the Abbey Theatre, which includes
relevant details of the predecessors of the Irish National Theatre Society, is Ann
Saddlemyer, 'Stars of the Abbey's Ascendancy', in *Theatre and Nationalism in
Twentieth Century Ireland,* ed. Robert O'Driscoll (London, 1971), pp. 21–39.

[2] John Masefield, 'John M. Synge', *Contemporary Review,* Apr. 1911, 470–8
(quoted in entirety in Stephens's TS. 1505–14, 2695–6, and 2700–1).

he returned to Crosthwaite Park.] I went up to his room to watch him unpacking; as he took out of his portmanteau the knife and fork and the little frying-pan that he had used in Paris, he showed them to me as if they were things he regarded with affection. I asked him whether they had ever been cleaned; he replied: 'A thing that is used by me only is never dirty'. . . .

He did not explain very clearly why he had given up his room in Paris,[1] and he did not mention that he had written plays. After-wards, when I heard of his dramatic work, I attributed his silence about it to his fear that his mother would object on religious grounds to his telling me anything about the theatre. . . .

When John was in London, Cousin Emily had given me the set of tools that she had used for wood-carving years before. They were beautifully arranged in a leather case in which I had found room for six more chisels that my father and mother had given me at Christmas. . . . One wet Saturday morning, when I had a holiday from school, I found John sitting by the dining-room fire and un-rolled my splendid case of tools on the table for him to admire. I told him that it was a present from Cousin Emily and that she had also given me White's *History of Selborne*. John was glad that ⟨she⟩ was encouraging me to learn a craft and to study natural history and admired the tools as much as I could have wished.

As we talked on about other things, he took up an old portfolio and began to show me some reproductions of pictures and to tell me something about old masters of painting and where they had lived. I was fourteen, and to me pictures were illustrations. He made no attempt to explain their importance, yet I felt that he was talking with intensity about things I did not understand and trying to find out whether I could appreciate pictures that he valued. I felt so much embarrassed that without thinking I seized one of my carv-ing tools from the case, which was lying open on the table, and felt the edge as if to test its sharpness. John seemed surprised and asked me if I did not like the pictures. I said that I liked them very much and, covered with confusion, put down the tool. . . .

[During the summer of 1903, Mrs. Synge moved to Tomriland House; unfortunately, John found that whenever he went to see her, he suffered so badly from asthma that he had to return to Dublin. Thus, apart from his usual long day trips, and a few days

[1] According to Stephens (TS. 1514), Mrs. Synge had asked him to give up the Paris room as he was making friends in London.

spent at Glanmore with his brother Robert, John stayed at Crosthwaite Park for the summer. He continued his reading and also
worked hard at his new play, *The Well of the Saints*. Towards the
end of the summer, he felt that he needed a holiday, but was uncertain where to go. In the middle of August, Robert returned from
an enjoyable fishing trip to Kerry and suggested that John might
find Kerry an interesting place to visit. He also recommended a
place where he could stay, Philly Harris's cottage at Mountain
Stage. John was delighted with the idea and left for Kerry at the
end of the month.]

When he arrived at Philly Harris's cottage, ⟨John⟩ was at once
aware that he had come among people whose life had the qualities
that he had valued in the . . . people of Aran and Wicklow. Their
life was not as primitive as ⟨that⟩ of the islanders, but it had less
contact with the outside world than that of any other mainland
people he had known. Irish was not generally spoken in their
district but they had preserved, in English, much traditional
lore. . . . [The richness of John's later plays and poetry owes a lot to
the material he noted during his visits to Kerry.]

Philly Harris's cottage, though it was not far out on the Kenmare
peninsula, overlooked part of the deep water of Dingle Bay;
John wrote of it: 'There is no village near this cottage, yet many
farms are scattered on the hills near it; and as the people are in some
ways a leading family, many men and women look in to talk or
tell stories or to buy a few pennyworth of sugar or starch.'[1] . . .
[This made it an ideal lodging place for John and he made notes of
many of the stories he heard. But he was also beginning to draft
passages of dialogue for a new play which he called 'The Fool of
Farnham'. This was to become *The Playboy of the Western World*,
and it seems likely that it was John's experiences in Kerry which
inspired him to start work on it. The story he had heard in Aran
several years earlier: the detailed plans and dialogue seem to date
from this period.[2]

[When John came home from Kerry, he was looking well.] He
was glad to tell stories of his stay ⟨there⟩ and to talk about the people
of the cottage where he had lodged, their neighbours, and the local
tramps who came in to talk and sometimes to sleep the night by
the fire. On his bicycle he had ranged over most of the unfenced

[1] *C.W.* II. 260.
[2] Stephens's dating is conjectural: see *C.W.* IV. 293–365.

mountain roads of the district near Glenbeigh. Bulls there wandered
at large with herds of cows, and were often dangerous. Once, John
said, when he was coasting down a long hill, he had turned a bend
at full speed to find an angry bull standing across his road, bellow-
ing and pawing the ground. For a second it had seemed that no
escape was possible, but by a quick swerve ⟨John⟩ had passed the
bull's nose and left him roaring behind. . . .

[Meanwhile, in Dublin, preparations were advancing for the
production of *The Shadow of the Glen* which was to open on 8
October in the Molesworth Hall. Willie Fay, who was to produce
the play, asked John to work with him in training the company
because they found considerable difficulty with the dialogue. It
was only after much hard practice that the actors could say the
lines as John wanted.

[The first performance of *The Shadow of the Glen* was an event
of considerable importance in the history of the Irish literary
revival, as well as in John's own life. The refusal of Yeats and
others connected with the dramatic movement to subordinate
artistic values to those of nationalism and moral uprightness had
laid them open to attack from those sections of Irish society most
vigorously committed to the ideals of Irish nationalism, as well as
those sections determined to uphold moral values. On the morning
of 8 October, the *Irish Independent* contained an article attacking the
dramatic movement and stirring up against it illiterate hostility.
The writer maintained that Irish drama should be 'true, pure and
national' and accused the Irish National Theatre Society of staging
'unwholesome productions' and of perverting the society's avowed
aims; he also asserted that the 'new writer, Mr. J. M. Synge . . . did
not derive his inspiration from the Western isles' but implied that
the idea for John's play came from 'the gaiety of Paris'. Thus John
found himself at the centre of a political, moral, and nationalist
uproar; the production of *The Shadow of the Glen* was to raise a
storm of press controversy that he could never have anticipated.

[The first-night audience received the play with both cheers and
hisses. Next morning, when John and his mother] came down to
breakfast, they read the account given of the play by the *Irish
Times* critic, ⟨who⟩ . . . 'while admitting the cleverness of the
dialect and the excellent acting of Nora and the tramp' . . . found it
'excessively distasteful'. . . . 'Mr. Synge has distinct power,' ⟨wrote
the critic,⟩

both in irony and in dialogue, but surely he could display them better in showing in some other way—a way that should above all cast no slur on Irish womanhood—the wrong of mercenary marriage. . . .

Mrs. Synge wrote in her diary: 'Very wet morning but cleared early—from breakfast. John's play reviewed.' All she read in the *Irish Times* perplexed her. She had thought of John as being over-persuaded by his literary friends into praising everything Irish but, now that a play of his had been acted, the newspapers were censuring him for attacking Irish character. She disliked the kind of publicity his work was getting, she was sorry that he should have adopted a form of dramatic writing that was likely to prove no more remunerative than the Aran book, and she was sorry that any of his work should be connected with the stage.

As I knew that she would never enter a theatre, I asked her, with some anxiety, what she thought about his writing plays. She said that she was sorry he should so occupy his time, but that a connection with an amateur company acting in the Molesworth Hall was quite different from an association with an ordinary theatre, an association which might countenance the immoral and worldly lives of actors and actresses. I did not attempt to hide my perplexity, and she went on to explain that there were in literature good plays, such as the plays of Shakespeare, read by many good people, but that putting even these on the stage created temptations for the people who acted. I asked her if she thought that the people who went to a theatre to see a good play were responsible for the way the actors and actresses lived. She said that if by reason of meat our brother stumbleth, it is better to do without meat. 'People', she said, 'are very weak and those who are strong in Christ must think of the weaker brethren.'

At the performances of *The Shadow of the Glen* given on Friday and Saturday evenings, demonstrations of disapproval continued. On Saturday, after the performance, John stayed to have tea at a gathering of the company and their friends, where the protests that had been made against his play were a main topic of conversation. He was a solitary writer who had not been involved in the organization of the dramatic movement, and did not see as clearly as Yeats and his other colleagues the danger to which opposition from extreme nationalists exposed their enterprise. With them he talked so late that the last train for Kingstown had left nearly two hours before he set out for home. The night was wild while he walked the seven miles from Dublin to Crosthwaite Park. ⟨Next day,⟩ his mother wrote in her diary: 'After a dreadful storm last night, I had a headache from lying awake listening to the storm and watching for Johnnie who was not home until 3.30. . . .'

[The hostility felt by Irish nationalists, particularly supporters of Arthur Griffith's paper *The United Irishman*, towards *The Shadow of the Glen*—and towards its author—was slow to quieten down. It had not fully subsided when the members of the Irish National Theatre Society decided that they would go ahead with plans for the first performance of the other play John had given them, *Riders to the Sea*. Initially, the reading committee had thought that the play was too slow-moving at the end, but this criticism was now set aside and it was decided to present it during the spring of 1904; the first performance was arranged for 25 February. As the date drew near, John became increasingly restless: he spent much of his time in town, helping with arrangements at the theatre and supervising the details of production, and he also went for long bicycle rides and walks, either alone or with Rosie Calthrop who happened to be staying with Mrs. Synge at the time. He was not really in good health, and complained of a cold and of toothache. On Thursday 25 February, the day of the performance, Mrs. Synge wrote in her diary:

A dull, rainy kind of day. Johnnie feeling his face sore, but went out—took a long walk with Rosie in the afternoon. I was not out at all. Johnnie in town late. His play on.

Though Rosie had walked and bicycled with him all over Wicklow and listened to his talk of the ideas that had taken shape in his plays, he did not take her to the first performance of *Riders to the Sea*. She would have been greatly interested in seeing his play, but she thought that as a visitor she should respect Mrs. Synge's disapproval of the stage.

The audience at the Molesworth Hall did not fully occupy the seats. On the programme, the first play was Æ's *Deirdre*, the production of which at St. Teresa's Hall in 1902 had made the link between Fay's company and the writers of the literary movement. It was followed only by *Riders to the Sea*. As *Deirdre* had been produced before and *Riders to the Sea* had been printed in

Samhain,[1] neither play was a surprise to the press reporters. The supporters of the Irish National Theatre Society applauded both plays
and called the authors before the curtain; but the audience generally,
though appreciative of *Deirdre*, was divided in its criticism of *Riders
to the Sea*.

John was unable to attend the other performances, for on Friday he was confined to his bed by an abscess at the root of a tooth
and a high temperature, which was probably aggravated by the
strain and excitement of the previous night. The *Irish Times* that
was sent up to his room contained a hostile criticism of his play.
Its reporter wrote:

... The idea underlying the work is good enough; but the treatment of
it is to our mind repulsive. Indeed the play develops into something like
a wake. The long exposure of the dead body before an audience may be
realistic, but it certainly is not artistic. There are some things which are
lifelike, and yet are quite unfit for presentation on the stage and we think
that *Riders to the Sea* is one of them.

I had heard very little discussion about *The Shadow of the Glen*
when it had been acted, but everyone in the family circle talked
disapprovingly of *Riders to the Sea*. I do not believe that any of
John's relations at Crosthwaite Park read the play, but they elabora-
ted the *Irish Times* review. They said that a realistic picture of a
poor fisherman's cottage after a drowning accident was not a play
because it had no plot. My father said that when he went to the
theatre he wanted to be amused and did not want to see on the stage
reproductions of depressing incidents from ordinary life. 'If they
want to act an Irish Play,' he said, 'why can't they act *The
Shaughraun*?'[2] My mother said that she did not think it was nice
to bring a drowned man in a dripping sail on to the stage and that
she did not know why John had made the company do it. ...

John talked little about his critics, but said that he did not expect
understanding from the vulgar and that he would not write any
'pot-boilers' to catch popular applause. The reception of his plays
in Dublin had been disappointing; but he had the satisfaction of

[1] *Samhain* No. 3 (Sept. 1903).
[2] *The Shaughraun* by Dion Boucicault was later described by Synge as being full
of 'good acting comedy'. In the same note, he pointed out that the absurdity of
Boucicault's plots and pathos had driven 'people of taste' away from his plays.
(*C.W.* II. 397–8.)

looking forward to seeing their production before an audience less affected by local bias, ⟨for⟩ the Irish Literary Society ⟨in London⟩ had invited ⟨Willie⟩ Fay to take his company to London and had secured the Royalty Theatre for a matinée and an evening performance on Saturday 26 March. John was anxious to recover his strength quickly so that he might go to London in time to see his plays and stay there for some weeks to build up his connection with publishers and editors. . . .

[By the middle of March he was much better and he travelled to London a few days before the performances were due and took lodgings. His two plays were to appear with Yeats's *The King's Threshold* in the afternoon and plays by Yeats and Padraic Colum were planned for the evening.]

For each performance the house was filled by a fashionable audience that took a real delight in the plays and their presentation. The visit of the Irish National Theatre Society to London proved a great success, but to Yeats and John it brought very different experiences. Yeats had been familiar with artistic coteries and theatre audiences for most of his life. He had achieved a great success with *The King's Threshold* and *The Pot of Broth*, but he was accustomed to public acclamation. John was not part of the city life around him. He had watched his friends from Dublin interpreting, to a great concourse of strangers, his deepest personal experiences, symbolized in the life of Aran and Glenmalure.[1] When, on Sunday evening, he said farewell to the weary but triumphant company and returned alone to his lodging, he had passed through a crisis in his career. . . .

The press comments on the performances . . . occupied considerable space in leading literary periodicals as they appeared. They treated John's plays as dramatic literature of consequence. Some were necessarily more sympathetic and appreciative than others but all were free from the superficiality expressed in the *Irish Independent* reporter's reference to *Riders to the Sea* as 'a one act trifle'. On Monday after the performances, an article in the *Westminster Gazette* commented on *The King's Threshold* and continued:

Far more effective from the purely theatrical point of view was *Riders to*

---

[1] Stephens maintained that the setting of *The Shadow of the Glen*—'The last cottage at the head of a long glen in County Wicklow'—was Harney's cottage at the head of Glenmalure.

the Sea, a singularly beautiful and pathetic piece of hopeless fatalism. . . .
Mr Synge's other effort is humorous but his humour is grim and cannot
get away from death and the tyranny of nature. . . .

John had been recognized as a dramatist by leading critics; in
their comparison of his work with that of Yeats, they had seemed
to view Yeats as the poet who used dramatic form and John as the
dramatist who had the imagination of a poet. It was little more
than a year since his last stay in London; then his plays had not been
acted and had been read and recognized only by Yeats, Lady
Gregory, and a small circle of their friends. His recognition by a
London audience and by the London press did not bring him
financial success, but it brought him encouragement and reassured
him in his belief that he had found his proper medium. . . .

4

[John came back to Crosthwaite Park on 1 May. It was] a
curious experience for him to return from London where his plays
had impressed a great audience and evoked serious comment from
the press to settle into the quiet routine of Crosthwaite Park where
the members of his family circle were serenely unaware of the
importance of his work. He told me of the applause with which it
had been greeted at the Royalty Theatre, and seemed excited by
the recognition that he had received. I was greatly perplexed and
asked him whether it was not strange for him to seek appreciation
for Irish plays in London. He said that it was not in any way
strange because literature was for cultured people everywhere. I
was silenced, but I did not feel satisfied. . . .

[In the summer of 1904, when Mrs. Synge again took Tomriland House, she invited Fanny and Lucy Synge, distant cousins
from Australia who were visiting Europe, to join her.] Fanny, the
elder and quieter of the two, was thirty-six years of age. As a
result of spending some time in the South Sea Islands as a missionary, she was not in very good health. Mrs. Synge was glad that her
niece had inherited the missionary spirit but suspected her of High
Church tendencies, and did not express unqualified approval of
her work. Lucy was thirty-two. She was incapable of being an
evangelist, but her cordiality and her unbounded enthusiasm for
Wicklow endeared her to Mrs. Synge, who told me that when, on
the Tuesday after their arrival, she had taken her two nieces to

visit Glanmore, Lucy had seemed like one walking on enchanted ground. . . .

[One afternoon, when we had finished tea and Mrs. Synge and our two cousins were out for a short walk,] John rode up on his bicycle. He had some tea, and then asked me to take a stroll with him in the fields. . . . Before long, we saw the others walking up the avenue and returned to the house. There we found them talking with Mr. Halligan, ⟨the clergyman,⟩ who had come to pay a parochial call. John was introduced to his cousins and soon afterwards, when Mr. Halligan left, sat down to chat with the family party. He had decided not to spend the night at Tomriland for fear of asthma, but stayed to supper, and did not set out for home until 8.30. . . .

When he had gone, Lucy talked about her meeting with her gifted cousin in an enthusiastic way that embarrassed his mother who was pleased by praise of John's work but felt that she should express disapproval of his opinions and of his connection with the stage. She demurred slightly but said very little, for she could not feel certain of being understood.

It was not only on the subject of the theatre that Lucy did not seem to comprehend her aunt's beliefs. Mrs. Synge regarded all demonstrativeness as unbecoming and expected the propriety of this view to be assumed by her household. Lucy challenged it by accident. While she was reading a novel in the drawing-room, she took my hand with almost absent-minded affection. I noticed that my grandmother became uncomfortable, but did not at first move.

Next day as we were walking up the avenue she expressed her disapproval. 'I saw Lucy hold your hand,' she said; 'that is only the way of a gushing Australian.' I do not know whether she was conscious that in a chance touch there was power to shake to its foundations the whole structure of her teaching, but there was tenseness in her voice as if she were afraid.

Lucy had brought her camera and sketch-book to Tomriland. She wanted to know every by-way in the neighbourhood and to make sketches of thatched cottages with pigs in front, of the mill of Annamoe and of everything else that she thought characteristic of the country. When I took ⟨the dog⟩ out for his regular exercise in the rain, Lucy came and enjoyed the mist in her face and the singing of the yellow-hammers on the telegraph wire. . . .

[A few days later, Sam, who was home from China on leave with his wife and baby daughter, arrived at Tomriland to spend some time with his mother.] She welcomed him with an enthusiasm that she rarely showed, and introduced him to his two Australian cousins. He was to be a member of John's family circle again for more than two years, as he did not leave for his mission hospital in China until 2 October 1906. . . .[1]

The strangeness of Sam's being back in Wicklow...⟨soon wore⟩ off, and no time seemed to me to have elapsed since the summer ⟨of 1892⟩ when he was learning Chinese in the woods at Castle Kevin. My recollection of his appearance had not faded. His religion was, as I had assumed, the evangelical faith of the family and it had not acquired any tinge of liberalism from his life in China. Gradually I was to become aware that his beliefs, though founded on his mother's logic, had none of the happy inconsistencies that relieved the rigidity of her dogma.

He did not wear the usual clerical collar lest he should be mistaken for a Roman Catholic priest. Instead he wore the low collar and white tie used by Protestant clergymen of the last generation. His manner was grave and, though he was not ill-humoured, he did not suffer frivolity gladly.

It became his custom to walk up and down the avenue of beech trees, like a monk in a cloister, reading. Once, when he turned opposite the garden gate where my brother and I were sitting he paused, pointed to a bee buzzing in the crevices of a whitewashed wall and said slowly: 'That is the *bombus Lapidarius*, I've just been reading about it. You can always recognize it by the dark red colour of the lower half.' Erect, with even steps and with his head slightly bent over his book, he continued his walk. His forehead was high and his thick hair and pointed beard were turning grey. In appearance he conformed to the family type described in the words *vir gravis admodum et doctus*, written on the tomb of the first Synge who had come to Ireland.

Sam had not been long at Tomriland before he began instructing my brother and me. He said that time should never be wasted in idle talk and that conversation should be concerned with useful knowledge. As a practical application of his theory he began

[1] Synge was very much attached to his brother Sam; he later wrote that Sam was '. . . one of the best fellows in ⟨the⟩ world . . . though he is so religious we have not much in common' (*Letters to Molly*, p. 43).

teaching us astronomy at meals and illustrating the movements of the heavenly bodies with the salt cellar and the pepper pot. He asked us to learn by heart the names of the planets in their order from the sun and recited them slowly so that we might commit them to memory. When Sunday came he said that it was not a day for acquiring secular knowledge and that we should learn the names of the lesser prophets. As there are twelve, he suggested that we should learn four each Sunday and so know them all at the end of three weeks.

'Hosea, Joel, Amos, Obadiah,' I said on the first Sunday. During the week I learnt the names of the planets, but my patience became exhausted. He asked me to recite them, but I mixed their names with the names of the lesser prophets and he abandoned my education in disgust. . . .

[On another occasion when I was visiting Mrs. Synge, and Sam and his family were also staying with her, I remember that we were having afternoon tea] with Mrs. Synge on the gravel sweep before the hall door. She was wearing a new black straw sailor hat that she had bought as a protection against the sun. As she gave Sam his tea she said: 'How do you like my hat?' He said: 'Well you know, Mother, it is a nice Christian hat.' Unwisely I asked why ugly things should be called 'Christian'. Mrs. Synge was visibly annoyed. 'It's not an ugly hat,' she said, rather abruptly, and changed the conversation.

Generally, she and Sam agreed perfectly about the practical application of their beliefs. ⟨One⟩ evening the baby's food was a little sour so Sam, having in mind the scriptural aim—that nothing be wasted—ate it for supper. When I put sugar on stewed rhubarb, he said that God would have put sugar in rhubarb if it had been necessary. Mrs. Synge said nothing, but she smiled approval. She and Sam seemed to be at one in a mood to give their theories a more fantastic application than any that I had known them to adopt at other times. I could not share their mood. . . .

[Meanwhile, John had gone to visit Lady Gregory at Coole Park.] The change to the big house with its shady avenues, woods and lakes relieved the restlessness that had been growing on him. . . . ⟨He⟩ walked with his friends in the woods or by the lake and rowed the boat from which Lady Gregory and her son Robert used to fish for pike. . . . [From Coole, he went on to Mountain Stage to spend a month with Philly Harris and his family, but he returned earlier] than he had intended because he had been suffering at night from asthma. His pleasure in being on the Atlantic coast seemed to have been spoiled, not only by loss of sleep but also by a restlessness of mind which blurred impressions and interrupted his work on his new play. He hoped to recover from his attack of asthma quickly enough to visit the west coast again before the winter but was uncertain as to where he should go. . . . He had heard much of Sligo from Yeats and ⟨George⟩ Russell so, [when the effects of his asthma had worn off, he planned to spend the last two weeks of September touring the counties of Sligo and Mayo.] On 16 September, his mother hastily mended his clothes and next day he left by the morning train for the west.

The few notes that he left of his visit to Sligo do not mention the house at which he stayed. It was probably Siberry's cottage in Glencar, and was certainly in the neighbourhood of Benbulben, a district . . . where the sides of flat-topped limestone hills fall as cliffs to the dry shores of a long-receded ocean, and then as steep banks of rubble, once submerged, to a narrow coastal plain. From reading *The Flight of Diarmuid and Grania*, John knew it as the setting of saga. The place had stirred the imagination of the Celtic people, ⟨and⟩ it was marked by Stone Age remains. . . . In its lakes were little islands where lake dwellings had stood, and its local lore was rich and powerful. . . .

⟨But John's⟩ visit seems to have been one of mental tumult; the country in which he was had furnished Yeats and Russell with lore for their fairy faith, and it seemed to recall to his mind old speculations about the spirit world. The emotions of early manhood seemed to him to be receding and the impressions they had inspired to be losing their brilliancy; he was restless and uncertain, and could not foresee the future shape of his work. . . .[1]

When he had spent some days seeing so much of Co. Sligo as was within his range on a bicycle from Benbulben, he left for his first visit to north Mayo, one of the Congested Districts described in the series of articles that he afterwards wrote for the *Manchester Guardian*. He decided to stay in Belmullet, a town where prosperous shopkeepers served the people of a surrounding wilderness that lacked fertility to support its population. In his early plays, John had used the delicate shades of his experiences in Wicklow

---

[1] This judgement seems to be based on entries in Synge's notebooks.

and Aran; he was to find in Mayo a life that had remained primitive but was characterized by a harsh quality that, in his restless mood, impressed his mind with peculiar force. It was the life of Mayo that was to provide him with the setting for his new play. . . .

[John returned from the west at the beginning of October.] ⟨He⟩ had not been many days at home before he decided to move for the winter nearer Dublin so that he might write undisturbed by the affairs of the family party[1] and be able to join with his colleagues in preparations for the opening of the Abbey Theatre.[2] On Saturday 8 October ⟨he⟩ went to see a furnished room that was to be let at 15 Maxwell Road, Rathmines, and ⟨he⟩ moved there on Monday. His lodging was within a mile of his old home at Orwell Park on a quiet road along which there were respectable little two-storied red-brick houses and some unused building-sites. . . .

While John was staying in Rathmines I heard nothing of his work unless he chanced to mention it when he came to see his mother. He came regularly on Sundays, usually after a long walk in the hills, and returned to town by the evening train. His mind was so much occupied with practical arrangements for the opening in December of the new theatre and the first production, in the spring, of *The Well of the Saints*, that even if he had been free of business it is probable that there would have been a pause in his dramatic work, for the rich material of his new play was taking shape very slowly. . . .

The opening of the Abbey Theatre ⟨on 27 December⟩ must have appeared to be the result of unified effort by all who were interested in the Irish dramatic movement. In reality the measure of agreement between them was so small that, for the rest of John's life, his association with the new theatre drew him into continual controversy. . . . ⟨This centred mainly around⟩ conflicting interpretations of the word 'National' in the title of the society for which the Abbey Theatre was provided.

For ⟨the Society's patron⟩, Miss Horniman, an Englishwoman concerned in the art of the stage, the word formed part of a distinguishing name and had no further significance. The principal

[1] Sam's wife Mary had come to stay with Mrs. Synge bringing her baby daughter, Edith.

[2] The building known as the Abbey Theatre was financed for the Irish National Theatre Society by Miss Annie Horniman.

writers of the dramatic movement regarded it as referring to a special inspiration that gave character to their work. Among the members of the company and of the audience, there were wide, ill-defined differences of opinion. Very few, if any, accepted Miss Horniman's view: the more accomplished tended to agree with the writers, and others, led by Maud Gonne, clamoured that the application of the word 'National' to the theatre implied that it was popular and propagandist. . . . The success of the Irish National Theatre Society in establishing itself in a special theatre did not over-awe but inflamed those who were inspired by intense nationalism to oppose its work. . . .

[None of this hostility was visible, however, on the opening night.] Lady Gregory was not able to be present owing to illness, and Miss Horniman had found it necessary to return to London; so at the opening of the theatre, Yeats and John were the principal representatives of the dramatic movement, other than the company. It was a strange experience for them both, a wonderful fruition of their efforts. They saw in a new Dublin theatre dramatic art with which they had associated themselves without reserve. The place was crowded and in the audience the different phases of thought then active in Dublin were well represented. The plays[1] were very well received: Yeats made a speech and when the audience scattered John went out by train to Kingstown and stayed the night at Crosthwaite Park.

Next day there was an account in the newspaper of the opening of the Abbey Theatre. My mother said that it had been paid for by an Englishwoman and that she did not know why any English-woman should want to finance an Irish nationalist theatre. She added: 'She must be a little mad!' . . .

[During January 1905, the company put into rehearsal the third of John's plays to be produced, *The Well of the Saints*. This, as a play in three acts, was his most extended dramatic work so far.] The unhesitating willingness of Fay and the members of his company to put it on the stage was an expression of loyalty to a playwright of their society. Any company enjoys the unanimous ⟨admiration⟩ of a crowded house, and they knew that *The Well of the Saints* would evoke no such response. . . .[Willie Fay asked John to modify the tone of the play somewhat, and make some of the

---

[1] *On Baile's Strand* by W. B. Yeats and *Spreading the News* by Lady Gregory.

characters 'good-natured' and 'lovable'; but John refused.[1]]

After the named characters, John had included among the people in the play other men and girls and, to act as one of them with no spoken part, Fay had enlisted Sara Allgood's younger sister Molly, who afterwards became famous as Maire O'Neill. She was only nineteen and so excited about appearing in a play that when she heard the ordinary stage call 'beginners please', she regarded it as a reference to her inexperience and wept with indignation—so she told me years afterwards. Her walking-on part in *The Well of the Saints* was the beginning of her acquaintance with John whose devotion to her later was to have an important influence on his work. . . .

[At the opening night of *The Well of the Saints*, the audience was large and generally enthusiastic. However the press reports made depressing reading. The nationalist press, led by Arthur Griffith's *United Irishman*, attacked the play, while other critics seemed confused and inconsistent. But no journal ignored the play and John's relations were now forced to take some notice of the controversies that raged in the newspapers over his work. One day in February 1905, soon after John had returned to live in Crosthwaite Park and given up his room in Rathmines, he took me out for a bicycle ride with him. I remember that] his mind was full of the controversy that had raged round *The Well of the Saints*. I asked him what he thought of the disapproval that the members of his family felt towards his play, a disapproval which they had probably never expressed clearly to him. As he generally appeared quite unmoved by their differing from him in opinion, I was surprised when he seemed stirred by what I said. He answered in a very emphatic voice: 'What do they know about it', and went on to tell me that he had the support of all the literary people and that George Moore, for example, had written a letter to *The Irish Times* in praise of the play.[2] I said: 'Isn't George Moore an awful ass?' John said that perhaps he was not a classical writer but that he was a novelist of considerable reputation and that he could criticize literature in a way that would be impossible for any of the family party at Crosthwaite Park.

I did not pursue the conversation at that time but the first evening

[1] Stephens explains this attitude by relating it to his view that all Synge's work sprang directly from the experiences of his personal life.

[2] *The Irish Times*, 13 Feb. 1905.

that I found John alone in Mrs. Synge's dining-room I asked him to explain why his play had been attacked. He said that people accustomed to the commercial stage wanted plays with plots and happy endings and they didn't like realism. I said: 'What is realism?' He replied that it was a way of conveying impressions by mentioning significant details instead of attempting to describe feelings. 'For example,' he said, 'suppose you wanted to convey an impression of a very wet day in town, you might say: "The drops were falling one by one from the point of the policeman's helmet"; that would be far more effective than any description of how wet the day seemed to you. . . .'

Since John had given up music for writing, his relations had tried to maintain the tacit assumption that his work was a hobby that could never attract much attention. Their assumption became increasingly difficult to maintain when first *The Shadow of the Glen* and then *Riders to the Sea* were produced and criticized. It became quite absurd when journalists were publishing sketch drawings of him and long criticisms of his three-act play. As his relations neither went to the Abbey Theatre nor, so far as I know, read his plays, they were dependent on newspaper reports for their knowledge of his work. They discussed his choice of it among themselves, but had to be content with regarding him amiably as incomprehensible. . . .

[In May, John received an offer] from the editor of the *Manchester Guardian* who proposed that ⟨he⟩ should tour the Congested Districts of the west to write a series of articles about the distress there and that Jack Yeats[1] should accompany him to illustrate his articles with line drawings suitable for newspaper reproduction. The editor proposed to pay all their expenses and to pay them for their work as well. . . .

[The partnership between the two men] was as well balanced as a marriage made in heaven. Both . . . possessed highly trained powers of observation and both enjoyed seeing anything that was beautiful of land or sea, or anything that was unclassified, personal and rich in character. Each understood how full and whimsical the other's enjoyment was, and yet they were in character and early experience strangely different.[2] I have heard charity defined as the quality of

---

[1] Jack B. Yeats (1871–1957), perhaps the most distinguished of Irish artists, was younger brother of the poet.

[2] Jack Yeats's father encouraged his children in their artistic development.

soul that produced the *Canterbury Tales*: and that quality inspired them both. . . .

[They set out from Dublin on 3 June and were away for a month. Their tour took them through south Connemara and north and east Mayo and resulted in a series of twelve articles which appeared in the *Manchester Guardian* in June and July;[1] each one was accompanied by one or two sketches by Jack Yeats and the series as a whole formed a striking and memorable account of life in the Congested Districts. Though John greatly enjoyed the trip, he was saddened by much of what he saw.

[After a month at home, John decided to go to the west again. This time he went to Kerry, to Ballyferriter, and then on to the Blasket Islands where he spent one of the most enjoyable fortnights of his life. When he returned, I remember helping him to develop the photographs he had taken.] The negatives were good, so we printed them at his bedroom window ⟨in Crosthwaite Park⟩ one bright afternoon. The fixing solution was on the dressing table and the press, in which he kept his collection of butterflies, his fishing tackle, and his photographic materials, lay open. He was as excited about his photographs as I was. Suddenly a picture of fisher people on the shore caught his eye. He picked it out of the fixing solution and slapped it wet on the inside of the press door, saying: 'There's a masterpiece! Look at that for a photograph! Why can't you take photographs like that?' When he had admired it enough he picked it off the door and put it back in the fixing solution.

While we worked we talked about his stay in Kerry. The substance of what he said he afterwards published in his articles on west Kerry,[2] but they did not include the boasts and exaggerations that gave colour to his conversation. He said that he had been staying with the King of the Blasket Islands, and that it was not everyone who had a princess to call him in the morning! Once, he told me, when she opened the door, hens that had been roosting in the kitchen fluttered across his bed to get out of the window. I asked him whether the people of the islands recognized their king. John said that he was looked up to as the head man, and that the

[1] Reprinted in *C.W.* II. 183–343. These articles were later the cause of friction between W. B. Yeats and George Roberts, the publisher of Synge's collected works. See *C.W.* II. xiii–xiv.

[2] See *C.W.* II. 237–82, particularly 246–57.

police sergeant would have a drink with him and remind him to
license his gun, instead of requiring him to do it under threat of
prosecution.

When the prints of his photographs were being washed, John
took out of his press and showed me some little grey pamphlets.
These, he told me, were copies of *The Shadow of the Glen* from an
edition published to secure his copyright in the United States by
John Quinn, who had given great help to Irish writers.

As a schoolboy I had no conception of a writer's life and work.
John's solitary and retiring habits had given me an impression of
him as more obscure than the professional members of the family.
This impression had been deepened by his mother's melancholy
reflections on the way in which she believed him to be wasting his
life. The people whom I heard spoken of as important were those
in high places. John, the youngest of my uncles, who talked about
antiquities and natural history, and argued about photographs,
seemed to me more like a person of my own generation than one
of the Olympians.

It was at the beginning of the football season that I became, by
chance, aware of him as a well-known author. One of my school
fellows, Edward Hatte, who never seemed to read anything that
he was required to learn, spent much of his time in the public
library and had some knowledge of literature. I was walking home
from the football field at Eglinton Park with him one evening at
the head of a troop of boys ... carrying their muddy football boots
slung on knotted laces over their shoulders. At the corner of Mul-
grave Street we met John, who greeted us as he turned down
towards the railway station. He was wearing a wide-brimmed hat
under which, in the evening light, his moustache and imperial
looked thick and dark. His cape hung to his knees, and he carried
one of his heavy walking sticks. He looked like a figure from a
foreign city. (I remembered his saying that it was the duty of
everyone to make himself as picturesque as possible.) Hatte
whispered: 'Is that the playwright?' and I realized suddenly that to
him John was a public character of importance. Without stopping
to speak to us he walked on down the street. ...

5

[The second half of 1905 saw the most serious of the rows which
erupted so often at the Abbey Theatre during the early years. The

success of the company had been such that Miss Horniman offered to guarantee salaries for the company which had, until this point, been entirely amateur. But a considerable number of the actors, some of whom were finding it difficult to work with Willie Fay in any case, objected strongly to the direction in which the company seemed to be going, and to Miss Horniman's suggestion. Ironically, it was the very success of the company which most annoyed them, as they felt that the original, political purpose of the company had been sacrificed and that the company should concentrate entirely on furthering the cause of Irish freedom. For them the delight of London audiences and the praise of English critics were signs of betrayal rather than of triumph.

[The row led to a secession; many of the actors, including the fine actress Maire Walker,[1] walked out and soon formed their own company 'The Theatre of Ireland'. But the Irish National Theatre Society survived this defection, for among those who remained were the two Fays and Sara Allgood, who was to replace Maire Walker and to become, in her own right, one of the great actresses of her generation. Willie Fay used his considerable talents to create a new company from the ruins of the old and changes were made in the way the Society was run. Both Fay and the actors lost their right to decide on what plays were to be performed and the Society became a limited company with three directors, Yeats, John, and Lady Gregory; these directors were, in Yeats's words, to be 'absolutely supreme in everything'. Thus John, despite his dislike of business and of political intrigue, found himself—as the only director permanently living in Dublin—responsible for the administration of a professional theatre company.]

Of the three directors, Lady Gregory, with her knowledge of the world, was probably the most skilled in dealing with people and certainly adopted the attitude of a kindly Mother-superior towards the other two. John, though he always applied sound judgement to the problems that came to him, avoided personal discussions as much as possible. Yeats, who could always reveal a business capacity of which poets are not usually suspected, felt exasperated by the wasting of his time and thought on trivial controversies but applied himself to getting definite decisions from the

[1] Maire Walker (d. 1958) acted under the name of Maire nic Shiubhlaigh. See *The Splendid Years* (Dublin, 1955), her reminiscences of early years at the Abbey Theatre.

dissatisfied members of the company and to reducing the relations of those who decided to remain under the control of the National Theatre Society Ltd. to contracts in writing. . . .

[However, though the Abbey Theatre now absorbed much of John's energy, a more potent influence on his personal life and artistic development during the last three years of his life was that of Molly Allgood. Soon after her appearance in *The Well of the Saints*, she and John were attracted to each other; despite the disapproval of both their families and of Lady Gregory,[1] the relationship continued until John's death. Molly inspired not only much of the dialogue and characterization in the play he was working on when he met her—*The Playboy of the Western World*—but also his last unfinished tragedy, *Deirdre of the Sorrows*.

[Molly's first important appearance on the stage of the Abbey was as Cathleen in the revival of *Riders to the Sea* which took place in January 1906. The production was the first given by the re-formed company and was thus of particular importance to them all. John, who was hard at work on *The Playboy*, took a hand in directing rehearsals for *Riders to the Sea* and so got to know Molly well. She] was quick to appreciate the way in which ⟨he⟩ wanted her to act her part and used her rich voice wonderfully in the speaking of his rhythmical prose. In the pleasant and personal social life of the Abbey Theatre, ⟨John⟩ lost much of the shy formality that limited his intercourse with strangers and found opportunities for improving his acquaintance with her. . . .

In ⟨*The Playboy*⟩ he had begun to dramatize himself as an adult in experience, as one who had been willing to defy authority and form himself in imaginative devotion. In writing it, he had turned a little from his delicately tinted youthful impressions of the Wicklow hills and the Aran Islands to harsher impressions of the western mainland. . . . From Molly he was creating the image of the new woman to whom he could relate himself in adult life, and was gradually to unite it with his earlier imaginings to form the composite conception of woman dramatized in his closing works. . . .

[It was not until February that John allowed any signs of his feelings for Molly to appear. The Abbey players were on tour in Wexford and one fine afternoon,] John strolled out with some

[1] The families disapproved of the match for religious and social reasons; Lady Gregory felt that, as a director of the Irish National Theatre, Synge should not be too closely involved with any member of the company.

members of the company and sat by an old tower on a grassy hill overlooking the harbour. His companions had not known until then of his attachment to Molly and were surprised by noticing that he sat with his arm half round her. As he accepted his mother's code of propriety, his slight demonstrativeness towards Molly, in the presence of their friends, must have been intended to indicate to them that her affections were not free. . . .

[A few weeks later, John was again helping to train Molly for a part in one of his plays, this time that of Nora Burke in *The Shadow of the Glen*.] Her temperament suited the part exactly for, though she was very young, she had a wistfulness like that of a woman who had grown accustomed to loneliness without becoming indifferent to life. For John, her acting seemed to link his current experience of her with his early imaginative experience that had inspired *The Shadow of the Glen*. Because he would never abandon the highest standards of his art, he had remained poor. He saw himself without worldly comforts to offer a wife, and pictured Molly turning her back on conventional success to walk through the world with him. In the realm of his symbols, the house, from which they were to be driven by hard words, was the house of vulgar values and the road, on which they were to go together, was the road of marriage made lovely, not by riches, but by accord in the appreciation of all they might find beautiful. When he corresponded with her afterwards, he signed himself 'Your Old Tramp'.

The new emotional experience that, since Christmas, had been spreading its illumination over John's mind was to make his life one of strange turmoil during the year 1906. In that year he was to finish *The Playboy of the Western World*, a play that had taken definite shape under the influence of a phase of experience that was over. He had become so far established in a world, rich with ideas, that he could look back to the artistic sterility of . . . his early environment as 'The naked parish where I grew a man'. Such was his artistic success that he could think of himself as the expected playboy, 'Winning all before him at the sports below'. He could realize that he had woven great stories of his struggle with parental authority and of his love for his 'Holy One'. In mind he had been through terrible experiences. He had not really killed family opinion, he had lost the girl of whom he had dreamed, but his experiences had left him free to create literature.

His roughly-formed play had given symbols to his life. They

seemed valid and complete, but they were in danger of disturbance by a new emotional current before they had formed a final dramatic pattern. The fascination of a dream image and puritanical isolation had left him without experience of women. In his devotion to Molly, he had to relate himself to a woman he met frequently. Their attachment to each other was to grow very strong but their tacit assumptions, formed in different schools and during different periods, were to prove irreconcilable. During the year they alternated rapidly between the delight of unity and the pain of conflict. John wrote under a mental strain that gave a vivid quality to his words, and later, with a feverish anxiety lest the structure of his play might break as he worked.

John was thirty-five years of age. For him love implied a unity in appreciation of all that he valued most with a unity in ambition to express it adequately. Such was his idea of harmony. Marriage for him meant the maintenance of a home and the rearing of children under its influence.

Molly, not yet of age, was slight and elegant. Large brown eyes gave her face a seriousness that was in constant competition with a look of madcap fun. Her face was interesting, but its beauty depended more on phases of expression than on special features. She had natural dramatic gifts that made her a star on the stage and gave her a great power of personal attraction. At the end of a national school education, she had worked for a short period in Switzer's drapery house before going to the Abbey Theatre to win immediate recognition on its stage and to capture John's affections. She enjoyed success, power, and attention and sought them passionately.

The evolution of ⟨their⟩ relationship ⟨as⟩ lovers ⟨brought⟩ her and John . . . experiences of joint exaltation and also of intense emotional conflict. At times his power of suggestion overwhelmed her sensitive and dramatic mind and as he showed her, in sunlight or twilight, places that he loved, she felt transported to a new world. He assumed that because she shared his vision, she would regard its literary expression as his first duty and, quiet as a nun, would wait, while he wrote, for such occasional delightful excursions together as his work allowed. Self-abnegation of the kind that his evangelical upbringing had led him to expect was not to be found in a young girl who longed to hold the first place in his mind. Between her wish for his companionship and other claims on his time she felt competition; but he felt none because he regarded his devotion to her as a fresh incentive to work. He had entered on a new emotional experience that was to provide the inspiration for *Deirdre of the Sorrows*, but in the meantime it was to put in jeopardy the synthesis of his past that had inspired *The Playboy of the Western World*. . . .

[Early in February, John moved into lodgings closer to the theatre, as he had in 1904. This time he took rooms] at 57 Rathgar Road, a house nine doors from a Roman Catholic Church dedicated to St. Patrick, St. Brigid, and St. Columcille, the three patron saints of Ireland. He moved from Crosthwaite Park because of its distance, not only from the Abbey Theatre but also from Mary Street, where Molly lived. As he had not spoken to his mother about his attachment to Molly, he had been unable to invite her to Crosthwaite Park and longed to increase his opportunities for seeing her. This he could do when he was living near Dublin although, as his engagement was not public, he would have thought it improper to bring her to his lodgings without a chaperone. . . .

[My father and mother had decided to move from Crosthwaite Park to a larger house near by, Silchester House, Glenageary. Mrs. Synge, who wanted to retain her close connection with our family, decided that she also would move and was lucky to find a suitable house only two or three hundred yards from the garden gate of Silchester House. She laughed at its name—Glendalough House— for it was a small semi-detached house, but she thought that it might suit her needs. During May, we moved to Silchester House and Mrs. Synge followed with her possessions to Glendalough House.]

Meanwhile John, as his mother did not need him at home, stayed at his lodgings in Rathgar Road, but went out sometimes on week-days to help her with preparations for her move and to pack books. He tended, as he usually did in May, to lay aside his work and go out to the hills. Molly went with him whenever she was free from her work at the Abbey Theatre. Though he could devote but little time to writing, *The Playboy of the Western World* was gaining new material and new force. At this time, he was not in doubt concerning its structure, Molly's choice of words and her coining of living, original phrases enriched his dialogue, and her presence revived the inspiration of the places he had known from childhood. She had an untamed and passionate nature and was living under the immeasurable strain of rising to fame in her art and developing an intimacy with a man whose modes of thought and

feeling were long formed in a mould of which she had no experience. Sometimes his way of talking roused her to uncontrollable
fury; once, she told me, she tore up her pocket handkerchief from
sheer rage as she walked with him down through Glen Dubh[1] and,
she said, he only laughed.

He had grown jealous with a passion that took fire at her slightest
friendly gesture towards any other man.[2] She, a young girl who
had left national school a few years before, could swing thought-
lessly from the arm of one of her stage companions; but John's
standards of social behaviour and his ideas of propriety were those
of his mother's house. With Molly in the hills, far from the rest of
the company, he could be free from anxiety and serenely happy, so
happy that he sometimes forgot that she had not had training like
his in walking, and took her distances that taxed her strength. He
tried to draw her into the world of his imagination by teaching her
to identify plants, insects, and the songs of birds and to appreciate
the changing face of the hills in sympathy with his moods. . . .

[During the summer, John went with the company on an extended tour of England, Wales, and Scotland. He was able to see a lot
of Molly, but also found himself feeling jealous several times at her
playful behaviour with other members of the company. The tour
was only a limited success and in Edinburgh the acting seemed to be
considerably below its usual standard. But there was little that John
could do to help. He had given up his lodgings in Rathgar Road
before the tour and when he returned, he came to live in his
mother's new home But, as she was spending the summer in Co.
Wicklow, he took his meals with us in Silchester House.]

From the time of his return to Glendalough House until he went
to Kerry, on 25 August, John tended to follow a daily routine.
After breakfast, dressed in an old jacket and waistcoat, his cycling
knickerbockers, and thick knitted stockings, he used to sit at his
typewriter opposite the window of his bedroom, facing Dalkey
Hill, and revise *The Playboy*. Near lunch-time, he used to put on
his old felt hat, which looked a little odd over his knickerbockers,
and walk up Adelaide Road to the garden gate, for which my
mother had lent him a key carefully tied on a loop of string. I used

---

[1] A valley near the southern suburbs of Dublin, one of Synge's favourite haunts.

[2] In particular, Synge was jealous of a young actor named Udolphus (Dossie)
Wright who, in later years, used to tell stories of putting his arm around Molly at
the theatre merely for the fun of seeing Synge's annoyance.

to watch for him strolling up the path twirling the key by its loop on his first finger. . . . I remember this very well because the key ⟨once⟩ flew off his finger into the strawberry bed and I had to find it. . . .

After lunch he sometimes sat on a rustic seat that I had made under a tree at the end of the south border, but more often he sat in a deck chair near the roses and in a patch of sunshine. There he used to sit quite motionless with his hat pulled down to shade his eyes. Once, when I brought out a chair and sat near him, he said that I had frightened a robin that had perched on the toe of his shoe. I said to John, who seemed half-asleep: 'You don't seem to be doing much work.' He replied: 'You are quite wrong: a man cannot work with the cream of his brain for more than six hours a day.' . . .

[For his visit to Kerry in the summer of 1906, John stayed three weeks at Mountain Stage with Philly Harris. He wrote to Molly constantly, alternating ecstatic descriptions of the beauty of the country and the life of the people with complaints of his loneliness and distress at being separated from her.[1] But he suffered from asthma at nights and found it impossible to work at *The Playboy*, which he had taken with him. Even after his return, much of his time was taken up with the affairs of the theatre and he was beset by problems over the play—this time with its structure. During the autumn, his relationship with Molly was also going through a difficult phase as they dared not make their engagement 'official' although it was, of course, suspected by all their friends at the theatre.

[The opening of the new season at the Abbey was to be preceded by a *conversazione* at the theatre early in October and, rather to our surprise, John said that he would take my brother and me,] if we thought we would enjoy it. I said that I would like very much to go if it would not make trouble at home. He said that no play would be acted and that he did not think that my grandmother or my mother would object to a *conversazione* because it would be held in a theatre. . . . ⟨Thus it was that⟩ I saw the Abbey Theatre for the first time. Yeats was to open the *conversazione* with an address on the aims of the Irish theatre, Henderson[2] had arranged a programme of songs and recitations by members of the company

[1] See *Letters to Molly*, pp. 15–26.
[2] W. A. Henderson, business secretary of the Abbey Theatre. He took up his duties at the beginning of October, and the *conversazione* was the first event that he organized.

and their friends and there was to be tea in the greenroom.

John sat with my brother and me near the back of the stalls. Many of the people who streamed in and took their places in the theatre greeted each other as friends. Yeats wandered backwards and forwards between the front seats and the door, his black hair drooping from his forehead and his black tie drooping from his neck.

When he came out on the stage he was greeted with applause. He spoke, it seemed to me, as if he were reciting poetry and described the work of creating an artistic drama in Ireland and of the nature of the opposition that he and his colleagues had to meet. I cannot now recall his address very clearly but I do remember his giving from the stage, it may have been that evening, a remarkable explanation of hostility in Dublin to the work of the National Theatre Society, an explanation which, because of my religious upbringing, impressed my mind particularly. He said that in other countries the Roman Catholic Church had been one of the great powers that encouraged the drama but that a Protestant cuckoo had got into the Church of Rome in Ireland ⟨and had⟩ made it puritanical.

When Yeats's speech was over, the entertainment on the programme began. John sometimes left his seat quietly, went up a short flight of stairs to the left of the stage, and vanished for a while through a little door that led to the greenroom.

I remember Sara Allgood walking out on the stage, standing next the silent piano, looking round the house with large brown eyes and singing, unaccompanied, Todhunter's 'Aghadoe'. Her voice was strangely clear and she sang with quiet confidence. There was a hush over the audience and at the end of her song a burst of applause. John did not mention that he had been responsible for persuading her to sing.[1]

Frank Fay, in costume, recited 'The Death of Cuchullain'. He was very impressive, but the items on the programme most memorable for me were two recitations given by Joseph Holloway,[2] ⟨one of which was⟩ 'Conn's Description of a Foxhunt' taken from

[1] Stephens writes (TS. 2262–3) that Henderson had told Holloway (the Abbey architect) that 'Synge had made her sing'.

[2] Holloway, a dedicated supporter of the Abbey Theatre (although an opponent of many individual plays—including most of Synge's work), kept a comprehensive daily chronicle of the affairs of the theatre. See *Joseph Holloway's Abbey Theatre*, ed. Robert Hogan and Michael J. O'Neill (Carbondale, Ill., 1967) and *Joseph Holloway's Irish Theatre*, vols. I–III (Dixon, Calif., 1968–70).

The Shaughraun by Boucicault. There was something over-whelmingly droll in his solemn delivery. I laughed until I was afraid to look at him and I felt John watching me with amused anxiety. I wondered whether laughing could become dangerous.

At the end of the entertainment, tea in the greenroom was announced and the audience began to pass up the narrow stairs and through the little door to the left of the stage. I saw a very pleasant-looking old gentleman with a pointed beard, wedged by the crowd against the handrail opposite the door. Someone called him 'Mr. Yeats,'[1] and I heard him say: 'Strait is the gate and narrow is the way that leadeth to tea and coffee.' The words gave me a queer shock. In a theatre, a place that Mrs. Synge regarded as bad, I had heard someone quoting as a joke one of the texts called 'guides to salvation', texts that I had been taught to regard as specially sacred like the Holy Name.

The greenroom was crowded. Members of the company and their friends were passing round tea and cake. John stood with his back to the wall talking to Sara and Molly. I do not remember whether he introduced my brother and me to them. Molly stood very close to him, and as she talked, looked at him in a way that made me ask my brother afterwards whether he thought they were in love. . . .

[Towards the end of 1906, the fact that John and Molly were engaged to be married became gradually more widely known. Earlier in the year he had told his brother Sam about Molly and had shown him her photograph; however he had asked Sam not to mention Molly's existence to the rest of the family. In November, when he was suffering from a bad attack of influenza and was too ill to leave the house, Molly wrote that she would like to visit him; on 22 November, she came to Glenageary and spent an hour or so with him. Mrs. Synge, who let her into the house, greeted her in a friendly way. As John wrote to Molly: 'It is much better to let my mother get used to the idea by degrees than to spring it on her suddenly.'

[To recuperate after his 'flu, John arranged to spend a fortnight with his cousin Edward Synge, the engraver, in Surrey.[2] He found the change most relaxing and, as *The Playboy* was now almost completed, he began to think about a new play. . . . While he was

---

[1] John Butler Yeats, father of W. B. and Jack B. Yeats.
[2] Edward Millington Synge (1860–1913), whom Synge had known in Paris.

away from Dublin, John also felt more inclined to tell the world of his engagement and he planned to write to both Lady Gregory and his mother with the news. Although he actually postponed telling Lady Gregory, he did write to his mother and posted the letter on 7 December; she replied with what he described to Molly as 'Quite a nice letter for a first go off.'

[John returned from England in the middle of December. Again, the affairs of the Abbey Theatre engrossed his attention, but now that *The Playboy* was finished and about to go into rehearsal—the first performance was scheduled for 26 January—the details of theatre administration seemed far less important to him than his play. But his work as a dramatist] had put the morality of theatre-going in issue for the argumentative members of the family circle at Silchester House. It was agreed that the Abbey Theatre must not be confused with the ordinary stage and that John was as strict in his behaviour as any of his relations, but the question remained as to whether going to the Abbey Theatre should be regarded as countenancing theatre-going in general. ⟨My cousin Ton Traill, who was staying with us,⟩ said that acting was an art and that it was as important to see good plays as to read them. I said that useful as theatrical life might be, in some ways, its spiritual consequences were the most important and that it was bad for the morals of those who made it their profession. Ton replied by mentioning a large number of English actors and actresses, who were, he said, highly respectable people. This confused me for I knew neither their names nor mode of life.

None of us tried to involve John in any of our discussions for we knew that he would not argue against the religious and political teaching of our elders. He had told us about his book on the Aran Islands, soon to be published,[1] and we had seen his article in *The Shanachie*,[2] about people we knew and places that we well remembered; the fact that some of his writing about them took the form of plays did not connect him very closely in our minds with the life of the stage. . . . [However, despite our prejudices, we did not all shun the theatre, and one evening at about this time Florence Ross,[3]

[1] Published jointly by Elkin Mathews of London and Maunsel & Co. of Dublin, 1907.

[2] 'The Vagrants of Wicklow', *The Shanachie*, No. 2 (Autumn 1906), 93–8. *The Shanachie* was a journal published by Maunsel & Co.

[3] Florence Ross had returned to Ireland after many years of living abroad, first

Ton Traill, and my brother Frank went] to see *The Hour Glass* and *The Mineral Workers* at the Abbey Theatre.[1] Mrs. Synge had disapproved of Florence going to any theatre from her house, but Florence had disregarded her aunt's wishes. Mrs. Synge entered in her diary: 'Frank, Ton and Florence went to the Abbey—not home till after 12. I lay awake a great deal. . . .' ⟨But despite Mrs. Synge's feelings,⟩ my brother and I accepted John as our authority in the sphere of art and literature (so far as we realized its existence) and Mrs. Synge as our authority in the sphere of religion. . . .

6

[During January 1907, John was occupied almost every day with the rehearsals for *The Playboy* but I often saw him for a few minutes when I went to visit Mrs. Synge. He looked tired and unwell, and Mrs. Synge was also, as she made clear in her diary, feeling depressed. On Sunday 20 January she wrote:]

A cold day, but fine. I did not go out, read and meditated. I felt poorly so I played a number of my old hymn tunes on the piano for nearly an hour and it did me good. Frank came from 2 to 3. . . . Annie came in for a short time, and Robert came for tea. Florence went to Church and had supper at Silchester. John home after 8. . . .

John was suffering from a slight cough, he was tired after a hard week's work and had a week of great anxiety before ⟨the first performance⟩. He required rest on Sunday, but his walks with Molly had become his greatest happiness and relaxation and he found difficulty in restricting their length. Molly had met him at Carrickmines railway station from which they walked to Glencullen, the lonely rock-strewn valley that had a character like the country of the west, deserted and desolate in the middle of winter. They sat for a while on a sheltered bank. The view of Sugarloaf and its line of hills was wonderful, but the air was keen. For John the last Sunday before the production of *The Playboy of the Western World* was happily spent, but in a way that tended to aggravate a cold at a time when he could not rest.

---

in Tonga as her brother's housekeeper and later in New Zealand, Australia, and South America.

[1] *The Hour Glass* was by W. B. Yeats and *The Mineral Workers* by William Boyle.

When he had finished his play, he had lost no time in handing over the typed script of it to his publisher.[1] The proofs had been corrected and the pages printed but he had not furnished the preface. It was short, but the result of much thought, and contained all that he was willing to tell the public about his aims or the source of his play. He signed the preface on Monday 21 January. . . .

The play had not been long in rehearsal before Willie Fay became convinced that parts of it would excite indignation. It was his business to secure good receptions for the plays he produced and to him features likely to evoke protests seemed unnecessary. In his account of his work at rehearsals with John he wrote:

Frank and I begged him to make Pegeen a decent likeable country girl, which she might easily have been without injury to the play, and to take out the torture scene in the last act, where the peasants burn Christy with lit turf. . . . Frank and I might as well have saved our breath. We might as well have tried to move the Hill of Howth as move Synge.[2]

Fay seems to have believed that John was made inflexible by a grudge in his mind against those who had attacked his earlier work and, in support of this belief, quoted one of John's joking threats that he would make sure to annoy them with his next play. The truth was that for John *The Playboy of the Western World* embodied a phase of his life. He would no more change its structure than he could change the past; but . . . through all the frenzied controversy that was to follow the production of his play, he refrained from disclosing ⟨this⟩ to anyone.

Though the directors ⟨of the Abbey Theatre probably⟩ expected disturbance of the kind they had experienced before, they were so unprepared for serious trouble ⟨at the first night of *The Playboy*⟩ that Yeats had gone to lecture in Scotland and Lady Gregory [only came to Dublin for the performance because Yeats wanted her to discuss the theatre management with John.]

Before the performance began, the theatre was full . . . [and as usual the audience was composed primarily of people who were nationalist in outlook.] In the stalls there was . . . a group of people who had been interested in the Irish literary renaissance from its beginning and had sufficient cultural education to appreciate

[1] George Roberts of Maunsel & Co.
[2] W. G. Fay and C. Carswell, *The Fays of the Abbey Theatre: an Autobiographical Record* (London, 1935), pp. 212–13.

literary plays. In the general body of the audience were some who,
without any special interest in politics, had been attracted to the
Abbey Theatre by its growing fame and good work and enjoyed
plays of the kind they saw there, and some who looked intensely
purposeful, as if they were there to support a cause. One evening
some years later, when I chanced to sit next a college friend who
had never been in the theatre before, he said: 'This is an extraordinary place, quite unlike the Queens or the Tivoli; look where
you like, there's not a glad eye in the house, not a girl you could
pick up.'. . . .

First, *Riders to the Sea* was acted and received with general
applause; then the curtain rose on *The Playboy of the Western World.*
The first two acts were played successfully, and the third act was
half over when demonstrations against the play began. . . . [Soon
the hooting and hissing became deafening and the theatre became
'a mass of angry swaying humanity'.[1] There had been nothing
unusual in some politically-minded young people starting a disturbance at the Abbey Theatre, but the dimensions to which it
grew and its results were so fantastic as to baffle explanation[2]. . . .

John went home ⟨that⟩ night exhausted by the strain of seeing
the first production of his play rudely interrupted. His chief
concerns were to shake off his cough, which seemed to be growing
worse, ⟨and⟩ to get rest sufficient to allow him to meet the difficulties of the coming week. . . . At home, ⟨he⟩ said very little about the
row that broke out in the theatre. . . . It was not until the newspapers came . . . that his family knew how great an uproar had
greeted his play. The *Irish Times* published a long account of the
first performance: it patronizingly referred to John as 'a playwright
who had already proved himself possessed of ability to present an
effective stage-representation of Irish people', but concluded:

It is open to serious question whether the author has been well advised in
regard to some of the dialogue. A large section of Saturday night's
audience very properly resented these indiscretions on the part of the

[1] Mary Colum, *Life and the Dream* (New York, 1947), p. 138.

[2] Stephens considers the riots caused by *The Playboy* in considerable detail (TS.
2415–2501), partly because when he wrote, little was known about them. The
details are now more familiar and it seems unnecessary to repeat them here. For a
summary of the affair, see Hilary Berrow, 'Eight Nights at the Abbey', in *J. M.
Synge: Centenary Papers,* ed. Maurice Harmon (Dublin, 1971), pp. 75–87 and references.

author and brought what in other respects was a brilliant success to an inglorious conclusion.

There was no doubt that my mother was shocked by what she read; soon after breakfast she went out ⟨and⟩ Mrs. Synge noted in her diary: 'Annie came in early, going to see Mrs Darling. I was troubled about John's play—not nice; talked to her about it.' John must have reassured his mother by telling her that there was nothing improper in the play and that the disturbances had been organized by extreme nationalists for, when she mentioned the disturbances to me, she seemed satisfied that they were made by people who objected to John telling the truth about life in Ireland. . . .

I remember that on one afternoon at about this time, John and I set out on our bicycles for the hills. As we walked up from Kilternan, we stopped occasionally to rest and look back at the view that was opening out behind us of the coastal plain and the bay. Where the road to Glencullen turned abruptly to take advantage of an easy gradient, we pushed on up the narrow Killigar lane. At its highest part, where we mounted our bicycles, we were suddenly enfolded by the hills and were gliding for a short way on a smoothly gravelled road between scented golden gorse and listening to the larks that soared singing from the moorland. For a stretch the lane grew rougher and ran between uncemented granite walls, then again we were travelling between gorse bushes and soon were facing the range from Great Sugarloaf to Bray Head. When, on our way home, we were nearing Kingstown, we stopped at the top of Johnstown Road before turning into Roches-town Avenue and leaned on our bicycles to look over a gate to-wards the Three Rock. Our talk had turned on *The Playboy* row, of which, until then, John had spoken but little. I asked him whether he knew who had organized the disturbance in the theatre. He said that it had been organized by Gaelic Leaguers and their friends, but that it did not matter, for *The Playboy* would live when they were all forgotten. Voltaire, he said, had been received in the same way. . . .

While dissension raged round John's work wherever it was acted, the happy family relation that differences of opinion could not interrupt—between John and the other members of his home circle—had tended to grow in strength. They had accepted the fact

The Stephens family, with Synge, at Castle Kevin. (From left) Edward Stephens, his mother, his uncle John, his father, and sister Claire.

Synge's Paris: The playwright's room in the Hotel Corneille, where he lived in 1896, and (below) Parisian bookstalls early in the century, from photographs found among Synge's papers.

A wool-buyer weighing wool in the west of Ireland, from a photograph possibly taken by Synge. (Below) Synge's photograph of Aran islanders waiting for the steamer at Kilronan pier on Aranmore.

Rehearsal room of the Irish National Theatre Society in Camden Street, Dublin, 1903. Portraits on the wall include ones of Synge and Lady Gregory; the blackboard announces a rehearsal of The Shadow of the Glen. (Inset) Molly Allgood (Maire O'Neill) in Riders to the Sea.

that in spite of all their advice he had become a writer. As they had prophesied, literature had not provided him with a lucrative occupation but, on the other hand, it had not lured him into bohemianism; his way of life remained as orderly as that of his most exacting evangelical relations. Although he did not go to church, nothing he said about religion was flippant or irreverent and press reports of his plays showed very clearly that he had no leanings towards Romanism. . . .

[However John's health, which had apparently been improving, was now beginning to cause his family, and himself, some alarm. The glands in his neck had begun to swell again and he was also suffering from pains in his legs and back as well as from various other symptoms. But since the Abbey Theatre company was planning a tour of England during which *The Playboy* was to be produced in Oxford and in London—and, they all hoped, to be received without hostility—he was determined to go to England to be present, at least, for the London performance.

[At the end of May he had recovered sufficiently to leave for England, but he went first to stay with Jack Yeats quietly in Devonshire before going on to London. He was able to attend the performance at the Great Queen Street theatre at which *The Playboy*, acted with the greatest skill and appreciation by the company, was received with great enthusiasm and good humour by a distinguished London audience. Afterwards John was called before the curtain and when he returned to his lodgings, he must have been aware that, in this triumph, his greatest hour had arrived.

[Several reviewers praised not only the play but also its leading actress.] John was delighted by Molly's success in his plays; but it was a success that ⟨also⟩ brought him anguish because it made her the centre of attraction for all the young men in the gatherings to which the company was invited. ⟨Molly⟩ resented John's unwillingness to join the groups that gathered round her and his preoccupation with . . . his ⟨more distinguished⟩ friends. With all the zest of youth, she threw herself into the social life that surrounded her and seemed to John like one who had withdrawn herself into a world where he had no part. . . .

[It was during this visit to London that John spent some time with John Masefield. One of their meetings took place in John's lodgings where he showed Masefield a typescript of his ballad 'Danny'.]

He told me the wild, picturesque story ⟨of a murder in Connaught⟩ which had inspired the ballad. His relish of the savagery made me feel that he was a dying man clutching at life, and clutching most wildly at violent life, as the sick man does. . . .[1]

Masefield was right in thinking that John's frame of mind was very different from what it had been in those days early in 1903 when Cherrie Matheson had, by her marriage, freed his imagination from his dream of her and his dramatic work was beginning to win recognition in London. In treating the mood in which John wrote his ballad 'Danny' as that of a dying man, clutching at violent life, Masefield was mistaken. John was not well, but he was expecting shortly to recover his strength and to make final arrangements for his marriage. The ballad, founded on a story that had dwelt in his imagination since he heard it in the Mullet in 1905, expressed too much real vitality to have been the product of any such mood as Masefield described. He was accustomed to meet John as a sensitive, individualistic writer, in urban literary circles, and may not have recognized in him a quality which was never well described by either his friends or his enemies. John shared with his brothers a hard core that was in the Synge family. . . . They had a tough quality so much part of their nature that they employed it without modifying the quiet demeanour that was usual in their home. Robert had accepted, as part of his ordinary life, mounting with his lasso for a rodeo or living in waggons when he was building stations on the South American railways. Edward had slept with money and a revolver under his pillow when he travelled round on Irish rent-collections, and Sam had faced life as a missionary in China soon after the Boxer rising. Though John, as a sensitive naturalist, gave up bait-fishing because he would not hurt earthworms by putting them on his hook, he had the quality that made him attack a bull with a walking stick on the way from Roundwood fair and battle with a rearing horse outside the forge at Annamoe.[2] John had acquired intellectual self-conciousness and a searching power of self-criticism, without losing his gift for joining imaginatively in the life of people more primitive than he. . . .

[For the summer of 1907, Mrs. Synge went to Tomriland House

---

[1] Masefield, 'John M. Synge', op. cit.

[2] Stephens refers to stories of incidents in Synge's life at Castle Kevin, told earlier in the TS.

taking as her companion Florence Ross. For some time, Florence had been living with us at Silchester House, but she was considered rather a bad influence on my brother and me as, despite the well-known views of Mrs. Synge and of my mother, Florence made it clear that, to her mind, neither dancing nor the theatre was sinful.] She read Yeats with delight and tended to find in the new Irish literature some relief from the suburban monotony of life in Kingstown. . . . [She was also very interested in John's work, even though she had retained her evangelical beliefs.] We had so long been accustomed to hearing John's friends deprecated by our relations that, until Florence came, ⟨my brother and I⟩ had failed to form a clear conception of his work as one of a group of writers concerned in creating a new Irish literature. . . .

[Despite the fact that he was pleased to be able to see Florence again, John decided that he would not accompany his mother to Tomriland in 1907. He had heard from Molly that she had arranged to go with her sister to Glencree, in the Wicklow mountains, for a fortnight in June and July. He soon found that he could lodge with a Mrs. McGuirk in a cottage about half a mile from Mrs. Dunne's cottage, in which Molly and Sara were staying, and he moved there on 28 June.]

For the next ⟨two weeks,⟩ John and Molly wandered through the whole valley ⟨of Glencree⟩ and along the mountain roads. They went down to the stream below the cottages, through the fields to the oak wood, down below it to Lackendaragh and up again by the little road that . . . ⟨ran⟩ among boulders and heather. The wood gave them shade from the sun and nooks in the rocks shelter from flying showers. In the evening they walked along or sat by the unfenced roads, listening to the whirring of the night-jar and the sound of water, and watched the stars come out. . . .

[Then Molly had to return to Dublin with her sister: but a fortnight later, she came up from the city again, this time on her own, to stay at Mrs. Dunne's for a further two weeks. Again John and his changeling[1] were able to wander all over the hills together and forget about the outside world. These two holidays] provided John with the best opportunity he ever knew for fulfilling his longing to unite, as if in one emotion, his love for places of inspiration and his love for a woman. Though he often took Molly to

---

[1] Synge's pet name for Molly: a changeling is a child substituted by the fairies for one that they have stolen.

places with which he sought to associate her in his mind, at no other times did they dwell in one of those places and there enjoy together summer days and evenings and their changing lights on the hills. . . .

[They both returned to Dublin on 4 August, Molly to the Abbey for rehearsals and John to Glendalough House, where he hoped to work on his play. But his health was not good; he thought that the glands were getting even larger and he was suffering from a cough and from asthma. He also had a constant slight fever. Not surprisingly, he was depressed and decided to put off plans he had made for a visit to Brittany; instead he arranged to have a further operation for the removal of his glands in September.

[The operation was to take place in the Mount Street Nursing Home] where he had gone for a similar operation nearly ten years earlier. He found it provided with a new operating theatre, ⟨a⟩ lift and other equipment of a private hospital. In the decade that had elapsed since he was there before, the technique of anaesthesia had advanced so much that he suffered no experience like the one he described in 'Under Ether', but he did talk with some excitement as he regained consciousness and heard voices saying that the operation had been successful.

[On the Sunday morning after the operation,] ⟨his brother⟩ Robert went to town to enquire for John and brought back a good report to their mother. As the swelled glands that had occasioned the operation had been next the spot from which others had been removed and no second operation had been necessary for almost ten years, neither John nor his relations thought that the disorder from which he suffered might manifest itself in other parts. . . . [Soon after the operation,] I called with ⟨a⟩ book to see him for a few minutes and found him very cheerful. . . .

[When he returned home, Molly came to see him.] Their spirits were rising so much that they talked of being married very soon. . . . In a few days he was well enough to meet Yeats again to discuss plans for work in the autumn. . . . [He was also planning his new play.] He had decided to turn from peasant life and to use an ancient, heroic tale, ⟨that of Deirdre and the sons of Usna⟩, as the medium for dramatizing his new experience—a medium that would yield a stately leading part for Molly. In selecting great figures from ancient lore for his characters, he had avoided the difficulty of representing historical people truthfully, and believed that he would be able to use rhythmical dialect as their speech without attaching them to a particular time. . . .

In constructing his play, he embodied himself as he had walked through Glencree with Molly in the person of Naisi, and another phase of himself as the middle-aged man who lectured and directed her in the person of Conchubor; his old mother housekeeping for the family and careful of their needs he embodied in Lavarcham, and his two loyal brothers, who had their last bicycle ride with him just before Sam left for China, seem to have suggested Ainnle and Ardan.[1] In Owen John embodied the detached critical spirit of his own mind and used him as Shakespeare used his fools, to expound wisdom.

Some years before, he had written in his article 'A Landlord's Garden': 'If a playwright chose to go through the Irish country houses he would find material, it is likely, for many gloomy plays that would turn on the dying away of these old families.'[2] While he utilized his relations as material for drama, he seems to have thought of adopting his own suggestion of seeking dramatic material in the class from which he came; but in his new mood, he saw in it material not for gloomy tragedy, but for the comic tragedy that was his natural medium. . . .

[In October, John decided to go to Kerry for a few days and stayed at Ventry. He hoped that the change would do his health good, and was deeply disappointed when his asthma proved so bad that he had to return home after only four days. I went to see him and found him less] depressed . . . than I had expected. He showed me with pride a *súgan* chair[3] that he had bought in Kerry and pointed out the skilful way that the seat had been made by interlacing a hay rope. The chair was the first piece of furniture that he had bought for the new home that he hoped to establish with Molly before Christmas, but he did not mention that to me. . . .

On Sunday 27 October, Mrs. Synge noted in her diary: 'Molly came at 4 and stayed till 9. We had a talk on China.' Her entry recorded the first occasion on which she had sat down to a family

1 Stephens believed his theory that Synge consciously modelled his dramatic characters on members of his family fitted *Deirdre of the Sorrows* particularly conveniently.

2 *C.W.* II. 231.

3 A *súgan* chair, traditional in many parts of Ireland, is made with a rope of twisted straw.

meal with Molly, and the improving subject of conversation she had chosen for Sunday evening—a subject which, in so far as it related to Sam, was a family one, and in so far as it related to his work was a religious one without being controversial, as his mission was to the heathen. . . .

[John and Molly were seeing each other as often as possible, but John's mind was in a turmoil: so much in his life was unresolved. He wrote to Molly:]

I cannot live this way any longer—I nearly died of loneliness and misery last night while you ought to be here to comfort me and cheer me up. . . . I am working myself sick with Deirdre or whatever you call it. It is a very anxious job. I dont want to make a failure. . . .[1]

[But the play was developing, and his fits of depression soon passed. The company, including Molly, left for a short tour of England and Scotland late in November. The tour was beset with problems and John was extremely lonely without Molly. He consoled himself with thoughts of the future: 'You'll be coming home to me in 10 days now, and then we'll be together all ways my dear love.'[2] Obviously he and Molly were planning to be married very soon[3] and John started looking for a flat in which they could set up home. He also wrote to his cousin Edward Synge, who had himself just announced his engagement, to tell him of his plans, but asked Edward to keep the secret still. 'It may come off very soon, but owing to my health and finances, it is a little uncertain,' he wrote.[4] Yet he was still engrossed in his new play.] His whole imagination was devoted to dramatizing the experience that was changing his life. . . .

7

[During the first few months of 1908, John's personal affairs weighed heavily on his mind. The problems of the Abbey Theatre were serious as the Fay brothers had finally broken their links with the theatre and resigned. But John's health was a more serious worry and as the weeks passed, the prospects of an early marriage grew darker. However, he continued to look for a suitable flat and in January he wrote to tell Molly that he had found a set of

---

[1] *Letters to Molly*, pp. 213–14.   [2] ibid., p. 224.
[3] See also his letter of 27 November, ibid., p. 220.
[4] Synge to Edward Synge, 31 December 1907.

three rooms]—one with a place for a gas cooker—with attendance and cooking for 13/6 a week. The rooms were at 47 York Road, Rathmines. . . . After a long discussion, . . . he and Molly decided to make these rooms their home. . . . Mrs. Synge wrote to Robert:

Johnnie is on the move; he is at home today packing and sorting over books, clothes etc. . . . I feel his going *very* much: furnishing these rooms, trying to make a little home for himself on such a very small and uncertain income. I am giving him some old furniture etc. and he must buy some. . . . Johnnie says this move reminds him of his trips to Paris! Counting over his socks etc. putting away things he does not want! However, he adds, it is not so far. . . .

When I called at Glendalough House on Wednesday 22 January, . . . ⟨the day before John was to move,⟩ [I found him] busy packing his books. Florence⟨Ross⟩ had lent him indefinitely an old double bed that had belonged to her mother. Besides, he had the old furniture that his mother had given him, the *súgán* chair that he had brought from Kerry, a new wicker arm chair and a few pictures which included an etching entitled 'A Courtyard in Venice' by Edward M. Synge[1] and a small print of 'The Concert' by Giorgione. As we arranged his pictures together, John pointed to the central figure in 'The Concert'—a monk who has just struck a chord—and said: 'Look at that face'; and then, half to himself, 'perhaps you wouldn't see it.' It was one of his odd moments that were made memorable, not because of the words he used, but because of the depth of feeling from which they came. Some years later, in Florence, his comment gave force to the strange shock of recognition with which I saw the face again in the full splendour of the original.

On Thursday morning, I helped John and the driver of ⟨the⟩ cart to load. Left to ourselves, John and I could have done the work well, for we had acquired skill from Willie Belton when with him we had loaded Mrs. Synge's goods for her move to Castle Kevin; but the driver made the load crooked and covered it badly with a skimpy tarpaulin. We stood at the gate and anxiously watched the cart sway down the road on its slow journey to town.

After lunch, John and I went to Rathmines to receive and arrange his furniture and pictures. The house in which he had taken the upper rooms was one of a two-storied red brick row, the nearest

1 A gift from the artist; see *Letters to Molly*, p. 123.

but one to Upper Rathmines Road. His sitting-room faced in a northerly direction, but it had a bow window that caught the evening sun. Its view was the dull grey side and garden wall of an old house that opened on the main road.

We had not waited long when the cart arrived. The load had travelled safely, except that part of it had been wet by driving showers. John placed each piece of furniture as it was carried in and when the cart went away we hung the pictures he had brought. The rooms soon looked habitable and he surveyed the result of our work with deep satisfaction in having at last established a home of his own.

He said that as he was going to the Abbey Theatre, we could go together into the city, and that he would show me the new picture gallery on my way to the railway station.[1] As we walked down Harcourt Street he seemed in high spirits. At No. 17 he turned in with the air of one very familiar with the place. The man at the door touched his hat as we passed and John began showing me the rooms with proprietary pleasure. The familiar pictures that had formed the nucleus of Lane's collection were there, but much better hung than they had been in the museum. Besides, there were others that I had not seen before.[2]

John showed me Mancini's portraits. He had told me, one evening at Glendalough House, that Mancini was in Dublin and that he was a great anxiety to his friends because his imagination was so strong that if he saw a lame man in the street he would walk home lame himself. I asked John whether Mancini's portraits were good likenesses. He said that he thought they were, but that the question of whether they were or not did not matter very much, because a picture might be a good picture without being like the person whose portrait it was. 'A bad picture', said John, 'could not become a good picture just because a person happened to die and nobody could remember what he was like.' . . .

When we came to a picture of a house with lights shining from its windows into a grey evening, John stopped and said: 'Do you see the impression of evening light in that picture?' The question

[1] The 'new picture gallery' was the Dublin Municipal Gallery of Modern Art, imaginatively conceived and generously endowed by Lady Gregory's nephew, Hugh Lane. See Synge's article, 'Good Pictures in Dublin', C.W. II. 390–2.

[2] Stephens had visited the collection before it was moved to 17 Harcourt Street; it is now housed in Charlemont House, Parnell Square.

was a simple one, but I thought that he asked it because he found in the picture an interpretation of endless impressions of villages that he had seen at nightfall. . . .

In her diary for Sunday, Mrs. Synge wrote: 'Molly came out and went up to ⟨the⟩ little front room. We had tea together,' and for Monday: 'A windy day very cold but fine. Johnnie went away. Tied up a chair to go with his things. I felt it.' Though her house had ceased to be his home, his mother thought that he might still need her care and arranged to keep his room ready for his use.

As Molly was recognized as his betrothed and he hoped very soon to be married, he saw no objection to her visiting him without a chaperone. Sitting with her by the bow window of his new rooms, he began to find the inspiration for the last two lines of the poem 'Dread' of which the first six drew their inspiration from his loneliness in his lodgings at 57 Rathgar Road in the spring of 1906. The poem took shape afterwards when he was able to write:

> Now by this window, where there's none can see,
> The Lord God's jealous of yourself and me.[1]

There he saw Molly so often that he did not write her letters. He was happy about the move he had made towards his marriage and towards saving time in going to and from the Abbey Theatre, but his work there was still so heavy that he could devote but little time to writing his new play.

The theatre was not John's only anxiety. He had left his mother with two servants and with her niece staying in the house so she did not lack care; but her health was deteriorating. Two days after John left she wrote in her diary:

A nice fine morning, but colder in afternoon. I went to Dr. Beatty. He said he thought my lump is a rupture. I felt very nervous. He sent me up to Dr. Gordon who thought so also. Came home by 3.45 train. Wrote a note to Annie and told her. Wrote to Sam.

She consulted her surgeon again; he advised an operation, but some days were to elapse before it could be performed because no suitable room was immediately available for her in Elpis.[2] From

---

[1] See Professor Robin Skelton's comment on Stephens's dating of this poem, C.W. I. 40 n., and p. xxvi.

[2] The name by which the nursing home in Lower Mount Street was known at this time.

the time the family at Silchester House heard the surgeon's advice, we spent with her all the time we could spare and on Wednesday afternoon I found John at Glendalough House talking with her about her trouble. . . .

On Monday, 17 February, Mrs. Synge wrote in her diary:

A day to be remembered. I went to Lr. Mount Street at 3.30. Annie came with me. It was a trying time. We had tea and then she went home and left me. Harry came to see me and was very kind. I got through the evening.

And on the following evening:

The Day. Got on very well. Annie came to see me. Dr. Gordon was pleased to see me so well in the evening—very kind.

The surgeon had made a small incision from which no great length of time was required for recovery, but it had disclosed not a rupture but a swelling caused by a disease in some ways similar to that from which John was suffering—so I heard long afterwards. My mother said that my grandmother was wonderfully well, but that the lump that had been removed had proved to be different from what the doctors had expected, and that it might have been better to have left it without interference. . . .

[One Friday early in April, John came] out to Glenageary to spend the afternoon with his mother. He found her far from well, suffering (she believed) from rheumatism and neuralgia, but in reality . . . from an illness that was gradually undermining her health. She told him of her troubles and her plans for going to Tomriland House to recover her strength in summer and discussed with him the question of his marriage. ⟨After he had gone, she⟩ sat by the fire and thought over all that John had said. On Tuesday she wrote to Robert: 'Johnnie came to see me on Friday last; he is seriously thinking of being soon married . . . ⟨and⟩ as he is determined . . . it is no use opposing him any more and we must only trust that he may get on. . . .'

[But once again, it was John's health which upset his plans. Late in April he went to Glenageary to see his mother. When she] went out to meet him at the door ⟨she⟩ was shocked by his pallor. . . . ⟨After⟩ lunch, ⟨she⟩ took John up to her bedroom and there he told her the news that he had held back in order to save her for as

long as was possible from distress and anxiety. He had been growing
steadily worse, and lying awake until three in the morning with
pains in his stomach and back. He had been twice to Dr. Parsons,
but his mother said that he had borne the pain too long in a lonely
lodging with no proper food. John said that the doctor had found
a small lump in his side, but that the pain did not seem to be connected with it. It had been arranged that he should go into Elpis . . .
for examination. He left by the 3.15 train and [the next day entered
the nursing home]. . . .

Molly was very anxious but could not spend much time with
him for some days as [she was very busy at the theatre.] My mother
called to see John on Friday afternoon and found that he had gone
out for a walk. On Saturday morning my brother called to see
him and found him in bed awaiting a visit from Dr. Parsons who
had arranged to have a consultation with Sir Charles Ball on
Monday.

I knew very little about illness and operations, and did not
realize that John's life was in danger. My mother told me nothing
and I could not go to see him as I was to sit for the Junior Freshman
examination ⟨at Trinity College⟩ on Monday and Tuesday.

At their consultation on Monday Sir Charles Ball and Dr.
Parsons decided that an operation was necessary and arranged it
for Tuesday morning. . . . [The first news of the operation was that
it had been successful, but my mother], who had gone to Elpis
⟨on Wednesday⟩, returned at tea-time in tears to say that John was
not so well and was very restless. The remainder of the week was a
time of terrible anxiety for the members of John's family, particularly for Mrs. Synge, and a time of terror and grief for Molly who
was busy at the theatre. . . . On Saturday, news reached the theatre
that there was little hope of John's life. . . .

As the days of ⟨his⟩ illness passed, both supporters and opponents
of his work, as well as his relations, had called at Elpis to enquire.
⟨At last⟩ the news of him became more hopeful on Sunday, and
on Tuesday Mrs. Synge, with her mind greatly relieved, gave
Robert an account of the last terrible days. She wrote:

We have had a terribly trying time since I wrote last week. Things did
not go right after the operation and until last Sunday Sir C. Ball had no
hope of our dear boy's life; we did not know that. Miss Huxley[1] only

---

[1] The matron.

told Annie yesterday, then on Sunday the change came for the better
and Sir C. B. said 'he'll do now' so we are filled with thankfulness to
God for His great mercy; each day last week, one could see what anxiety
they were in about him; Annie went in on Wednesday, the day after,
and came home in tears, not able to speak for some time; some thing was
not right, but we did not know what. Then on Thursday night there
was such danger Dr. Parsons wrote to tell me. The letter came on Friday
morning. I got it before I got up. I felt it was just to prepare me for the
worst and I wept and prayed that God would not take him unless he first
came to know Him. I was enabled to give him up reservedly to God. It
was the only way of peace. Annie went in again on Friday or Saturday I
think and came back more hopelessly sad than ever. Miss H. would not
say anything, but said everything was a little worse. So we were in great
grief: Harry saw dear J. that evening, and then came to see me and told
me he was able to chat a little and was not as weak as he expected, but it
was very critical. I think they feared some blood poisoning of some kind.
On Sunday morning Dr. Ball took out the stitches, and immediately
the wound opened and a great discharge came from it, and that saved
his life. . . .

Johnnie would be gratified if he saw how everyone loves him and
what sorrow we have been in. I really did not know Annie loved him
so much she was in such grief; may God use it for drawing us more
together, and enabling us to show the love we feel instead of hiding it all
away till death comes.

The great sorrow of knowing he had not come to God was the greatest
of all. Frank used to go 2 or 3 times to Elpis during the day to enquire;
he looked quite ill with anxiety. I am still very poorly—weak and thin
and these pains come on each night. . . . I am longing for you to come
home. We want you. The summer is all uncertain. I am so very poorly
I ought to get away for a change, but if my dear boy is here and an invalid
of course he could not be left alone, so I am seeking to leave this also to
God to settle for me. . . .

[With the news of John's continuing improvement,] the pall
of anxiety had been lifted from his family circle. . . . I knew very
little about illness, and fully believed that John was on his way to
complete recovery. The change in his condition raised for his
doctors the difficulty of deciding what he should be told. When he
had seemed to be sinking, Dr. Parsons had written truthfully to his
mother telling her that the operation had disclosed a swelling which
could not be eradicated. As John's condition began to improve his
doctors, in order to prevent his being crushed by despair, thought
it necessary to give him a more optimistic account of the operation.

They told him that a tumour had been removed, but that its removal had made necessary a very large incision and a cutting of the bowel. In his low state of health, they said, healing might take time, but with the assistance of treatment there was no reason to think that it would not be satisfactory. . . .

[Once the crisis was over, John recovered quite rapidly. However, it was decided that his flat in Rathmines should not be retained and I attended to the moving of his furniture.] Molly had packed his small personal belongings, but she was not there when John's rooms were emptied. . . . Mrs. Synge wrote to Robert:

. . . We got ⟨Johnnie's⟩ furniture all back from Rathmines yesterday. . . . It was such a sad little flitting altogether. I remember now remarking how ill he looked when he was going away. He says those pains began in December! I think if he had been at home, I would certainly have thought there was something serious going on; but I saw him very seldom during the four months he was away, and I know he did not feed himself as he was accustomed and he used to be so very hungry for his dinners when he came. God has permitted it all to happen, so I can say nothing. . . .

[During June, John's condition definitely improved, though the wound was very slow to heal. However he was not allowed to leave hospital so Mrs. Synge, who was herself badly in need of a change of air, moved down to Tomriland House at the beginning of July. But she was not strong enough to undergo the journey.] She . . . suffered dreadfully from the unevenness of the road and the heat, but was so glad to be at Tomriland that she did not at first realize the seriousness of her fatigue. . . . In reality, Mrs. Synge's visit to Tomriland was to be her last and was to be peculiarly melancholy for her and her little party. She was much too ill for life in the country at a distance from her medical advisers. . . . [A month later she was brought home:] my mother and I were waiting for her when she drove up in a cab . . . from the railway station. It was difficult for my mother to hide her concern when she saw how ill Mrs. Synge looked and how feebly she walked with assistance into the house. As soon as I had carried in her small personal luggage, I went home. My mother, when she returned later, said that she had put my grandmother to bed and sent for ⟨the doctor⟩.

[Meanwhile, John had been allowed to leave hospital; he had not returned to Glendalough House, as Mrs. Synge had taken her maids to the country with her, but he had come to stay with us in Silchester House so that my mother could look after him.] In Elpis, John had been for his medical advisers and the nursing staff the perfect patient. In illness he had not complained. He had made no unnecessary demands and had with gratitude acknowledged the attention he received. When he reached convalescence, he had been to his nurses the interesting and conversational companion that he had been to his mother's visitors at Castle Kevin and had become the personal friend of several stationed on the landing where the door of his room . . . opened. . . . [He received cheerful, friendly letters from three or four of the nurses when he left.]

John's stay at Silchester ⟨House⟩ was to last a month. It was a period of melancholy convalescence in which he was recovering his strength after his operation. His medical advisers knew that he had no hope of ultimate recovery, but did what they could to conceal this fact from him. Those of his relations who knew, hid it from the younger members of the family; John himself clung to every hope held out by his doctors and maintained, in spite of his feelings, a sort of belief that he was working his way back to normal health. . . . He was glad to be ⟨at Silchester House⟩ and to enjoy the quiet of the garden, . . . but it was in some ways not a wholly suitable place for anyone so gravely ill. . . . He was filled with the contradictory feelings of an invalid: if the family were out, he felt lonely and deserted; and if any of their friends came to play tennis, he sought escape from numbers. . . .

[The day after his mother's return from the country, John himself moved back to Glendalough House. He continued working at the play as much as he could and gradually, as his strength began to return, undertook short excursions again. Sometimes he went to Bray, with Molly or alone, and sometimes he walked by the sea near home. He was less troubled by pain and really seemed to be getting stronger. One of the projects which now occupied his attention was the publication of his poetry. Yeats, who considered some of the poems 'very fine', encouraged him to give them to the press run by his sister Elizabeth at Dundrum, the Dun Emer—later the Cuala—Press, and he began to revise many of his verses and prepare them for publication.

[One Sunday late in September,] Molly came to see John and sat in the dining-room at Glendalough House going through, with him, the poems . . . for the Cuala Press. They talked with each other

on the assumption that he had only to recruit his health before
taking a house and being married, yet their minds were between
hope and despair, for they had the latent dread that he would not
recover. As he could not keep this dread unspoken, he asked her
whether, if he died, she would go to his funeral. Once mentioned,
the dread in her mind inspired a violent repudiation of the idea that
she could find a place in the silent procession or among the formally
devout at the grave. After Molly went home, John mused over the
fire and in his poem 'A Question' gave their thoughts powerful
expression that they could both appreciate. . . .[1]
[A few days later, he was able to tell her:]

I handed over the MS. of my poems to Yeats yesterday so I hope that will
go all right now. I did one new poem—that is partly *your* work—that
he says is *Magnificent*. . . .[2]

[The volume of John's verse did not appear until shortly after his
death, but he saw it through the press and, in his introduction,
stated clearly his theories of poetic diction; yet most of the poems,
as he made clear, were written before he had any ideas on poetic
diction. They had sprung from the incidents of his life.

   [One morning, towards the end of September, I remember going
in to see Mrs. Synge.] Her illness and her prospects of returning
health she discussed without emotion. She did not seem to suspect
that she was dying but she seemed to recognize in a new light the
value of natural expressions of feeling. Her recognition was not a
reluctant admission that she had held a mistaken view but rather
the acceptance of a new discovery with the surprise of a child.
Speaking of an old friend who had come to visit her, she said: 'She
put her arms round me when she was going away and, do you know,
it was very comforting.' . . .

   [John was now feeling well enough to long for a change of air
and, with surprising suddenness, decided to go to Germany to visit
the von Eiken sisters in Coblenz. He hoped that the trip would
'set him up' but was torn between the need for a holiday and the
loneliness he knew he would feel when away from Molly. However
he left on 6 October and arrived safely in Coblenz two days later.
He was warmly welcomed by the sisters and found the place 'a
good deal changed but very pleasant still. . . .' Later he continued

[1] *C.W.* I. 64.   [2] *Letters to Molly*, p. 283.

in a letter to Molly: 'All the von Eikens are very kind . . . but poor things they are most of them getting old.'[1]

[Though he could not undertake anything strenuous, John enjoyed taking gentle walks through the German countryside and the woods and his health continued to improve during the first part of his stay. However he missed Molly very much and he soon heard that his mother, whom he had thought was improving, was very much worse; on Monday 26 October, he received a telegram to tell him that his mother had died early that morning. He was deeply distressed, but after two days he felt able to write to Molly and tried to express his grief. Then he made plans to come back to Ireland: he did not return for the funeral but came on the mail boat ten days later. I called to see him.] He was looking ill and tired. In a quiet unemotional voice he spoke of Germany and his journey home, but of his home-coming he did not say anything. His eyes looked as if their focus was on something beyond physical vision.

8

As the lease that Mrs. Synge had taken of Glendalough House was unexpired, it had been arranged that John should stay on there in the care of her two maids until he should have time to make new plans. . . . [He was feeling, as he wrote to Molly, 'inexpressibly sad in this empty house,'[2] but Molly came to see him as often as she could, and sometimes they went out together.] He was trying to retain his belief that he was recovering his health, to build happiness on the idea that he was soon to be married, and to devote his working time to finishing *Deirdre of the Sorrows*. Often in the course of the next two months he nearly gave up his work in despair; but when he felt despondent, Molly used to act in the dining-room at Glendalough House fragments of the part he was writing for her, and so give him courage to go on again. . . .

The change that was taking place in John's health was gradual; the members of his family circle were sorry that he had not re-gained his strength but, if they noticed that he seemed more tired and looked more ill than he had been, they kept silent. John told me that he was disturbed about his symptoms, that a discharge was still coming through the intestine from the site of the operation, and that the doctors thought that it should disappear gradually if

[1] ibid., pp. 285, 287.   [2] ibid., p. 298.

the remains of the tumour became absorbed, but that if it should cease suddenly, trouble might follow. . . .

[Despite his hopes, and despite occasional days when he felt well, John was suffering almost constant pain. At the beginning of January, he and Molly decided that he should call in Dr. Parsons again and he also consulted the surgeon, Sir Charles Ball; but neither of them seemed to be able to do much to help.] On Thursday 21 January, Robert wrote in his diary: 'Went to see John; found him much the same—nights disturbed and feverish.' There was no doubt that John's health was declining, yet what should be done for him nobody seemed to know. Molly came to see him often, Robert and the different members of the family . . . called to see him when they could; but at night, except for the servants, he was alone in the house. He tried to maintain his interest in his work but, even with encouragement from Molly, he could do but little.

When Robert called on Saturday, he found that John had a temperature of over 100°. He called again on Sunday and decided that he would seek advice from Sir Charles Ball as John was not well enough to go to town. . . . After an interview with Sir Charles on Monday, ⟨Robert⟩ went to see John with instructions that he was not to go out when his temperature was over normal. On Tuesday and again on Thursday, Robert called at Glendalough House; but John could not report any change for the better. Next day, Robert entered in his diary: 'Went at 5 to see John. Found Molly . . . there. He seemed not so well after dinner; I returned and decided that he should write to Dr Parsons to come out to see him tomorrow, which he did. Had a talk to Annie.'. . .

[The doctor was unwilling to give a firm opinion on the nature of John's illness but decided, towards the end of the week, that he should return to the Elpis nursing home for further examination.] Nothing could be done on Sunday to carry Dr. Parsons's instructions into effect but on Monday Robert wrote in his diary:

Went to Dublin to Elpis at 12.30 to arrange for a room for John tomorrow; spoke to Miss Huxley. Came out 1.45 p.m. train to Glenageary station. Arranged to drive into Dublin at noon tomorrow with John. Watch fast by R.D.S. clock—2 m. 43 s.[1] Heard first blackbird singing at 5.20 p.m. in Monkstown House grounds. . . .

[1] Robert's obsession with details pervades all his diary entries; the R.D.S. is the Royal Dublin Society.

On Tuesday 2 February, after breakfast I went down to Glendalough House to help John with his preparations for going to Elpis. I found him in the dining-room where there was a fire. If I remember rightly, he was stuffing books into the lower part of his book-case, which stood between the window and the chimney-piece. He arranged things about the room silently; then he said that he would like to show me where he had left his papers. We went up to his bedroom. As the day was cold, he put a travelling rug round his shoulders. He opened the old painted wardrobe and showed me where he kept his manuscripts and letters. Everything we went through under the shadow of his unspoken belief that he would not handle them again. I went about with an awed feeling which I failed to interpret in the conscious knowledge that he could not recover.

Robert arrived and John left with him in a cab for more than an hour's drive to Elpis. It was not decided whether he should stay in Elpis or nearby in lodgings where, though living ordinarily, he would be near medical aid if he required treatment suddenly. He hoped to be able to work and brought with him the typed script of his Wicklow and Kerry articles and of *Deirdre of the Sorrows*. . . .

On Thursday . . . Robert and my mother met at Glendalough House to make plans for its care while John was in hospital. They arranged that the silver should be sent to the Royal Bank of Ireland for safe-keeping, that the maids should leave, and that Mary Tyndal should come as caretaker. Next day when Robert went to Elpis, John's condition seemed little changed. He was under Dr. Parsons's observation and Sir Charles Ball was to see him in the morning to consider whether another operation would be useful. On Saturday Robert noted in his diary: 'Sat a while with John. He was more cheerful as Charles Ball decided against an operation. . . .'

At Elpis, John was within a penny tram ride from the Abbey Theatre ⟨and⟩ for the first half of February, Molly called to see him every day. He had given instructions for the drawing of his will to my father who, on Saturday 13 February, brought it to him engrossed for signature. John signed it in the presence of two witnesses. That evening he said farewell to Molly who was going with the other members of the Abbey company to Manchester to play for a week at the Gaiety Theatre. . . .

Though from day to day when Robert or one of our family

party at Silchester House saw John there did not seem to be much change in his condition, he was losing strength. He was unable to work at . . . the Wicklow and Kerry articles and *Deirdre* . . . and when Molly was away could not even write letters to her. He asked my mother to tell her how he was and she wrote on ⟨17 February⟩:

Dear Miss Allgood: I saw John on Tuesday. He is going on much the same. The Dr had just been there and thought him rather better. My son Frank was with him yesterday and he was as usual. I am sure he misses your visits. I hope you are having a successful week in Manchester. Yours very sincerely,

ANNIE I. STEPHENS

The wonderful reception of his plays in Manchester was the greatest comfort John had during the lonely week in Elpis while Molly was away. . . . [The *Manchester Guardian* printed three most enthusiastic reviews of John's plays, in one of which Molly's acting was described as 'of extraordinary value'. The reviewer continued by praising without reserve her radiance and good looks.] ⟨The following⟩ Monday, John was overjoyed to see Molly ⟨back in Dublin⟩ and to hear from her direct about her success in his plays; but his strength had been failing. She was glad to cheer him with her youthful delight in the applause of full houses and did not realize that his hold on life was more uncertain than ⟨it had been⟩ when she left. Joseph Holloway noted in his diary for Wednesday 24 February:

I had a word or two with 'Maire O'Neill' in Nassau Street in the afternoon. She was full of the Manchester trip and its success. . . . She was on her way to daily visit to Synge in the Elpis. . . .

⟨By the beginning of March,⟩ John could write no more and could read but little. I have heard that he read the Bible regularly during the closing days of his life and that he kept it in brown paper lest his reading a religious book should provoke comment. Its contents had for him a meaning with its roots in his early youth; he had rejected not its wisdom but the theories of his relations about its teaching, and ⟨he⟩ did not wish anyone to suppose that contemplation of death had made them acceptable. . . .

My mother was very anxious about John and wanted to be near at hand if his condition became worse. But she had another

anxiety on her mind for my sister had been in . . . poor health
during the winter and was suffering from laryngitis and asthma.
Change of air had been recommended for her, and my mother had
planned to take her to St. Ann's Hydro in Blarney; but ⟨she⟩
hesitated to leave town while John was very ill. The doctors said
that his illness might be of long duration and that my sister should
have a change of air without delay, so my mother took her to
Blarney on Saturday 20 March leaving the two maids to keep
house for my father, my brother, and me. . . .

[The same day, Robert reported in his diary that John was 'a
little easier' and the next day he wrote: 'Ball and Parsons had a
third consultation.' For Monday, his entry reads:]

Went to Dublin to see Harry at noon and to Fox the wine-merchant to
choose a champagne for John. I got to Elpis at 1. Sat with him while at
his lunch. . . . He seemed weaker than when I last saw him and seemed to
have lost hope since the consultation.

[The same day Joseph Holloway wrote in his diary[1] that John]

. . . was quite despondent and melancholy and was calling to the nurse:
'What is the use of giving me anything? All's up with me; it is better to
let me die.' He was in great pain and would not allow any nurse but one
to attend him, and she sat with him for hours at a time. Miss Molly
Allgood calls each day to see him, and it was only a day or two ago she
realized how badly he was. With tears in her eyes she asked the nurse as
she came out in the passage what she thought of him, and she answered:
'What do you think yourself?' and then she knew for the first time how
hopeless his case is.

Joseph Holloway was mistaken in thinking that John was in great
pain; more than from actual pain, he suffered from digestive
discomfort and a sense of growing weakness.

Molly told me afterwards that, in a frenzy of despair, she had
gone to more than one priest seeking to have a Mass offered for
John's recovery. The priests, she said, had asked how she was
seeking to have a Mass offered for a Protestant; she had been
distraught and incoherent: nothing had come of her mission.

On Tuesday 23 March, I saw John for the last time. Robert had
asked me to take him the champagne that he had bought at Fox's

---

[1] Holloway reported what he had been told by a friend named Miss Clinch, who
was in the room next to Synge's.

the day before and a corkscrew tap that my father had for draining
it off in small quantities. A nurse on the landing at Elpis, when she
saw me going to the room where John had been, said: 'Mr. Synge
is in here,' and took me into a sunny back room from which there
was a view across house-tops to the hills.[1]

I was shocked by the change in John's appearance since the last
time I saw him but, as a student of twenty, I had very little experience of serious illness and did not fully realize how near he was to
death. At first he was too weak to talk; but the nurse screwed the
tap into the cork of the bottle I had brought and gave him some
champagne, and then he seemed a little brighter. He asked me
whether I had heard any blackbirds singing yet: I said that I had
heard thrushes but had not heard any blackbirds. For a few minutes
I chatted to him about home and college interests and left without
understanding that I would not see him again.

Next morning after breakfast, I saw a telegraph boy coming
up the gravel to Silchester House and ⟨I opened⟩ the door. In
spite of having seen John the day before, I felt a strange shock and a
sense of terrible finality when I read the words of the telegram:
'All is over. Huxley.' I said to the boy: 'There is no answer,' and
took the telegram upstairs to my father who was making ready to
leave for his office. He said that he had known for a long time that
John could not recover. I took out my bicycle and rode to . . . tell
Robert and . . . Edward that John was dead. Then I returned home
to work in a dazed way at the ivy leaves I was carving on a bread
board that I had left, with my tools lying next it, clamped to a
table in the front basement room that my brother and I used as a
study. Robert wrote in his diary:

Very wet day. Eddie Stephens came at 9 a.m. to tell me that poor John
had passed away at 5.30 this morning. I went to Dublin to Harry and
then to Mount Jerome[2] to arrange for the funeral. He will be laid in the
same grave with Aunt Jane Synge. Went to Waller's to arrange for the
removal tonight to Glendalough House.

My brother and I went down to Glendalough House some time
before the coffin was to arrive fearing that Mary Tyndal, the
solitary caretaker, might at such a time be feeling in need of our
support. We found her glad to be in charge of the house on a sad

---

[1] Synge had been moved the previous day from room 29 to room 31.
[2] A large Dublin cemetery.

occasion for the family that she had known since John's infancy. When we knocked, she hurried to the door and opened it: . . . 'I thought you were the men,' she said; and, as we went into the dining-room added: 'There's a fine strong table I left ready for the coffin.'

Next day Robert wrote in his diary:

Received . . . a visit from Yeats and the Sec. of Abbey Theatre with a request which I refused as impossible. I then went to Glendalough House; saw the coffin lying in the dining-room, brought from Elpis last night. Wrote to Samuel S. sending him the cutting from the *Irish Times*.

The request with which Yeats and Henderson came to Robert was for his permission to have a death mask of John made. Robert would have disliked it under any conditions but he definitely refused it because he believed John's face to have changed so much during his last illness that no real likeness of him, as he was in good health, could have been obtained. . . .

On the morning of Friday 26 March at half-past eight, my father, my brother, and I left the garden by the path behind the church to walk down to Glendalough House. Robert was there as well as Edward with his brother-in-law, Victor Price, and his two sons Hutchie and Millington. Willie Ormsby, 'the Judge', joined us and the rector, Edmund Robinson. No other people came. In front of the house ⟨were⟩ four black horses yoked to a tall hearse and behind it three or four mourning carriages. Robert soon told the men, who were standing near the door, that it was time to start. They carried out the coffin and slowly drove away followed by a small family party like the party that had followed Mrs. Synge's coffin to the grave from the same house a few months before.

It was half past ten when we reached Mount Jerome. There, at the gate, a group of those who had known John as a writer and as a director of the National Theatre Society joined the procession that followed the coffin up the main avenue to the chapel and, after a short service, to the open grave.

As the words of commitment were said, I noticed there the people John had known divided, as they had always been in his lifetime, into separate groups. His relations were together in black, carrying bowler hats; and, a little apart, ⟨stood⟩ the people among whom he had worked. I knew few of them, even by appearance; but I can remember seeing Sara Allgood and watching Padraic Colum's hair blowing in the wind. The grave was filled, flowers laid upon it, and those who had stood by it scattered.

From words that John used in praise of others can but be framed his epitaph: 'He wrote using his whole life as his material.'

INDEX